EFFECTIVE TEACHING IN HIGHER EDUCATION

EFFECTIVE TEACHING
IN HIGHER EDUCATION

GEORGE BROWN
and
MADELEINE ATKINS

For Elizabeth and John

First published 1988 by Methuen & Co. Ltd.

Reprinted 1990, 1993, 1994, 1996 by Routledge
11 New Fetter Lane, London EC4P 4EE

Routledge is an International Thomson Publishing company I(T)P

© 1988 George Brown and Madeleine Atkins

Set by Hope Services (Abingdon) Ltd
Printed and bound in Great Britain by
Biddles Ltd, Guildford and King's Lynn

British Library Cataloguing in Publication Data
    Brown, George 1935–
    Effective teaching in higher education.
    1. College teaching
    I. Title   II. Atkins, Madeleine
    378′. 125   LB2331

    ISBN 0–415–03675–5

Contents

Acknowledgements

We wish to thank our friends, colleagues, and students who have participated in our workshops. Special thanks are given to Dr David Mack and Dr Andrew Wilson of Loughborough University for their suggestions and support. We also thank Ben Brown, Joy Bryant, and Diana Simons for typing and word-processing. Most important of all, we wish to thank our respective spouses, Elizabeth Brown and John Atkins, for their patience and encouragement during the time of writing this book. It is dedicated to them.

1
Introduction

A wise man learns from experience and an even wiser man from the experience of others.

(Plato)

A PROLOGUE

Lecturers in universities and polytechnics have three functions: teaching, research, and management. This book is concerned with the teaching function. If you believe that teaching in higher education is a trivial non-assessable pursuit then this book is not for you, for the book is based on two interrelated assumptions. First, that effective teaching is a complex, intellectually demanding, and socially challenging task. Second, that effective teaching consists of a set of skills that can be acquired, improved, and extended.

Effective teaching is intellectually demanding in that it requires the teacher to know, in a deep sense, the subject being taught. To teach effectively you need to be able to think and problem-solve, to analyse a topic, to reflect upon what is an appropriate approach, to select key strategies and materials, and to organize and structure ideas, information, and tasks for students. None of these activities occurs in a vacuum. Effective teaching is socially challenging in that it takes place in the context of a department and institution which may have unexamined traditions and conflicting goals and values. Most important of all, effective teaching requires the teacher to consider what the students know, to communicate clearly to them, and to stimulate them to learn, think, communicate, and perhaps in their turn, to stimulate their teachers. In short, to teach effectively you must know your subject, know how your students learn, *and* how to teach.

But clearly, effective teaching is not solely dependent upon the teachers. Students too have responsibilities to learn. Sometimes these responsibilities need to be made explicit. Often an indirect but powerful way of improving your teaching is to improve the ways in which students learn. Hence a theme in this book, particularly the final chapter, is how you can help your students to learn. But whereas students' responsibilities to learn may be described as individual and personal, ours as teachers may be regarded as collective and professional. Hence the importance of developing, monitoring, and assessing teaching by individuals and by departments.

WHAT IS TEACHING?

Before embarking upon the study of various methods of teaching it seems appropriate to consider the following question: what is teaching? Teaching may be regarded as providing opportunities for students to learn. It is an interactive process as well as an intentional activity. However, students may not always learn what we intend and they may, sometimes alas, also learn notions which we did not intend them to learn.

The content of learning may be facts, procedures, skills, and ideas and values. Your goals in teaching, and therefore for the learning of your students, may be gains in knowledge and skills, the deepening of understanding, the development of problem solving or changes in perceptions, attitudes, values, and behaviour. (Students' goals may, of course, be more pragmatic – passing examinations!) Given that teaching is an intentional activity concerned with student learning, it follows that it is sensible to spend some time on thinking and articulating your intentions in teaching a particular topic to a group of students – and on checking whether those intentions are realizable and were realized.

The various methods of teaching may be placed on a continuum. At one extreme is the lecture in which student control and participation is usually minimal. At the other extreme is private study in which lecturer control and participation is usually minimal. It should be noted that even at each end of the continuum there is some control and participation by both lecturer and students. Thus in lectures students may choose what notes to take, whether to ask questions – or even disrupt the class. A student's private study is likely to be influenced by the suggestions of the lecturer, the materials and tasks that he or she has provided and the texts that are made available in the library.

Between the extremes of the continuum one may place, approximately, small group teaching, laboratory work, and individual research or project supervision. The precise location of these types of teaching is less easy. For each type of teaching contains a rich variety of methods involving varying proportions of lecturer and student participation. For example, small group teaching may be highly structured and tightly controlled by the lecturer or it may be free-flowing discussion in which the lecturer prompts or facilitates

Figure 1.1 A continuum of teaching methods

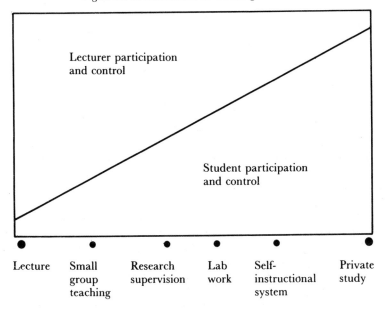

Lecturer participation
and control

Student participation
and control

| Lecture | Small group teaching | Research supervision | Lab work | Self-instructional system | Private study |

occasionally. Laboratory work may be a series of routine experiments specified precisely by the lecturer or a set of guided inquiries in which the student develops hypotheses to test, chooses methods, and designs appropriate experiments. A particular research supervision may be wholly lecturer directed, another may be wholly student directed. These notions are discussed in more detail in the relevant chapters. In the meantime you might find the continuum useful in helping to clarify your intentions with regard to student participation and control.

This book has been written to help you to reflect upon, experiment with, develop, and appraise your own teaching. In a sense the book is a starting-point for teachers in higher education who want to research their own teaching and how their students learn. The text focuses upon the major methods of teaching – lecturing, small group teaching, laboratory work, and individual research or project supervision — and it provides ways of helping students to improve their learning in class and in private study.

Chapters in the text contain brief outlines of relevant research, guidelines for teaching effectively which are based upon the research, and some practical suggestions for planning and assessing your teaching. At the end of each chapter are a set of activities which may be tackled individually, in informal study groups, or as part of a workshop or course. All of the activities have been used by the authors in workshops on teaching and learning. Notes and comments on the activities are provided at the end of the book (pp. 196–211) with some suggestions for organizing workshops based on the content of the book. The book does not consider student assessment or computer-based learning; these are considered in Beard and Hartley (1984) and McKeachie (1986). Nor does the book attempt to integrate systematically knowledge of particular academic subjects with knowledge of the processes of teaching and learning. Such a task is best assumed by the readers who, after all, know their subjects and their underlying values. The book does, however, provide examples drawn from different academic fields which may help you to see ways of using various approaches to teaching in your own subject – ways which you may not have previously considered.

The book may be used in at least four ways. First, you may simply read it. This will take most people no more than two or three evenings. It will be time well spent since you will learn of various strategies and activities that you can use, and of the research on which they are based. Second, you can read the book and try out the activities on your own or with small groups of colleagues. This will provide practice, reflection, and perhaps discussion of the issues involved, thereby deepening your understanding and developing your expertise. Third, you can use parts of the text as the basis of short courses on different methods of teaching and learning. The notes and comments as well as the activities are of value for this purpose. Used in this way you will learn from watching your colleagues at work and discussing with them various approaches. The fourth way of using the text is for organizing, and participating in, a systematic course on teaching in higher education. Such a course would take about twenty-one days and it might best be tackled in blocks of time distributed throughout the year. This approach would give participants time to learn new approaches, to reflect on them, to use them in their teaching, and to bring back to the course their new experiences and problems.

EFFECTIVE TEACHING

Effectiveness is best estimated in relation to your own goals of teaching. Thus what counts as effective in one context may not be so in another. A beautifully polished lecture which provides the solution to a problem may be considered effective if the goal was merely conveying information. If the goal was to stimulate the students to develop the solution then the polished lecture may be regarded as ineffective. However, you should be wary of the argument that bad teaching is effective teaching because it forces students to study more intensely. Leaving aside the differing views of 'bad' teaching, such an argument may be a rationalization for not improving your teaching. For us, bad teaching reduces motivation, increases negative attitudes to learning, and yields lower achievement. In our view it is better to teach clearly and stimulate the students to think by drawing their attention to particular issues than it is to be deliberately confusing.

Although effective teaching is best estimated in relation to your goals, there are some features of teaching on which there is both a consensus among lecturers and evidence from studies of student learning. Generally speaking, effective teaching is systematic, stimulating, and caring (McKeachie and Kulik 1975; P. A. Cohen 1981; Marsh 1982). Obviously the emphasis on these factors varies between lecturers and subjects and each of these factors is complex and, in practice, challenging.

Effective teaching is sometimes equated with successful teaching – that is, the students learn what is intended. While this argument has some appeal, it is not the whole of the matter. Effective teaching is concerned not only with success but also with appropriate values. A lecturer may teach Anglo-Saxon grammar so successfully that all the class pass the examination – and then drop Anglo-Saxon. Was the lecturer an effective teacher? The answer depends in part on whether you value attitudes more than short-term gains in knowledge. Thus in considering research on effective teaching it is important to consider successful teaching strategies in the context of what lecturers and students value. This procedure is adopted in the subsequent chapters of this book.

ACTIVITIES

These activities, and those in subsequent chapters, are designed to encourage the reader to think, discuss, and try out various suggestions. Some of the activities may be tackled privately, others are best tackled in small groups. There are notes and comments (pp. 196–211) on some of the activities. It is not necessary to tackle all the activities in each chapter but do tackle some. Obviously you may modify the activities for use with particular groups of colleagues.

1.1 Research is sometimes described as 'organized curiosity' and teaching as 'organized communication'. How far do you agree?

1.2 Teaching ability is often not estimated for promotion purposes on the grounds that there are no objective measures of teaching. Suggest a few ways of assessing teaching and explore their strengths and weaknesses. Compare the strengths and weaknesses with those of the usual approaches to estimating research ability.

1.3 What is 'spoonfeeding'? How does it differ from effective teaching?

1.4 Which do you prefer, lecturing or small group teaching? Why?

1.5 What are, for you, the characteristics of effective teaching? (You may find it helpful to specify various contexts when considering this question.) Jot down your list of characteristics and compare them with a few colleagues.

1.6 Three dimensions of teaching are:
    Systematic .... Slipshod
    Stimulating .... Boring
    Caring .... Uncaring

Which of these dimensions do you consider most important? Which do you think your students consider most important? How do you rate yourself on each of these dimensions? How does a class of students probably rate you?

1.7 Is teaching ever non-manipulative?

2

Studies of lecturing

The decrying of the wholesale use of lectures is probably justified. The wholesale decrying of the use of lectures is just as certainly not justified.

(Spence 1928)

It is sometimes forgotten that lectures are for the benefit of students. They have three purposes: coverage, understanding, and motivation. Without motivation attention is lost and there can be little understanding. Without information on a topic there is nothing to be understood. These purposes of conveying information, generating understanding, and stimulating interest are therefore interrelated. But in any one lecture one of these purposes is likely to be prime and thereby shape the structure and content of the lecture (see Activity 2.1).

Given the ubiquity of lecturing in universities and polytechnics – and its antiquity – it seems appropriate to spend some time exploring various studies of lecturing before considering the practical questions of how to make your lectures more effective. So in this chapter an outline of the origins of lecturing is provided followed by a model for understanding the processes of lecturing. This model is then used to provide a framework for a review of more recent studies of lecturing. The review in turn provides the basis for the subsequent chapter on the skills of lecturing.

AN HISTORICAL SKETCH

Lecturers may be traced back to the Greeks of the fifth century BC. In medieval times lectures were the most common form of teaching in both Christian and Muslim universities. The term 'lecture' was derived from the medieval Latin *lectare*, to read aloud. Lectures consisted of an oral reading of a text followed by a commentary. The method of reading aloud from a text or script is still used by some lecturers in the arts even though the conventions of written and oral language differ over time and across cultures.

In contrast, lecturers in medicine and surgery have long used the demonstration as part of the lecture. By the nineteenth century demonstrations, pictures, and blackboards were used in lectures in science as well as medicine. Today it is still the lecturers in science, engineering, and medicine who are the more active users of audio-visual aids.

Lectures are the most common method of teaching in universities throughout the world (Bligh 1980). Their continued use may be attributable in part to tradition and in part to economics. Classes of one thousand or more are not uncommon in countries which are anxious to minimize costs in higher education. In some countries the lecture may be the major source of information, and only the lecturers may have access to texts and articles in the major languages of the world.

These simple facts suggest that lectures are likely to be widely used well into the twenty-first century. Hence the importance of exploring ways of making lectures more effective as well as economical in the years ahead.

A MODEL FOR EXPLORING LECTURES

A full model of the processes of lecturing would necessarily take account of the personalities and ways of thinking of lecturers and students, their modes of communication and listening, and the nature and content of the lecture subject. All of these influence the processes of lecturing in diverse ways. Such a model is provided by Entwistle and Hounsell (1975). At its core is a simple, robust model of information processing which may be used to describe the processes of lecturing and to diagnose common errors in lecturing. The model is shown in Figure 2.1.

The key features of the process of lecturing are intentions, transmission, receipt of information, and output. Other important features are the objectives and expectations of the recipients (the students) and their intended applications and extensions of the information received. All of these features influence considerably the overall quality of the lecture as a method of teaching and learning.

Intentions

The lecturer's intentions may be, as indicated in the introduction to this chapter, to provide coverage of a topic, to generate understanding, and to stimulate interest. Undue attention to coverage can obscure understanding. A stress on understanding may require deliberate neglect of factual detail. A stress on interest *per se* may lead to inadequate understanding. Of course, handouts and carefully selected readings can be used to augment coverage. Not all lectures within a course need to be concerned equally with all three goals,

Figure 2.1 Model for exploring lectures

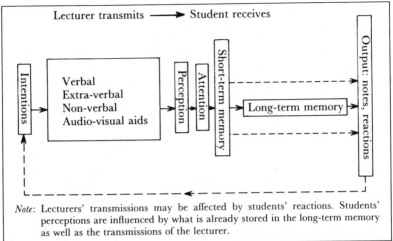

Note: Lecturers' transmissions may be affected by students' reactions. Students' perceptions are influenced by what is already stored in the long-term memory as well as the transmissions of the lecturer.

and other teaching methods may be used to generate understanding and interest. Consideration of the three goals of lecturing, together with a knowledge of the earlier learning of the students, are an essential constituent of lecture preparation.

Transmission

A lecturer sends messages verbally, extra-verbally, non-verbally, and through his or her use of audio-visual aids. The verbal messages may consist of definitions, descriptions, examples, explanations, or comments. The 'extra-verbal' component is the lecturer's vocal qualities, hesitations, stumbles, errors, and use of pauses and silence. The 'non-verbal' component consists of his or her gestures, facial expressions, and body movements. Audio-visual messages are presented on blackboards, transparencies, slides, and audio-visual extracts. All of these types of messages may be received by the students who may sift, select, perhaps store and summarize, and note what they perceive as the important messages. A lecturer does not only transmit information: his or her extra-verbal and non-verbal cues and the quality of the audio-visual aids used may convey meanings and attitudes which highlight, qualify, or distort the essential messages.

Receipt

The information, meaning, and attitudes conveyed by the lecturer may or may not be perceived by the students. Attention fluctuates throughout a one-hour lecture. After twenty minutes there is a marked decline in attention followed by a peak of attention just before the lecture ends. This decline in attention is less likely to occur if the lecture includes some short activities for students such as *brief* small group discussions or simple problem-solving. Any change of activity is, in fact, likely to renew attention. Messages that are received by the students are filtered and stored temporarily in the short-term memory. They are forgotten after about thirty seconds if they cannot be kept in mind or noted, or if they cannot be transferred to the long-term memory. The long-term memory most readily receives messages which are closely related to the network of concepts and facts which are already stored in the long-term memory and have been called up. For links can then be made between the new and the old. Sometimes this processing of the new information in the light of the old will profoundly affect the pre-existing networks and information and they will be 'returned' to long-term store in a different or modified form. A lecture can, therefore, radically change your perception of a topic or issue. The long-term memory will also store new messages which are only loosely associated with existing facts and ideas. But facts and concepts that are incomprehensible are not likely to be stored. Competing verbal and audio-visual messages are also difficult to cope with.

Output

A student's response or 'output' is not only a set of intelligible notes which may be understood and, if necessary, restructured and learnt; it also consists of reactions to the lecture and the lecturer. The immediate reactions are usually non-verbal signals and these may be received, interpreted, and perhaps acted upon by the lecturer. Herein lies an important difference between recorded and live lectures.

More important than the immediately observable responses to a lecture are the long-term changes in attitudes and understanding which may occur in a student. These changes are not easily disentangled from other learning experiences but it is likely that a student's attitude towards a subject and towards lecture methods is influenced markedly by the quality of lecturing he or she experiences as well as by the student's own personality characteristics. A lecture *may* change a student's perception of a problem or theory, it *may* increase a student's insight, and it *may* stimulate him or her to read, think, and discuss ideas with others. The probability of these events is dependent upon the student's knowledge, attitudes, and motivation to learn and on the lecturer's preparation, lecture structure, and presentation.

Using the model for error diagnosis

The model of lecturing may readily be used to analyse the potential weaknesses – and strengths – in your own lecturing. These are likely to be gaps between a lecturer's intention, the transmission, and the receipt of information. A common error is to try to close the gap between intention and transmission by reading aloud from a written script. This usually increases the gap between transmission and receipt.

The gaps between intentions and transmission may be explored by comparing your intentions and notes with a video-recording of part of your lecture. Transmission and reception may be explored by comparing a video-recording with students' notes and their discussion of the ideas presented. A simple but powerful test of the gap between intention and receipt is to compare the key points in your notes with the notes of your students. However it should be borne in mind that notes are not the sole criterion of 'good' lecturing.

Clarifying intentions is closely associated with strategies of lecture preparation. This theme is taken up in the section on lecture preparation in the next chapter. Transmission skills and problems, including the use of audio-visual aids, are also discussed in Chapter 3 where the particular problems of achieving clarity and generating interest are considered. Weaknesses in learning from lectures are considered in Chapter 8.

RESEARCH ON LECTURING

Studies of lecturing have been the subject of many reviews during the past sixty years (Spence 1928; Bligh 1980; Dunkin 1983). Other useful sources are Beard and Hartley (1984) and Brown (1987). Two major trends can be discerned in the reviews: a desire to compare the effectiveness of lecturing against other forms of teaching; and a desire to obtain the views and experiences of students and lecturers of lecturing.

Lecturing compared to other methods of teaching

A common question asked is 'Is lecturing as effective as other methods of teaching?' The evidence indicates that lecturing is at least as effective as other methods at presenting information and providing explanations. Practical skills are obviously taught more effectively in laboratories but the underlying methodologies and theories may be taught as effectively and perhaps more efficiently in lectures. Problem-solving skills appear to be taught more effectively in small groups.

However even these results depend upon the quality of the discussion or lecture. The few studies of attitude change also favour the small group although it is likely that a skilful lecturer does achieve attitude changes in a lecture.

Comparisons between lectures and newer methods of teaching should also be treated cautiously. Whereas newer methods such as computer-assisted learning, games, and tape-slide programmes are prepared carefully and evaluated systematically, lecture methods are rarely subject to such rigorous planning and analysis.

Comparisons of live lectures and televised lectures have also yielded equivocal results. Although there is a tendency for live lectures to be more effective in producing learning, the trends do not reach the level of statistical significance. However it does seem clear that students do prefer live lectures (MacKenzie, Eraut, and Jones 1970). The lack of differences may be due to defects in experimental design and to inadequacies in television production. Indeed, a distinction should be made between live lectures, live lectures which are televised but not recorded, televised lectures which are pre-recorded, and televised lectures which are produced and pre-recorded. Only the last category is likely to be more effective than live lectures. But the costs of this form of production and technical assistance should be borne in mind by any intending user.

Even allowing for the equivocality of some studies comparing lectures and other forms of teaching, it does appear that lectures have a role in higher education. But they should not be the only method used. As Spence (1928) observed in the first review of research on lecturing: 'The decrying of the wholesale use of lectures is probably justified. The wholesale decrying of the use of lecturing is just as certainly not justified'.

Views of students and lecturers

Figure 2.2 sets out the positive and negative aspects of lecturing as perceived by lecturers. Generally speaking lecturers appear to like lectures.

Students also like lectures although they do comment frequently on poor lecturing technique. A comparison of criticisms voiced by students and lecturers about lecturing is set out in Figure 2.3. Students are particularly critical of lectures from which it is difficult to take notes. Judging from the survey by Brown and Bakhtar (1983), most lecturers are aware of the importance of note-taking, although some lecturers prefer students not to take notes and some consider note-taking to be the sole responsibility of the students.

Both students and lecturers place high value on clarity of presen-

Figure 2.2 Common dislikes and likes

The most common reasons for dislike of lectures amongst lecturers were:
1 Unresponsive audiences.
2 Large groups.[1]
3 Effort and time involved in preparation.
4 Feelings of failure after a bad lecture.
5 Lecturing on topics disliked.

The most common reasons for liking lectures were:
1 Intellectual challenge in structuring a lecture.
2 Personal satisfaction in giving a good lecture.
3 Student responsiveness during a lecture and subsequently.
4 Arousing and stimulating interest in one's subject.
5 Motivation from having to give a lecture.[2]

Source: Brown and Bakhtar (1983).
Notes: 1 Large groups probably had different connotations for lecturers working in different subjects. Engineers had in mind classes of 300 students; some arts lecturers thought 60 students were a large group.
2 This is related to the intellectual challenge. Because you are forced to give a lecture on a particular topic you often become more involved with the materials and learn from it. Without this motivation you might not take up the intellectual challenge.

Figure 2.3 Some common criticisms of lecturers

STUDENTS' VIEWS	LECTURERS' VIEWS
1 Inaudibility.	1 Saying too much too quickly.
2 Incoherence.	2 Assuming too much knowledge.
3 Failure to pitch at an appropriate level.	3 Forgetting to provide summaries.
4 Not emphasizing key points.	4 Not indicating when making an aside (rather than a main point).
5 Poor blackboard work.	5 Difficulty in timing the length of a lecture.

Source: Based on Brown and Daines (1981a; 1981b) and Brown and Bakhtar (1983).

tation, structure, and interest. However there are differences between arts and science students on valued characteristics and between arts and science lecturers. This is not surprising given that the role of lectures is perceived differently. The experience of giving and receiving a lecture in arts is subtly different from the experience of giving and receiving a lecture in science. Science students value detailed, logically structured notes more highly than arts students (Brown and Daines' 1981a). Science lecturers value logical and structured characteristics more highly than arts lecturers. Science lecturers consider that features of lecturing, such as logical presentation, structure, use of aids, and selection of apt examples, can be learnt whereas many arts lecturers do not (Brown and Daines 1981b). On the other hand, arts students value gaining of insight and new perspectives. And whereas science students tend to see lectures as a way in to reading, for arts students lectures ideally follow reading and help them to interpret what they have read.

In an interesting study of thirty-three 'gifted' lecturers, Sheffield (1974) concluded that the most important aspect of lecturing was 'to stimulate students to become active learners in their own right'. The group of lecturers and their former students also stressed in their essays and comments the importance of caring for students, love of subject, preparing properly, and conveying principles rather than details.

The views of lecturers identified by Sheffield are echoed in the 'good' and 'bad' stories of lectures told by science students in discursive interviews (Ogborn 1977; Bliss and Ogborn 1977). 'Good' stories contained descriptions of involvement, enthusiasm, generating understanding, and human interest. 'Bad' stories described the opposite.

The research conducted on lecturing can also be analysed on the basis of the model of information processing presented in Figure 2.1.

Use of the lecturing model

Intentions and planning

Studies of intentions and planning are neglected research topics. While Beard and Hartley (1984) and Brown (1978b) provide guidelines for preparing lectures, there are no published studies of how lecturers actually prepare their lectures (see Activity 2.2).

Transmission

The key variables in effective transmission found by researchers are clarity and expressiveness. Land (1985) has summarized the main studies in the last decade on clarity of explanations as measured by student achievement. The results show that higher student achievement scores were obtained when explanations had fewer verbal mazes (false starts, redundant phrases, tangles of words), greater use of specific emphasis and clear transitions from one subject to another. Brown (1982) also identified four structuring moves which are related to high student ratings of clarity. These are discussed under the skill of explaining in Chapter 3.

Expressiveness, which includes enthusiasm, friendliness, humour, dynamism, and even charisma, has long been regarded as an essential ingredient of lecturing. A meta-analysis of twelve experimental studies of expressiveness (Abrami, Levanthal, and Perry 1982) suggests that expressiveness is more likely to influence students' responses to a lecturer and their attitude towards their subject of study than it is to produce marked changes in achievement. However the studies reviewed were rather extreme in their use of expressiveness and variation in content. Furthermore, favourable changes in attitude towards a topic are often an important long-term goal of lecturing.

The sequence and organization of lectures has not been studied in detail. Lecturers report that their most common method of organizing lectures is the 'classical' approach of subdividing topics and then subdividing the sub-topics (Brown and Bakhtar 1983). Linguistic analyses of lectures appear to have focused upon microsctructure and as yet they have not considered larger units of discourses in lectures (Pirianen-Marsh 1985).

Underpinning the sequence and organization of lectures are the skills of lecturing (Brown 1978b). Chapter 3 provides an analysis of these skills. Amongst the most important are: presenting information, explaining, and generating interest. These skills in their turn are based upon the specific skills of opening a lecture, using audio-visual aids, comparing and contrasting, narrating, varying activities, and summarizing.These skills are likely to be improved upon through training as are the skills of learning from lectures (Brown 1982; Hartley 1986).

Different styles of lecturing have been identified and these appear to be closely associated with subject content but not with length of experience or status. In one study (Brown and Bakhtar 1983), five styles were identified. These were the 'visual information giver'; the 'oral presenter'; the 'exemplary' who used successfully a blend of visual and oral approaches; the 'eclectic' who was less successful at blending visual and oral approaches, who has self-doubts but a strong commitment to his or her subject; and the 'amorphous' whose main characteristics are vagueness and arrogance. Visual information givers were most common in science and engineering, oral presenters in arts. Both exemplaries and eclectics were found in biomedical science and arts. Amorphous lecturers could also be found in all departments but were particularly common in science, engineering, and medicine (see Activity 2.3).

Receipt and output

Studies of note-taking in lectures are reviewed succinctly in Beard and Hartley (1984). In general it appears that note-taking aids learning and recall, and that reviewing one's notes soon after a lecture aids subsequent recall and understanding. There is a wide variety of approaches to note-taking and it appears that students in different subjects tend to have different approaches. Science, engineering, and medical students tend to take fuller, more structured notes than do arts students. This may be in part because objectives and expectations of learning from lectures vary across subjects. Some suggestions for helping students to take more effective notes are presented in Chapter 8.

There are also likely to be differences between students according to their personality characteristics, motivation to learn, and learning styles. For example Hodgson (1984) used the technique of stimulated recall to study how students had reacted during lectures. Three broad sets of reported experiences were identified: extrinsic, intrinsic, and vicarious experience. The first two appear to be related to the learning styles of surface and deep processing (see Chapter 7) and the third is related to the students' perception and understanding of the lecturer's view. Vicarious experience occurs when the lecturer is enthusiastic, committed, and provides illustrations and metaphors which strike home. Vicarious experience provides a link between studies of expressiveness and student attitude change. It is as if the student begins to identify and incorporate the lecturer's view into his or her own mode of thinking and appreciation of the subject.

SUMMARY

Lecturing and lectures are clearly portmanteau terms which require closer scrutiny. The term 'lecture' may have quite different meanings for science and arts lecturers and students. The experiences of receiving or giving lectures in different subjects have not been fully explored, yet it is clear that the structure and content of subjects have a marked influence upon the mode of lecturing. Students' learning styles may also have a marked effect upon note-taking and learning from lectures.

Overall, research over the past sixty years indicates that for some tasks lectures are at least as good as other methods of teaching. They are economical and fairly efficient but they should be augmented by other forms of teaching. The research has also shown that clarity of presentation, structure, and expressiveness are key factors in effective lecturing. However it is not yet clear how these factors operate upon the student's perception, understanding, and attitudes. Given that they do operate, it is worth providing some training in lecturing for lecturers, and in learning from lectures for students. Activity 2.5 provides a simple but powerful method of helping people to improve their presentation and structure in lectures.

ACTIVITIES

Here are a few activities and questions which are designed to help you to reflect upon, and analyse, your own approaches to lecturing. Some of the activities may be tackled independently or, better still, in small groups. Activity 2.5 requires technical resources such as video cameras and overhead projectors. Some notes and comments on the activities are given on p. 197.

2.1 Think of a lecture you have given recently. Which of the three goals – coverage, understanding, and motivation – took primacy in the lecture?

2.2 How do you prepare lectures? What problems, if any, do you have in preparing lectures?

2.3 What are your own strengths and weaknesses when giving a lecture? What is your usual style of lecturing?

2.4 What do your students expect to gain from a lecture in your subject? How do you know? How far do their expectations influence the way you structure and present facts and ideas in your lectures?

2.5 Prepare and give a brief explanation to a small group of colleagues on a topic from your own subject area. You may assume your colleagues are intelligent, but not necessarily knowledgeable about the topic. The explanation should take no more than five minutes. You may use audio-visual aids such as transparencies, slides, or the blackboard.

Each member of the group should give a five-minute explanation. The explanations should be video-recorded. Each member of the group should also take the role of time-keeper, camera operator, and note-taker. The time-keeper should signal at the end of four minutes that one minute is left and again at the end of five minutes. The camera operator should video-record the presenter and visual aids. If possible he or she should take some close-up shots of the presenter and the audience. The note-takers should take notes as if they were students.

When all the video-recordings have been made the group should view, analyse, and comment on the recordings. The presenter should first comment on his or her own recording. One person should comment on the body language, another on the use of audio-visual aids (if used), and another on the structure of the explanation. All comments should be directed at helping the presenter to improve the quality of the explanation.

Some examples of topics which have been used by lecturers in this activity are:

Why rotate crops?
Why do trees have roots?
What is tragedy?
Why did Dr Johnson dislike Dean Swift?
Was Queen Elizabeth I a bastard?
Is history just facts?
How hips are replaced.
Ultrasonic scanning.
Magnetic nuclear resonance.
How holograms are produced.
The basic concepts of architecture.
What is microeconomics?
Meat marketing.
What is a university?

This activity, but not necessarily the same topic, should be repeated after tackling Chapter 3 (see notes and comments).

3
The skills of lecturing

The technique of imparting knowledge in the special way
called lecturing can be learned and improved upon.

(Pear 1933)

The major skills of lecturing are explaining, presenting information, generating interest and lecture preparation. These skills are closely associated with the goals of coverage, understanding, and motivation and they are dependent upon component skills such as using audio-visual aids, varying student activities, comparing and contrasting, and getting the openings and endings right (see Figure 3.1).

Given the complexity of lecturing skills it is useful to identify the one skill which, if improved, will enhance consequentially performance in other skills. Without doubt the skill which is likely to have most carry over effects is explaining. So in this section we focus primarily upon explaining and then consider briefly some of the other skills.

EXPLAINING

Explaining is giving understanding to another. Understanding is the creation of new connections between facts, between ideas, and between facts and ideas. These apparently simple descriptions of explaining and understanding provide a basic framework for exploring research on explaining in various professional contexts (Brown and Atkins 1986).

There are several ways of classifying explanations (Hyman 1974; Ennis 1969; Brown and Hatton 1982) but perhaps the most useful for practical purposes is the typology of:

1 Interpretative   What are local anaesthetics?
                     What is optimality theory?
2 Descriptive   How do local anaesthetics work?
                     How is optimality used by economists?
3 Reason-giving Why are local anaesthetics used?
                     Why is optimality theory thought to be important?

Figure 3.1 The skills of lecturing

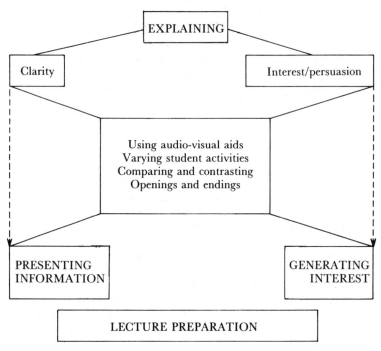

Note: Explaining, presenting information, and generating interest are major skills
related to the goals of understanding, coverage, and motivation. Lecture preparation is also a major skill. Other skills shown are important sub-skills. The
text provides further information.

These types of explanations approximate to the questions 'What?',
'How?', and 'Why?'. Together with the subsidiary questions 'When?'
and 'Where?' they may be used to provide a framework for an
explanation, a talk, or a lecture.

The processes of explaining may be conceptualized as:

A problem to be explained (problem identification)
↓
A series of statements (transmission)
↓
An understanding of the problem (outcome)

The problem may be expressed in the form of a question. In answering
it, the explainer makes a set of linked statements. These statements

may be quite lengthy and they may contain principles, examples, analogies, metaphors, qualifications, and reservations. Each of the statements should be capable of being understood by the explainees. The complete set of statements is then likely to yield understanding of the problem. A useful analogy for understanding the process of explaining is the proof of a geometrical theorem. There is a new statement to prove, and a series of statements which have already been accepted. The series of statements together create new knowledge and understanding. The analogy, like all analogies, is not an exact description of the process of explaining. In explaining, it is not always possible or necessary to provide the solution to a problem. What may be required is to provide an understanding of the nature of the problem.

It follows from the description of explaining that the explainer has to take account of both the problem *and* the likely knowledge of the explainees. Thus the explanation of DNA you would give to 14-year-olds may be very different from the explanation you would give to second-year undergraduate biochemists. This point may seem obvious. It is less easy to translate into practice. The essential tactic is to pitch the level correctly and this in turn requires you to analyse the variables implicit in the problem to be explained. Activities 3.3 and 3.4 provide some practice and guidance on pitching an explanation at an appropriate level.

Another implication of the three-part process of explaining is that we must know (fairly precisely) what the problem is that we are trying to explain. Again the point is obvious but not so easy to translate into practice. Indeed we may not arrive at a precise formulation of the problem until we have attempted an explanation of it. This observation explains in part why a second attempt at an explanation or lecture topic is often better than the first (Activity 3.1) and why a second draft of an article is often better than the first.

It is commonplace that the key features of transmission are clarity and interest. This is substantiated by the research cited earlier and accords with common sense. Unfortunately common sense does not necessarily provide clues on *how* to make an explanation clear and interesting. Some suggestions are given in the next sections.

The outcome of understanding is rarely checked in lectures although non-verbal signals of puzzlement, bewilderment, and so on can be monitored by a lecturer. Eye contact has two functions – establishing rapport and looking to check students' reactions. We can also use brief student activities in a lecture to check on understanding (see Activity 3.8) and of course we can use tutorials, small group discussions, and assessment papers to provide checks on understanding and give feedback to students.

Clarity in explaining

Clear explanations are, as indicated, dependent upon knowing precisely what you wish to explain. However intentions *per se* are not enough. In addition you have to consider the structure of the explanation.

Four important structuring moves, identified in one study which used independent observers, have been shown to be related to high ratings of clarity and to better note-taking by students (Brown 1982).

The four structuring moves are:

1 Signposts   These are statements which signal the direction and structure of a lecture. 'Today I want to examine four approaches to the management of tumours. First the use of surgical techniques, secondly the use of radiotherapy, thirdly the use of chemotherapy, and fourthly the use of psychological support – which some surgeons call "doing nothing". In tackling each of these approaches I will be indicating the strenghts and weaknesses of each approach and at the end of the lecture I will be presenting some case histories based upon a mixture of these approaches.'

2 Frames   These are statements which delineate the beginning and ending of topics and subtopics – 'let's turn now to the uses of chemotherapy. By chemotherapy I mean . . .'

3 Foci   These are statements which highlight and emphasize key points. 'The basic pharmacological principle underlying chemotherapy is this [pause].'

4 Links   These are statements that link the sections of the lecture together.They may also link the lecture to the experience, previously acquired knowledge, and observations of the audience. 'So you can see that chemotherapy is often as aggressive and invasive as the older techniques of excision and radiotherapy.' It should be noted that frames are a subset of links (see Activity 3.5).

Lecturers' advice to colleagues who are new to lecturing (Brown and Bakhtar 1983) also included suggestions to improve clarity. In descending rank order these were:

● Speak clearly, use pauses, don't go too fast.

- Plan, prepare, and structure to give a clear, simple (not simplistic) view of a topic.
- Make it understandable and clarify key points.
- Observe student reactions.
- Do not try to cover everything.
- Check you understand your own material.

In addition, repetition and paraphrasing of key points helps students to grasp the main points. The same information expressed in different forms can trigger ideas and associations that aid understanding. Since students learn in different ways, the greater the number of ways a lecturer presents key points the greater the chance that a higher proportion of students will understand.

Finally, even if perfect clarity cannot be achieved, vagueness can be minimized by using names and labels more frequently than pronouns. 'It', 'this', and 'that' with an airy wave of the hand towards a blackboard is a poor substitute for the use of correct terms and precise pointing at a diagram.

Interest

There is little doubt that this is the most challenging feature of effective explaining. It is also an important long-term goal of lecturing. If a student is motivated by a lecturer's approach to a subject then he or she is likely to become self-motivated and the lecture will have an influence long after the content has been forgotten.

Three strategies can assist in the generation of interest. First, the use of gesture, eye contact, and vocal inflection can increase expressiveness. This is not to advocate the manic body language of some TV commentators but rather to suggest that if we convey our enthusiasm for a topic through language and body language then it is more likely to become infectious.

Second, the use of apt examples and analogies can generate interest – and understanding. Aptness refers to both the topic and the audience, so examples that have personal or vocational relevance are particularly appropritae. The examples provided may be positive instances of the concept or process being explained or negative instances – what the thing is not. Such negative examples delineate the boundaries of a definition and so assist clarity as well as enhance interest. 'Rogue' cases can also stimulate intellectual curiosity as indeed can puzzles or problems (see Activity 3.7).

The order in which examples are presented is of importance. The usual order is positive, negative, and 'rogue'. In a study of explaining in biology (Brown and Armstrong 1984) it was found that when ideas which were new to a group were being explained then an inductive pattern of several examples leading to a definition or generalization was most effective. When the ideas were relatively familiar to the group the use of the deductive pattern of statement of principle followed by examples was more effective. The reasons for this finding are not hard to discern. Introducing new knowledge requires activation of examples already known so that the new connections may be made. When ideas are already known the deductive pattern restructures the existing knowledge of the students.

The third approach is to use an appropriate mode of explaining. Three modes have been observed: the narrative, the anecdotal, and the conceptual. In the narrative mode that lecturer explains an event or a set of research findings in the form of a personal story. In the anecdotal mode the lecturer uses humorous stories, perhaps drawn from his or her experience, to illustrate and make key points. In the conceptual mode, the lecturer provides a series of principles or facts in a logical order.The narrative mode is most likely to capture interest but it may not provide clear, precise knowledge. The anecdotal mode can be very entertaining but it is not always informative. The conceptual mode is likely to be clear but less interesting. A mixture of the three, beginning with the narrative, using anecdotes appropriately, and ending with a conceptual summary is likely to be the most effective way of generating interest and understanding (see Figure 3.2).

Figure 3.2 Suggestions for generating interest

---

1 Show your own interest/commitment to the topic.
2 Think of and use examples, analogies, metaphors, and models which are apt for the audience and the topic.
3 If the material is unfamiliar begin with several examples.
4 Use a mixture of modes of explaining, but particularly the narrative mode.
5 Play on the intellectual curiosity of the audience through the use of puzzles, problems, and questions.

Persuasion

The art of persuasion is akin to generating interest. Some lecturers might argue that persuasion is not part of their work. The facts or ideas will speak for themselves. Such a viewpoint is naive. The order and quality of presentation do have an effect upon an audience so you might as well be aware of the processes and use them to good effect. Furthermore there are contexts in which persuasive explaining may be necessary. For example you may wish to introduce a new approach, advocate an interpretation of conflicting theories, or challenge existing, and hitherto authoritative, assumptions. These tasks can occur in any subject. Nor is persuasion confined to lecturing. But the mode of persuading in, for example, research supervision may well be different from the mode used in lecturing.

In lecturing, persuasion depends in large measure upon the use of rhetoric. Atkinson (1984) provides an analysis of rhetorical devices used by politicians. Of these the most relevant to lecturing are the use of pairs of contrasting statements, the use of triple statements, pausing before important points, and summarizing with punch lines.

Studies of attitude change (e.g. Zimbardo, Erbeson, and Maslach 1977) conducted in a wide variety of contexts suggest some basic principles of persuasive explaining. These are summarized in Figure 3.3.

Figure 3.3 Persuasive explaining

---

1 Know your audience and estimate what kinds of arguments may be appealing and interesting.
2 People are more likely to listen to you and accept your suggestions if you are perceived as credible, trustworthy, and have expertise.
3 When there are arguments in favour and against a procedure, it is usually better to present both sides.
4 If you have to stress risks in a procedure, don't overdo the arousal of fear.
5 Say what experts or expert groups do when faced with the problem you are discussing.
6 If the problem is complex for the group, you should draw the conclusions – or give them time for discussion. If it is not too complex, let the group members draw their own conclusions.
7 If the suggestions you are making are likely to be challenged by others, describe their views and show how they may be wrong.
8 If the task you are asking a group to perform is complex, prepare them for the likelihood of failure. Never say a task is easy. Rather, say it may not be easy at first.
9 If a task is threatening, admit it and describe how they might feel and what they can do to reduce their anxiety.

COMPONENT SKILLS OF LECTURING

Using audio-visual aids

The main use of audio-visual aids in lectures is to improve clarity in explaining. It follows that visual aids should be easy to see and audio aids easy to hear. The point is obvious but, alas, not always followed in pratice. Aids may also sustain attention and enhance interest in a topic providing they are well presented and colourful. Effective use of audio-visual aids has been shown to improve learning in secondary school pupils (Turney 1983) and in higher education (Kozma, Belle, and Williams 1978). However the effectiveness of a particular medium depends not so much upon the medium *per se* but upon how it is used (Clark and Salomon 1986). Merely using a video-recording instead of a blackboard will not in itself enhance learning.

how it is used (Clark and Salomon 1986). Merely using a video-recording instead of a blackboard will not in itself enhance learning.

The good reasons for using audio-visual aids are associated with the process of learning. Lecturers provide linear sequences of information particularly in oral lectures. Students are given bits of information which they are required to deal with sequentially. Yet many topics have networks of connections which might be exemplified better by diagrams or maps. Networks or maps of information based on key nodal points may be a more accurate analogy for the way the brain works than coded computer tape (Lindsay and Norman 1972). Ideas which are linked through visual symbols are also likely to be retained in the long-term memory. It is therefore worth spending a little time thinking out a visual presentation for key concepts, relationships, and processes. The effort may well deepen your own understanding of a topic as well as providing meaningful connections for your students (Activity 3.9).

Audio-visual aids may be used (as the handout and blackboard summary often are) to confirm and reinforce the main points of a lecture, as an explanatory device in their own right, as an exemplar, or as a stimulus for thinking and discussion. However, for aids to be effective some basic guidelines must be followed:

1 Illustrations, diagrams, and summaries must be simple, brief and readable from the back of the class. If the illustrations are important, give the students time to look at them and, if necessary, time to copy them. If the illustrations are available in a book give the full reference. Don't feel that you have to speak while the audience is looking at the illustrations; indeed if you want them to look intensively, tell them what to look for and then shut up!

2 Handouts should be brief and well structured. They should contain key references and, if necessary, definitions of new terms. Lengthy handouts become substitutes for lectures, not adjuncts. It is probably best to give the students a few minutes to read

through the handout before you start lecturing. If the handout is likely to pre-empt the excitement of the lecture then distribute it afterwards. Many experienced teachers assert that 'skeletal' handouts, which require completion by students during the lecture, are better than comprehensive abstracts (Brown and Tomlinson 1980).

3 Slides, audio-recordings, films, and videotapes can be effective ways of maintaining interest and attention and varying the nature of input. But their excessive use may induce sleep. You should indicate clearly which features of the material to look for. If possible, pose questions for the students to answer while they are watching, give them an opportunity for brief discussion afterwards, and then summarize the main points and link them to the relevant parts of the lecture. These guidelines are important – without them a potentially valuable learning experience can be reduced to the level of home movies (Brown 1985).

When these guidelines are not followed the result can be confusion confounded (see Figure 3.4).

Figure 3.4 Next slide please

'I thought that in the eight minutes I've got I'd bring you up to date on what our group has been doing in the last year; in a sense this is a progress report and updates the paper we gave here last year; I won't go over the nomenclature again; could I have the first slide please – oh, I think you must have someone else's box – mine is the grey one with my name on the top, no, wait a minute, not my name, whose name was it now? Ah yes, you've found it; there's a red spot on the top right hand side of each slide – that is the side that becomes the bottom left when you project it. OK, you've got it now, let's have a look, no, that's the last slide not the first, yes, now you've got the right one but it's on its side, what about the red dot? There are two? Well anyway turn it through ninety degrees, no, the other way, yes now we're there, perhaps we could have the lights off. Well I'm sorry there are probably too many words on this slide, and the printing is a bit thin; can you read it at the back? You can't; well I'd better read it out; no I won't, it's in the paper which should be published within a month or so, and anyone who wants I'll give a preprint to afterwards. Anyway, for those who can read it, this slide is a block diagram of the publication process we used and before I go any further I should mention that there are a couple of misprints: on the third row, fourth box from the left, well, of course that's the second box from the right, if you can read it, it says alkaline, now that should be acidic; also you can perhaps see the word 'mebmrane', that should of course be 'membrane'; now if I can have a look at the next slide – now which one is this? Ah, yes it's the scatter diagram. I haven't marked the quantities but we are plotting

concentration against particle size; if I remember rightly this has been
normalised; perhaps I could have the lights for a moment to check in
the text, yes, here we are, well it doesn't actually say – we could work it
out but it's probably not worth the time, so if I could have the lights off,
let's look at the plot; well, I think you can see a sort of linear
relationship – there's a fair bit of scatter, of course, but I think the data
are at least suggestive; perhaps if I held up a pointer you could see the
relationship more clearly – I expect there's a pointer around
somewhere, no I won't need the lights. Yes here it is. Now I can see the
trend and there's just the hint of another trend running sub-parallel to
it through this other cluster of points, you may see that more clearly if I
slide the pointer across to the other – no, I wasn't saying next slide, just
that I would slide the pointer; anyway now the next slide is up let's
keep it on the screen. Now this is the sort of evidence on which the data
in the last slide were based; this is a thin section – it could take just a bit
of focusing – yes, that's better. It's difficult to get the whole slide in
focus at once, now the scale is, well that bar is one micron long. Hang
on, what am I saying? It's ten microns long – oh dear, the chairman is
giving me the two-minute warning. It's difficult to give you a clear
picture of this work in only eight minutes, but let's plough on, what was
I saying? Ah yes, the bar is ten microns long, now if we turn to the next
slide, please, this is the result of a chemical analysis of the dark region
that is near the centre of that thin section, is it possible to go back a
slide? Well not to worry, you can see in the analysis how dominant –
sorry what was that? Oh deviation, no it can't be, it must be the
standard error of the mean – oh dear, the chairman says my time is up.
Can I beg half a minute – are there any more slides? Really? Well let's
skip the next two, now this one is pretty important. It brings together
several of the threads that you've probably been able to discern
running through this talk, but rather than go through it in detail
perhaps I should have the lights up and just put up one or two key
numbers on the blackboard – the chairman says there's no chalk, well
it's all in the paper I was mentioning. Anyway perhaps I've been able
to give you the gist of what we've been doing. I guess that's all I've got
time for.'

(Reprinted, by kind permission of the editor, from *Nature* 272, 27 April 1978: 743)

Varying student activities

It does not follow that because you have a lecture class for one hour
that you have to talk for the whole hour. By varying student
activities during a lecture you can renew their attention, generate
interest, provide opportunities for students to think, and obtain
some feedback on their understanding.

Some lecturers react to this suggestion by saying that they do not have time to waste on student activities in lectures and that, anyway, students will not participate. The answer to the first objection is that what matters in lectures is what the students learn – and what encourages them to continue learning. The answer to the second objection is that students can be encouraged to participate. After a little practice most students adapt willingly to participative methods of learning in lectures. Some lecturers are also worried about losing control if they introduce activities into a lecture. Provided that the class is told what the signals are for the beginning and end of the activity there are unlikely to be any problems.

Buzz groups

A simple and effective method of involving students is known as 'buzz groups'. The lecturer sets a problem or a discussion topic and invites the students to form groups of three or four who discuss or solve the problem set. The solution to the problem or a summary of discussion points can then be shown to the class on a transparency or blackboard. Alternatively some buzz groups can be invited to offer their solution or discussion points.

Buzz groups take very little time. They give students an activity and a break so they return to listening and note-taking with renewed concentration. They can be used to link one section of a lecture to another and as a check on understanding. They encourage students to discuss and think. Students are also more likely to answer questions in a large audience if they have checked out their answers with a few fellow-students first.

Other suggestions for varying student activities are given in Figure 3.5. Bligh (1980) and Gibbs, Habeshaw, and Habeshaw (1983) provide further suggestions.

Figure 3.5 Some ways of varying student activity in lectures

1 Set a question or problem to be discussed in buzz groups.
2 Show a video clip – with instructions on what to look for.
3 Demonstrate a task – with instructions on what to look for.
4 Set a brief multiple choice questionnaire.
5 Ask the students to frame questions in relation to data or to make estimates (e.g. percentages of various crimes, costs of social services, range of accuracy of instruments). They can compare their ideas in buzz groups. Then show them the correct figures.
6 Solve a problem collectively.
7 Ask the students to discuss briefly (in groups of two or three) a research design or set of findings.

8 Ask the students to invent examples and compare them with those of
  another student.
9 Ask the students to consider briefly likely advantages and disadvantages, or strengths and weaknesses, of a procedure or theory. Then
  outline the advantages and disadvantages so they can compare their
  views.

All of the above are methods of getting students to observe and think in
lectures as well as varying what they do.

Varying student activities in lectures is a useful strategy but like
all teaching strategies it can lose its effect if it is overused. Hence it is
worth providing some lectures with student activities and some
lectures which rely on other strategies to promote understanding
and motivation.

Comparing and contrasting

Comparing and contrasting two or more viewpoints requires the
lecturer to identify and describe essential similarities and differences,
or advantages and disadvantages. The skill is a complex one that
requires careful preparation and the strength of purpose to keep to
the chosen path. These are two approaches that you can use: the
theme or topic can be divided into subsections and the similarities
and differences within each subsection noted, or you can describe
each viewpoint in turn and then summarize the similarities and
differences.

Comparing and contrasting is challenging for both lecturer and
students. It is easy to confuse and to be confused. Building up a
summary on the blackboard or overhead transparency as you lecture
helps to reduce the likelihood of confusion and keeps you on course.
In the introduction it is advisable to spell out clearly what you
propose to do and to indicate briefly the criteria or themes of the
comparison. The method is particularly useful for showing students
how to tackle comparative problems. It is also useful for drawing
together and comparing different approaches or theories that may
have been presented during a course.

Openings
(see Activity 3.10)

The opening stages of a lecture or lecture topic are crucial. Not only
are you creating impressions (unintentionally as well as intentionally)
but also you are providing a framework in which attitudes to a topic

and to learning are created. First impressions count. One study (Kohlan 1973) showed that the first impressions of lecturers accounted for two-thirds of subsequent impressions of the same lecturers.

Effective openings are based upon three simple but important principles:

1 Gain and hold attention.
2 Establish a relationship with the lecture class.
3 Indicate the content and structure of the lecture.

There are many ways of implementing each of these principles. An obvious way of gaining attention is to stand still, look around, and say 'I'm ready to start now'. Some lecturers suggest that the first few sentences should be an unimportant preamble to give students time to tune in to the content. Others suggest switching on the overhead projector and showing a transparency of the structure of the lecture.

Establishing a relationship with a lecture class is of obvious importance in the early stages of a course or a one-off lecture. Introducing yourself and indicating that you know something about the audience's interests is not only courteous but also likely to gain attention. If eye contact and rapport are established at this stage a lecture class is more likely to appraise a lecturer as interesting and accessible even if, in the remainder of the lecture, eye contact may be infrequent. (Despite what some texts say, it really is difficult and counterproductive to attempt to maintain frequent eye contact *and* use a blackboard!)

Giving an indication of content and structure provides students with a framework for note-taking and learning, reduces uncertainty, and increases their confidence in the lecturer's professional skills.

Endings

The skill of closing a lecture or lecture topic is often neglected yet evidence suggests that summarizing and linking helps recall and understanding (Dunkin and Biddle 1974). In essence a summary should emphasize the key points, show the links within the topic and, if appropriate, between the topic and other knowledge and experience. The summary may be provided on a prepared transparency or handout or built up on a blackboard.

Some lecturers ask what they should do if students close their notebooks (or even depart!) as soon as they hear the words 'in summary'. In the early stages of a lecture course you can stress that the summaries are important, and then ensure that they are. Alternatively you can set a 'summary exercise' as a student activity.

In some lecture courses, particularly in science and engineering, lectures are not unitary events. A lecture topic may spill over into the next lecture in the series. Openings and endings of this type of lecture are then different from openings and endings of lecture topics. However, the same principles apply although the opening and ending of a lecture topic should be provided in more detail than the opening and ending of individual lectures. But it is still important to end on time. Coffee breaks, and time to get to the next lecture, are appreciated by students as well as lecturers.

PRESENTING INFORMATION

Coverage of a topic is the most commonly expressed goal of lecturing. Some of the advice on clarity in explaining is particularly relevant here (see p. 21). The advice suggests that even if coverage is the primary goal then some attention to understanding and motivation is necessary. So the skills of opening and closing, using audio-visual aids, comparing and contrasting, and explaining are relevant. But the essential ingredient of presenting information is structure. Hence the importance of planning (see Preparing lectures, p. 35), of the use of the four structuring moves – signposts, frames, foci, and links – which were described on pp. 21–2, and the structure of the lecture.

Three common methods of structuring lectures are described by Bligh (1972). These are the classical, the problem-centred, and the sequential. Sometimes all three may be used within one lecture.

The classical structure

The lecture is divided into broad sections. Each broad section is divided into separate subsections, and, perhaps, each subsection into smaller units. Each of the subsections may be what we call a key because it unlocks understanding. It will contain main points, and perhaps examples, qualifications, elaborations, reservations, and a brief summary.

The classical method is by far the most common form of lecture structure (Brown and Bakhtar 1983). It appears to be easy to plan, it is probably the easiest to take notes from, and it is particularly useful for the outlining of topics. Thus it can be used with topics as diverse as renal functions or Johnson's views of the metaphysical poets.

A variation on the classical method is the iterative-classical method. In this case the lecture is again divided into broad sections, but within each section there is a similar structure. For example a lecturer in medicine might consider four related diseases by examining: 'Presenting symptoms', 'Signs evident on examination',

'Provisional diagnosis', 'Planned management', and 'Statement of prognosis' for each disease in turn. If this method is to be used it is helpful for students to be told so at the beginning of the lecture. It is also helpful if you do not deviate from the iterative loop or, if you do, that a signpost statement warns the students that you are doing so.

Good use of the classical method is not as easy as it may first appear. First, you must have a good grasp of what you propose to tackle – and ignore. Second, you need to frame each main section clearly. Third, you need to indicate when you are beginning and ending each section; this may be done with a blackboard summary, an overhead transparency, or by verbal markers such as: 'So [pause] the main point is . . . . Now let's turn to the next subsection on . . .'. Without these simple signposts or frames the classical structure can easily become a confusing mish-mash.

One further pitfall for the unwary is boredom. Because it is fairly simple to list facts it is easy to grind on relentlessly, generating ennui rather than presenting information. Thus you need to use apt examples and illustrations, and to present them in a lively and interesting way.

Problem-centred structure

This is useful for examining views on, and solutions to, such problems as: the body–mind problem; the relationship between truth and meaning; what is history?; definitions of limits; changing processes of manufacturing electronic components.

All problem-centred lectures contain a statement of a problem; then various solutions each followed by an evaluation of that solution – its strengths and weaknesses. If the indications are stated explicitly, confusion can be minimized.

The solutions may be presented in the form of keys as in the classical method. Figure 3.6 shows an outline of the problem-centred approach. A necessary, but not sufficient, condition of success is a clear, brief statement of the problem. Without this the structure of the lecture crumbles. The problem-centred method also requires selection of the main alternative solutions and clear statements of the main points for or against each solution that is considered. The approach can be intellectually stimulating, particularly if it is combined with expressed enthusiasm for the problem and with the use of rhetorical devices such as, 'So, Pasteur demonstrated to his own satisfaction that . . . . Now [pause] some of you may think he was right. But was he? Let's take a look at what Koch had to say . . .'.

But the problem-centred method is not only potentially intellectually stimulating, it is also easy to fudge. The most common errors

Figure 3.6 A problem-centred structure

Topic: Methods of analysing and studying human stress

1 What is stress?
   Three approaches:

   ● Responses to environment – examples.
   ● Stimulus characteristics of 'anxious' environment – examples.
   ● Lack of 'fit' between person and environment – examples.

2 Research based on responses.
   Response-based models; physiological response; psychological response.
   Weakness of models and approach.
3 Research based on stimuli.
   Stimuli-based models; the engineering analogy of stress and data.
   Characteristics of stressful stimuli; weakness of models and approach.
4 Research based on interaction models.
   Interaction model.
   Examples of explanatory power of model – stress and the work situation; stress and diabetes.
   Advantages and disadvantages of model.
5 Summary and conclusion.

---

are: unclear, excessively lengthy statements of the problem; confused statements for and against a solution; the introduction of several asides; and frequent cross-referencing to alternative solutions. If you use this method you should stick to the main lines of enquiry. It is also helpful for students if you summarize at the end of each alternative and again at the end of the lecture.

Sequential structure

This consists of a series of linked statements which usually lead to a conclusion. This method is used in historical accounts, which may be given in virtually all subjects: mathematics, science, and medicine as well as history and literature. It is important to highlight and emphasize the main points; a lecturer who merely recites the research literature in chronological order without indicating the importance of various contributions is likely to be neither interesting nor illuminating.

The sequential method is the common one in mathematically based topics. In these subjects it looks easy. In fact this is the most difficult method to make meaningful, and it is the easiest to get wrong. To make it meaningful you have to ensure that the steps are within the students' grasp. You may also have to summarize the main steps and procedures frequently. Making it interesting can also be difficult; to do this you can show the relevance of the proofs or procedures to other topics and problems, or indicate their historical origins, their applications, and even their elegance.

GENERATING INTEREST

This skill has been discussed under 'Explaining', p. 19. If the primary goal is generating interest then you should pay particular attention to the opening sequence, use high quality aids, and lively, perhaps intriguing examples. A narrative approach interleaved with a problem-centred structure is likely to reveal your own enthusiasm for a topic – itself a motivator – and play on the intellectual curiosity of the audience. It is worth emphasizing that interest will be short-lived unless there is some substance and intellectual stimulus in the lecture. If students want to rush away and read the texts you have been discussing or try out with renewed vigour some approaches to a topic, then you can feel modestly satisfied that you have achieved this goal.

If the primary goal is persuasion to a viewpoint or the adoption of a new approach, then it is particularly important to establish rapport with an audience – so you must know and state something about the audience including any relevant recent experiences. 'I know you have already had a busy, exhausting day . . . so what I propose to do is . . .'. It is also important *not* to use a bevy of highly sophisticated aids in the early stages lest the audience is swamped with too much information. Later on in the lecture you might use stimulating aids and quotations. Audio-recordings of other people's views and comments are often a useful way of conveying feelings and attitudes. The use of 'before' and 'after' audio interviews can be very effective.

A temptation when attempting to persuade is to go on for too long. It is much better to take less time than that allotted rather than more.

PREPARING LECTURES

The essential skill of effective lecturing is preparation not presentation. Obviously presentation is important but without a clear, co-herent lecture structure which emphasizes key points and examples, a presentation may have a short-lived effect. Further, if we know our own strengths and weaknesses we can take steps to minimize weaknesses during the preparatory stage. (We might also practise strategies to overcome weaknesses.) For example a common error in lecturing is covering too much ground too quickly. Since most people speak at about sixty to seventy words a minute it follows that even if you wrote down every word you were going to say, then you should have no more than about ten pages of typescript (3,000–3,500 words).

Lecture preparation was found by many new lecturers at Nottingham and Newcastle universities – and no doubt other universities too – to be much more time-consuming and frustrating than they had anticipated. Hence we were asked to provide a workshop on lecture preparation. What follows is based upon that workshop which many lecturers, both new and experienced, found useful.

Ten steps of preparing a lecture can be identified but, in reality, you will probably zig-zag or backtrack during the process. However too much backtracking is inefficient.

Step 1   What is the topic?

The topic may have been given to you, laid down in the syllabus, or left for you to decide upon.

Step 2   Free associate

Write down any ideas, facts, and, particularly, questions which spring to mind. A useful trick is to put the topic in the centre of a blank page and jot down the ideas, facts, and questions as they come to you (see Figure 3.7). Try and group them as you go along and then cross out those that seem irrelevant for the particular audience you have in mind and ring those that seem important.

Step 3   State a working title

Look at the points you have ringed and decide upon a working title. This may be in the form of a statement such as 'The potential uses of magnetic nuclear resonance in medicine' or in the form of a question such as 'Was unemployment in the 1930s a political issue?'

Step 4   Analyse the 'hidden' variables in the title

Look at the working title and analyse the key factors or variables hidden in it (see Activity 3.13).

Step 5   Prepare a rough structure of the lecture

This structure should be done on no more than one page. At this stage you should, if time allows, stop and read. So far, there has been

Figure 3.7 Beginnings of a free association

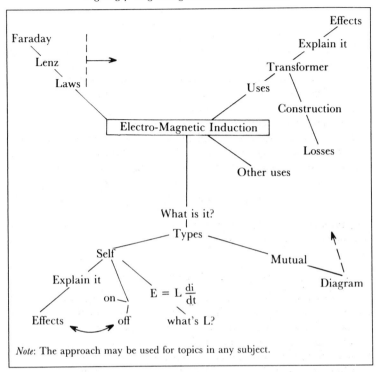

Note: The approach may be used for topics in any subject.

no mention of reading. Indeed steps 1 to 5 may be summarized as 'Think before you read'. A common error in lecture preparation is to read so much that you become overwhelmed and still unsure about what you are going to say – so you are tempted to read more and the cycle continues.

Step 6   Directed reading

Steps 1 to 5 provide direction for your reading. Read only the relevant sections from a few texts or articles. Look at the headings and layout to see if they suggest any ways of structuring your lecture. As you read and take notes, jot down any other suggestions, questions, or important areas that you may have missed earlier.

Step 7   Structure the lecture

Set out the lecture, preferably in note form, leaving plenty of space
between major sections and clear headings. Make sure that structuring moves (signposts, frames, foci, links) and examples are built
in. Prepare the audio-visual aids and any handouts and activities
that you are going to use. Summarize the main points of the lecture
on one sheet. (This might also be a useful handout.) On the same
sheet list the resources needed (slide projector, slides, OHP, spare
transparencies, etc). Some lecturers read aloud from a complete
script. Such a procedure is not recommended for it can lack credibil-
ity, it is often difficult to take notes from, and it minimizes contact
with an audience. Often such scripts are more like elegant reviews
than an oral discourse. If you are so nervous that you feel you cannot
depart from a script then the script should be written in spoken
language rather than said in written language. (The use of transparencies and slides can act as useful prompts for a lecturer who is
afraid of losing track.)

Step 8   Check the opening and ending

Examine the opening and ending of the lecture carefully to see if it
links clearly with the main body of the lecture. Similarly check that
the ending draws the themes of the lecture together. Often a good
opening to a lecture (or article) cannot be written until you know
what you are going to say and do. Figure 3.8 sets out a check-list
that can help at this stage. A little mental rehearsal of the opening,
the main points, and the conclusion is also useful.

Figure 3.8 Structuring a lecture

Here is a check-list of questions that you could use when you have
prepared your lecture:

1 What are the central questions of your lecture?
2 What do you expect the students to learn or understand from your
   lecture?
3 What lecture methods will you use?
4 Will the opening be clear and interesting?
5 Are the sections of the lecture clearly organized and clearly linked?
6 Are the main keys clear and accurate and linked?
7 Are your examples and illustrations apt?
8 Will any reservations and qualifications you plan to make be clear
   and apt?

9 Will your section summaries and final summary be clear and coherent?
10 What activities will the students have to carry out in your lecture?
11 What possible weaknesses are there likely to be in your presentation?
12 How do you plan to combat these possible weaknesses?
13 Are any audio-visual resources you might need going to be available?
14 Will the group of students that you are going to lecture to understand your lecture?
15 How do you plan to find this out?

Step 9   Give the lecture

Check the equipment is working before the lecture. It is normal to be a little anxious just before a lecture or during the early stages. Once this is accepted, you can, paradoxically, relax about being anxious. Give the lecture. Talk to the audience of students, rather than at them, and watch for their reactions during the lecture. If you are particularly anxious about timing, rehearse the lecture. About 35 minutes' audio-recording in private is equivalent to 50 minutes of lecturing to a live audience.

Step 10   Reflect and note

Soon after a lecture, when the adrenalin flow has subsided, think about the lecture and note down any changes, omissions, or amendments that should be made before giving the lecture again.

Lecturing can be a stressful experience – particularly in the early years of your career. While the anxiety and stress can never be eliminated, it can be minimized by following the steps, modified if necessary, indicated here. Furthermore by following these steps you are likely to enjoy the intellectual satisfaction of having given a good lecture.

EVALUATING LECTURES

The main purpose of evaluating lectures, or any other form of teaching, is to improve them.

It is often said that you cannot evaluate lecturing or any other form of teaching but you can evaluate research, by counting research publications, grants awarded, and peer evaluation. So we often do not even try to evaluate teaching even though there is a wide range of methods available (Elton 1984) which are at least as reliable and valid as those used customarily to evaluate research.

Where evaluation of lectures differs from evaluating articles is that lectures are a transient, live experience – more akin to musical performance than music scores. None the less there are ways of evaluating lectures, given that the goal is to improve lecturing. Here are a few suggestions:

Student learning

As indicated in Chapter 2, the notes that students take during your lectures provide a powerful measure of your skills. From time to time it may be worth borrowing a sample of your students' notes and comparing them with your own. Examination results clearly depend on many factors besides lectures but consistently poor or outstanding results can be useful indicators. If you wish to measure student learning from a particular lecture or set of lectures then you can devise your own tests, perhaps of multiple choice items. These could be used during a lecture to check understanding and to stimulate interest in the next stage of the lecture. You can include in a test items which require students to recall key information, identify essential principles, and apply information and principles to solve a problem.

Student reactions

These are based on the principle that if you want to know if a restaurant is good you ask the customers, not the cook or proprietor. Student reactions can be gathered casually in conversation or, more

---

Figure 3.9 Example of a simple rating schedule

Please rate the lectures on this course on the following items. On the whole the lectures were:

	Agree strongly	Agree slightly	Disagree slightly	Disagree strongly
Well-structured	4	3	2	I
Interesting	4	3	2	I
Easy to take notes from	4	3	2	I
Thought-provoking	4	3	2	I
Relevant to course	4	3	2	I

Comments:
Thank you for your help.

Figure 3.10 Example of a rating schedule

Please rate the lecture you have just received on the items below. Please indicate the following:

Subject .... Topic ....
Year (1st, 2nd, 3rd, etc) .... Today's date ....

Give your reaction to each separate item on the six-point scales below. Do not omit any item.

6 = very highly favourable   3 = slightly unfavourable
5 = highly favourable   2 = unfavourable
4 = favourable   1 = extremely unfavourable

Put a ring round the number which most clearly describes your view on that item.

1 The lecture was clearly structured	6	5	4	3	2	1
2 The lecturer indicated when he or she had come to the end of a major section	6	5	4	3	2	1
3 The main points given were clear and understandable	6	5	4	3	2	1
4 The minor points and reservations given were understandable and clear	6	5	4	3	2	1
5 The examples given were relevant	6	5	4	3	2	1
6 The examples given were interesting	6	5	4	3	2	1
7 The pace (speed) of the lecture was right for me	6	5	4	3	2	1
8 The amount of material covered was right for me	6	5	4	3	2	1
9 The lecture was clearly audible	6	5	4	3	2	1
10 The blackboard and other aids were used effectively	6	5	4	3	2	1
11 The lecture seemed well prepared	6	5	4	3	2	1
12 The lecture was well presented	6	5	4	3	2	1
13 The lecture held my attention most of the time	6	5	4	3	2	1
14 The lecture was interesting	6	5	4	3	2	1
15 The lecturer usually looked at and talked to the lecture group and not to the furniture fittings	6	5	4	3	2	1
16 The lecturer summarized the main points of the lecture effectively	6	5	4	3	2	1

Figure 3.11 Explanations evaluated

ORIENTATION

1 Does your opening gain the group's attention   Yes/No
2 Does it establish rapport with the group?   Yes/No
3 Does it indicate what you intend to explain?   Yes/No

THE KEY POINTS

1 Are your key points clearly expressed?   Yes/No
2 Are your examples apt and interesting?   Yes/No
3 Are your qualifications of the key points clearly stated?   Yes/No
4 Is each key point clearly summarized?   Yes/No
5 Are the beginnings and ends of the key points clearly
   indicated?   Yes/No

THE SUMMARY

1 Does your summary bring together the main points?   Yes/No
2 Are your conclusions clearly stated?   Yes/No
3 Do you come to an effective stop?   Yes/No

PRESENTATION

1 Can the group hear and see you?   Yes/No
2 Do you use eye contact to involve but not to threaten?   Yes/No
3 Do you use audio-visual techniques effectively?   Yes/No
4 Are you fluent verbally?   Yes/No
5 Is your vocabulary appropriate to the group?   Yes/No
6 Do you make use of pauses and silences?   Yes/No
7 Do you vary your intonation?   Yes/No
8 Is the organization of your material clear?   Yes/No
9 Do you avoid vagueness and ambiguities?   Yes/No
10 Is the presentation as interesting as you can make it?   Yes/No

Any 'No' answer indicates that your explanation is not as good as it might be – but everybody gives quite a lot of 'No' answers if they're honest!

---

preferably, systematically through the use of check-lists, questionnaires, or rating schedules. Questions on structure and presentation are more likely to yield useful feedback than on likes and dislikes. A space for open comments is useful. There are likely to be wide variations in responses so if you use rating schedules you should inspect standard deviations as well as means. Examples of rating schedules are given in Figures 3.9, 3.10, and 3.11 above.

Peer evaluation

Pairs of lecturers or groups of lecturers can undertake evaluation of each other's lectures. An important step in this process is to agree upon a set of criteria. The method is valuable but it is important that the structure of the lecture is explored, not just the content, and that observations and written comments are constructive.

Self-evaluation

This is based upon recall and reflection. It may also include evidence gathered from your fellow lecturers and from student reactions and learning. A variant is to conduct self-evaluation based on video feedback. Check-lists and questions are useful aids to viewing video-recordings. Video-recordings based upon 'micro-lectures' are often more useful and economical for exploring your skills in structuring material, presentation, and timing than excerpts from a lecture.

SUMMARY

This chapter has presented the basic skills of lecturing. The goals of lecturing may be coverage, understanding, and motivation. Clarity and interest are the key variables and these are also central to the skill of explaining. Clarity may be enhanced by careful preparation, the effective use of audio-visual aids, and the use of structuring moves. Interest is dependent largely upon lecturer expressiveness, upon the use of examples that are apt for the audience, and the topic. An essential skill of lecturing is lecture-preparation. All of these skills require practice and feedback and all can be learned and improved – if you so desire.

ACTIVITIES

3.1 Repeat Activity 2.5 but on a different topic. Reverse the order of presenters. The check-list given in Figure 3.11 provides discussion points. In addition it is useful to discuss in what ways the structure and presentation have been improved or changed.

3.2 Draw up a list of good and bad tactics of explaining. What are the essential characteristics of effective explaining in your subject?

3.3 Invent three levels of brief explanations suitable for:

- An intelligent 7-year-old
- An intelligent 12-year-old
- An intelligent adult

The question to be explained is:
Why do people drown underwater?
Compare your explanations with those of a few colleagues.

3.4 Now choose a topic or question in your own subject and prepare three levels of explanation of increasing sophistication. Discuss your explanations with a few colleagues.

3.5 Which of the four structuring moves – signposts, frames, foci, and links – do you tend to neglect?

3.6 Read through the two tapescripts which follow. Decide which is the better explanation and why. Each tapescript is divided into sections marked by a line drawn across the page. Re-read each tapescript. Decide what was the central question the explainer claimed he was explaining and then look at each section and try to decide what he explained in each of the sections. Write down the questions and statements for each section and the question the explainer claimed to be explaining. Did the explainer explain what he intended to explain? How can the order and content of the sections be improved?

Compare your analyses and comments with those of a few colleagues.

Tapescript 1

Er – the – the title of my talk today is why nude mice are important to biologists.

Okay

Well, the thymus as most of you probably know is – er – a large – er – organ that's located in the – em – upper part of the chest, it's referred to as a lymphoid organ because most of the cell – cells processed by the organ – most of the constituent cells in this – in the thymus are lymphocytes – a specific cell type. Its importance lies in the fact that lymphoid cells processed by this – by this organ – erm – are cells which control the mechanism of graft rejection this is important in transplantation. Erm – they also have a specific role in immune responses – erm – and the role here is one of control – it's the thymocytes, the lymphoid cells rising from this organ which determine the pattern of an immune response. Now, one way of studying the importance of such an organ is to remove it and see what happens in its absence. So the surgical ablation of thymectomy as it's known in this particular instance has become quite a widespread procedure normally combined with irradiation – er – irradiation of sufficient intensity to destroy – erm – other lymphocytes present in the body since lymphocytes are particularly sensitive to irradiation – erm. The procedure doesn't unduly affect other cell types but – erm – in particular instances where irradiation has to be given of – erm – a lethal quantity of irradiation has to be given then the – erm – problem is that the – erm – animal has then to be reconstituted with marrow cells and kept on a variety of antibiotics to prevent infection since lymphocytes have such a – a – an important role-function in – erm – in immune responses an animal deprived of these lymphocytes then has to be kept artificially to ensure its survival, by the administration of antibiotics and so on.

Such a mouse, anyway, is known as an immunologically deprived animal and it's an extremely valuable – erm – it's an extremely valuable – erm – animal to the biologists because it provides a sort of tool whereby the role of other cell types can be assessed. You've destroyed the lymphocytes in – in this particular animal you can then re-inject other – erm – specific cell types and see how they function in – when various stimuli are given to them. Organs, for instance, can be – erm – transplanted back into the animal and their role can be assessed in the absence of other interfering factors.

So where does the nude mouse come into all this? Well, in 1966 – erm – Flanagan first described a creature, "the nude mouse is a homozygous recessive condition", and I think one ought to explain here using the blackboard – erm – the nude condition – erm – is governed by a single gene and since each gene is – is – is represented by two in each cell of the body you have three possible combinations. You have a d-a plus, plus combination [writes on board] this is known as the wild type.

Tapescript 2

The title of my talk is why nude mice are important to biologists.

The term the "nude mouse" is used to describe a strain of mouse which arose by mutation from normal laboratory mice – um. It's a condition which is characterized by two main features. These are, first of all, absence of hair hence the term "nude mouse", and the second feature is the absence of a thymus and it's the second property, the absence of a thymus, which is the subject of my talk. Now, the basic point is going to be summarized on this first table. So, there are two conditions possible, either the thymus is present or it's absent. Thymus present, a naturally occurring condition, leads to an ability to respond. (Perhaps I should stand on this side.) The absence of a thymus which either can be experimentally induced or it can occur naturally in the nude mouse leads to inability to respond immunologically. The question then rephrased is why is the absence of a thymus a useful condition and the answer – um – simply that animals without a thymus cannot respond immunologically and therefore such animals can be injected with foreign cells – um – and the role and the function of these cells can then be studied without the interference of immune responses.

Second table then once again summarizes this main, this – um – this statement of mine. No thymus results in no immune response therefore there is no interference from the immune response, hence injected cells can survive and can be studied. A very useful experimental situation.

Going back to the first table – um, the last point which I want to make is that the natural condition, i.e. the nude mouse, is preferable to the experimental condition – um – because in order to achieve the experimental condition complex surgery is involved. This needs to be followed by prolonged drug treatment and such a combination – um – is highly lethal to the animal resulting in mortality of – um – experimental groups.

So to summarize the, the nude mouse is an important – um – is important to biologists because – um – first of all it's easy to obtain relative to the experimentally induced condition and since it doesn't have a thymus it's a useful animal because it doesn't respond immunologically and it's this last condition which is in much demand in biological research.

3.7 Think of a principle or theme in your subject. Note a few examples or analogies of the principle or theme. If it is possible note also a few instances when the principle or theme does not work and a 'rogue' case.
    Explain the principle or theme to someone who is not in your own department.

3.8 Introducing interaction in lectures.
Set out below is a list of elements which are commonly found
in lectures. Place a tick in the first column if your lectures
contain these elements. Put a tick in the second column if you
think the elements could usefully be made interactive for your
students. 'Interactive' means that students may talk to each
other or to the lecturer.

Element	Found in my lectures	Could be interactive
1 Explanation of key principles		
2 Demonstration of proof or theorem		
3 Practical demonstration or experiment		
4 Generation of hypotheses		
5 Problem-solving		
6 Narration of sequence of events		
7 Steps in a causal explanation		
8 Comparison of theories		
9 Evaluation of theories		
10 Analysis of case histories		
11 Presentation of evidence		
12 Provision of examples		
13 Commentary on research findings		
14 Summarizing the main findings.		

Compare your views with those of a few of your colleagues.

3.9 Select a small segment of a topic which is suitable for expressing
in a simple diagram. Prepare the diagram and an explanation of
it. Draw the diagram on a transparency, blackboard, or large
sheet of paper *as you give the explanation* to the group.
The discussion afterwards should be concerned with the
clarity of the explanation and the diagram, and with how well
the lecturer maintained contact with the group.

3.10 Looking at an opening.
Read through the following transcripts of brief presentations
to first-year students then decide:

● What are the good and bad points of each?
● Which was the better one?
● How could each have been improved?

Transcript 1

[Lecturer paces up and down room]
'Freud. What a fascinating man he was. Freud. An intellectual giant who bridged the nineteenth and twentieth centuries in a way which no other man did, and indeed no other man could. Freud. A profound genius. His genius lay not in the fact that he was a founder of the school of psychoanalysis, not because he was a skilful psychotherapist, nor because he was a brilliant physiologist. No, the major contribution was that he created an absolutely [lecturer turns away from the audience] magnificent mythology of the mind.

But of course in so doing he drew upon a vast erudition, for Freud was a scholar in the western tradition. Those of you who read his collected works, his twenty-two volumes, will find in them absolutely golden nuggets of wisdom. Profound insights into the nature of Man. You will also discern the hand of Herbart, the subtleties of Spinoza, and the wisdom of that veritable sage, Plato. All these are enshrined in Freud.

Now let me not give the impression that Freud was . . .'

Transcript 2

[Lecturer stands and faces the audience]
'Good morning, ladies and gentlemen. My name is Professor McKeating of the Department of Sociology. This is, I think, your second lecture in the series on "Some modern thinkers"? Is that right? [Students in the front row nod.] Good. Well, my task today is to introduce to you the study of Marx. What I'm going to do is first describe *very* simply the core of Marxist thought. Secondly, go on to examine the assumptions and background to Marx's ideas. Thirdly, go on to tell you what some modern critics think of Marx. Towards the end of the lecture I'll give you an opportunity to talk amongst yourselves and to ask me questions about Marx. I will be giving you a brief annotated bibliography at the end of the lecture.

Well, Marx's basic idea was very simple . . .'

Compare your views of these transcripts with those of a few colleagues (see notes and comments).

3.11   What do you do in the opening stages of the first lecture that you give to a group of students? Compare your approach with those of a few colleagues. What are the principles underlying your approach to opening lectures?

3.12 How do you end your lectures? Compare your approach with those of a few colleagues. What other ways of ending lectures are there? How might your approach be improved?

3.13 From the following list of working titles of lectures choose a topic you know little or nothing about. Plan the structure of the lecture using some of the steps indicated in the chapter. Spend about five minutes on this activity and then discuss your proposed structure with a few colleagues.

1 The influence of the Catholic Revivalist Movement upon late-nineteenth-century French literature (French literature).
2 New techniques of handling non-Newtonian fluids (Chemical engineering).
3 'Tools maketh man' (Anthropology).
4 Ultrasonic scanning and the human embryo (Anatomy).
5 Physiological effects of starvation (Physiology).
6 Physiological effects of starvation (Paediatrics).
7 The Frontier Thesis (History).
8 The use of drugs in psychiatric practice (Psychiatry).
9 Some applications of optimality theory in ecosystems (Biology).

3.14 Prepare and structure a lecture you are going to give (or have given) on one of your courses. Prepare a summary sheet of the lecture. Discuss your approach with a few colleagues. Your colleagues should comment on the structure and offer suggestions and appraisals of the lecture content and structure.

3.15 You have been asked to give a public lecture on your research. Use the information given in this chapter to prepare and structure a lecture which would be interesting and understandable to an intelligent audience from diverse backgrounds. Discuss your proposed lecture with a few colleagues. If you get the opportunity, give the lecture . . . .

4

Effective small group teaching

> Discussion in a group does for thinking what testing on
> real objects does for seeing.
>
> (Abercrombie 1969)
>
> The problem of developing small group teaching depends
> as much on student training as on teacher training.
>
> (Stenhouse 1971)

Effective small group teaching is a much more challenging task than
is often realized. It is relatively easy to have a vague meandering
discussion. It is much more difficult for students to discuss coherently,
to question, and to think.

The underlying themes of this chapter are getting students to talk
– to each other as well as the tutor – and getting students to think. In
this chapter we look briefly at some of the relevant research, at some
methods of facilitating discussion, and various methods of small
group teaching. We then explore the skills required by students as
well as tutors if small group teaching is to be effective. The chapter
ends with guidelines for preparing for small group teaching and
some suggestions for evaluating your own small group teaching.

The common labels for small group teaching are tutorials, seminars, and problem-solving classes – although these terms are used
differently by different subjects, departments, and institutions. The
key characteristic of these groups is probably size not teaching
method. Rather than enter into a scholastic discussion of the precise
differences between tutorials, seminars, and problem-solving classes
we propose to use the generic term 'small group teaching' to cover
all the types already mentioned. We also suggest, as a rule of thumb,
that tutorials contain up to five students, seminars perhaps as many
as twenty, and problem-solving classes may have up to thirty students. Of course the size of the group can affect its intimacy and
interaction. But even with the smallest group the effectiveness of the
teaching and learning depends upon the strategies and skills of the
tutor and students. Tutorials of four can be a turn-off as much as
large problem-solving classes.

STUDIES OF SMALL GROUP TEACHING

Small group teaching has a long history. Its great proponent is reputed to be Plato's teacher, Socrates, who valued the development of attitudes as much as critical thinking. Subtle questioning was the core of Socrates' method and his strategies still deserve study. In the Middle Ages Socratic dialogue became formalized as disputations between assailants and defendants who used syllogisms to express their arguments (Broudy 1963). Small group teaching as we know it did not emerge until the late nineteenth century. Yet the Socratic goals of enhancing intellectual and oral skills, of developing attitudes and of improving understanding of oneself and others are as relevant today as they were in the fifth century BC.

Figure 4.1 Socratic dialogue with a quip

Socrates: You said, I think, that the troubles among the gods were composed by love of beauty, for there could not be such a thing as love of ugliness. Was not that it?
Agathon: Yes.
Socrates: And if that is so, Love will be love of beauty, will he not, and not love of ugliness?
Agathon: Agreed.
Socrates: Now we have agreed that Love is in love with what he lacks and does not possess.
Agathon: Yes.
Socrates: So after all, Love lacks and does not possess beauty?
Agathon: Inevitably.
Socrates: Well then, would you call what lacks and in no way possesses beauty beautiful?
Agathon: Certainly not.
Socrates: Do you still think then that Love is beautiful if this is so?

(Plato, *The Symposium*, from the translation by W. Hamilton (1951) Harmondsworth: Penguin.)

Studes of small groups *per se* have long been the hunting ground of social psychologists (Homans 1951; Sprott 1957; Kelley and Thibaute 1970; Argyle 1983). Their work suggests that the best group size for complex issues is five or six and that twenty is the approximate upper limit for group interaction. Their findings also suggest that, in general, heterogeneous groups are more effective at group decision-making than individuals of the same personalities or abilities. Interaction and decision-making is affected by the style of management of the leader, the task and its definition, and last, but not least, the layout of the seating used for the group.

The major theme of research on small group teaching in the past fifty years has been the question of when small group teaching should be used. A review of over a hundred studies which used examination results as the sole criterion (Dubin and Taveggia 1968) suggested that small group teaching is only as effective as other methods of teaching – and more costly. These findings may tell us more about the examinations than the teaching. The reviews by more recent writers (e.g. Kulik and Kulik 1979; Bligh 1980; Jaques 1984) show that small group teaching is usually better than other methods at promoting intellectual skills including problem-solving, and at changing attitudes, and about as effective as other methods at presenting information. But small group teaching is not an efficient method of imparting information – its potential lies in the interplay of ideas and views that develop a student's capacity to think.

The research comparing small group teaching and other methods seems to be based upon the assumption that there is one stable phenomenon known as small group teaching. In fact there is a rich variety of small group teaching methods (Bligh 1986) and within each method there is potential both for competence and for incompetence. So you should be wary of assuming that a particular method of small group teaching is necessarily superior to other forms of teaching for developing thinking or attitudes. Rather than compare small group teaching with other methods it may be more useful to study small group teaching *per se* to identify the goals and strategies of tutors and students.

Research of this kind is still relatively rare. Baumgart (1976) in his observational study of seminars identified various tasks of the tutor. Amongst these were instructor, commentator, stage-setter, prober, and 'reflexive judge'. The 'reflexive judge' appraises a contributor and probes. Baumgart found that students made more thoughtful responses when the tutor appraised and probed. Thoughtfulness was measured in terms of the number of interpretative, evaluative, and speculative utterances. The sessions in which there was more thinking displayed were also the sessions which received more favourable student ratings.

Goldschmid and Goldschmid (1976) in their review of peer group teaching (groups without official tutors) show that such groups, when used in conjunction with other methods of teaching, increase participation and develop the students' responsibility for their own learning. Kulik and Kulik (1979) in their thorough review of small group teaching also show how methods of small group teaching promote discussion skills and higher order cognitive responses.

In spite of the potential strengths of small group teaching for

developing thinking and discussion skills, there are a number of
studies which show that small group teaching is dominated by tutor
talk and low levels of thinking. Ellner (1983) in a study of small
group teaching in North American colleges noted that transmission
of information was the major mode of transaction, that the level of
questions rarely soared beyond recall of information, and, not surprisingly, that the quality of thinking was low.

Foster (1981) in a study of tutorials found tutor talk to be as high
as 86 per cent and student–student interaction as low as 8 per cent.
Lecturers used students' ideas less than 2 per cent of the time. Luker
(1987) in a study of small group teaching in a British university
found that the proportion of time spent on lecturing in small groups
varied from 7 to 70 per cent and the proportion of time devoted to
asking questions varied from 1 to 28 per cent. The mean time spent
by tutors talking was 64 per cent. Physics, production engineering,
and education had the student groups who made most contributions.
Interestingly the tutors involved were all using problem-solving
methods of teaching.

In two studies which focused upon levels of thinking displayed in
small groups it was found that over 80 per cent of the utterances
were concerned with recall and clarification rather than with interpreting, evaluating, or speculating (Hegarty 1978; Barnes 1980).

Other studies of small group teaching *per se* have been impression-
istic rather than analytical. Bliss and Ogborn (1977) provide students' descriptions of 'good' and 'bad' experiences in small group
teaching in science. The good experiences may be characterized as
lively, stimulating, and full of learning. Bad experiences related to
tutors' attitude – from careless to coercive – ill-defined goals and
uncertainty. Rudduck (1978) and Abercrombie and Terry (1978)
made a series of video-recordings in various subjects and used these
to discuss the problems and processes of small group teaching and
the reactions of students and tutors. Their sensitive and illuminating
work raises one's awareness of the problems and issues involved in
small group teaching, but it leaves the reader with the difficult task
of extricating guidelines and suggestions which would enhance his
or her small group teaching.

The Nuffield Foundation (1976) and Abercrombie (1969) do however provide descriptions of various forms of small group teaching
which may be used in various subjects. Jaques (1984) also describes
a range of approaches as do Habeshaw, Habeshaw, and Gibbs
(1986). Luker (1987) has explored tutors' and students' views of
small group teaching and analysed the patterns of interaction in
tutorials and seminars. Figures 4.2 and 4.3 encapsulate some of her
findings.

Figure 4.2 'What I like about small group teaching'

TUTORS

1 'The informal atmosphere – opportunity to get to know students at a personal level and for them to get to know me.'

2 'Their attainment is not constrained by pressures of curriculum, difficulties associated with large group inflexibility, and above all passive lethargy in a mass lecture environment.'

3 'Feeling of informality and, when things go right, that students have learnt something and – even in Statistics – enjoyed themselves.'

4 'Seeing a student suddenly grasp an idea for the first time, which makes, for him, a number of other disjointed areas simultaneously fall into place.'

5 'I can be stimulated by students' ideas.'

6 'Hearing the spontaneous insights of students.'

7 'Opportunity for providing instantaneous, personal feedback on their own thoughts and efforts.'

8 'Being able to give praise.'

9 'The educational goals are readily defined, almost as a contract between myself and the group.'

10 'Talking. Contradicting superficial ideas!!'

STUDENTS

1 'I personally have a greater influence on what is being discussed. I can actually remember, and feel I understand what we are discussing.'

2 'You can discuss issues together rather than be told them.'

3 'Being able to participate and to find out other people's ideas.'

4 'Being able to discuss and having queries sorted out there and then.'

5 'It is less formal, less intimidating. There is the possibility of asking questions. I think you learn more.'

6 'You get more individual attention.'

7 'I like the flexibility of a small group. We aren't bound to a rigid schedule.'

8 'It teaches you how to converse in a literate manner.'

9 'Helps develop your power of analysing problems and arriving at solutions.'

10 'By being in a smaller group, one feels part of the class rather than just another face in a sea of faces. I actually feel more part of the university.'

Source: Luker (1987).

Despite the growing interest in research on small group teaching we still have little precise information on how tutors prepare for small group teaching or what strategies and methods they use and

Figure 4.3 Difficulties and dislikes

TUTOR'S DIFFICULTIES

1 'Keeping my mouth shut.'
2 'Getting a discussion going.'
3 'It often requires considerable skill to direct discussion in fruitful directions.'
4 'It requires considerably more mental alertness and flexibility than a formal lecture, and can be a bit of a strain.'
5 'Keeping on your toes all the time. Perhaps I'm getting old, but it's tiring.'
6 'Getting students to see me as an equal, talk to me as they would to their peers, and lose their inhibitions about displaying ignorance in front of me and their peers.'
7 'Very difficult to establish the kind of atmosphere in which students will begin to talk. They tend to be very much afraid of *not* saying the right thing.'
8 'Shutting up the vociferous.'
9 'Bringing in the meek.'
10 'How to deal with a poor or irrelevant answer.'

STUDENT DISLIKES

1 'A small group can easily be dominated by one person.'
2 'When members of the group will not talk.'
3 'Long silences.'
4 'You can't hide out.'
5 'Being asked to contribute when you don't want to.'
6 'Being directly asked vague questions.'
7 'I am sometimes frustrated at being held up by the problems or queries of other group members.'
8 'A feeling of being assessed by the lecturer through your answers to questions and your attitudes.'
9 'Sometimes you feel threatened by the closeness of the lecturers.'
10 'You have to have completed a certain amount of work to understand what's going on.'

Source: Luker (1987).
Note: Most students said 'None'.

what approaches are most effective for encouraging students to think and participate (Bligh 1986). Hence the suggestions and guidelines on effective small group teaching are based on our experience and that of colleagues as well as on the relevant research. Readers interested in conducting research on small group teaching or in analysing their own teaching will find the section of this chapter on evaluation helpful.

THE GOALS OF SMALL GROUP TEACHING
(see Activity 4.2)

Put simply the immediate goals of small group teaching are to get students to talk and to think. The long-term goals are personal growth and competence. These goals may be expressed in the form:

1 The development of communication skills.
2 The development of intellectual and professional competencies.
3 The personal growth of students (and perhaps the tutor?).

These three goals are interconnected in practice and each has implications for the role of the tutor in small group teaching. If he or she spends most of the time talking there is little opportunity for students to develop their communication or intellectual skills. For the goals to be achieved the tutor has to consider the students involved as well as the task. Indeed the tutor's role is threefold: managing the learning task, the individuals, and the group processes.

Communication skills

The skills of listening, explaining, questioning, and responding are important in themselves as well as being crucial for the development of intellectual skills. Discussion also develops skills that are central to most professions: the ability to communicate with others (both professional and 'lay'), and the sensitive and precise handling of the language of the subject. This language contains not only concepts, facts, and processes but also explicit and implicit attitudes and values. For example many physicists value quantitative measurements, pure mathematicians are concerned with rigour of proofs, and historians with the quality of various types of evidence. So one of the goals of small group teaching may be to socialize students into the values and perspectives of your own subject, discipline, or profession. It may be important, therefore, for the tutor to be 'his, or her, subject' when small group teaching. In other words to show, discuss, and encourage certain ways of thinking, of using evidence, and of structuring ideas and procedures.

Intellectual and professional competencies

Most of us want students to think and, in particular, to think about and within the framework of the subject we teach or profess. Every subject probably has its own style of thinking but also features in common with other styles. Figure 4.4 lists the main types of thinking

Figure 4.4 Some types of thinking

- Analysing
- Logical reasoning
- Evaluating evidence or data
- Appraising and judging perceptively
- Thinking critically
- Seeing new relationships
- Synthesizing
- Speculating creatively
- Designing
- Arguing rationally
- Transferring skills to new contexts
- Problem-solving

across the spectrum of subjects. The value and precise nature of the type of thinking varies from subject to subject.

Of course, not all professional competencies are concerned with thinking – practical procedures may be at least as important. And small group teaching is only one way in which intellectual and professional competencies may be developed. However small group teaching is, potentially, a powerful method of encouraging students to think generally and in the specific modes of the subject. Thus small group teaching may be used to develop proficiency with data and evidence whether in history, anatomy, or electrical engineering. It may be used to remedy deficiencies in understanding, as a guide for activities in private study, and to provide practice in thinking. Perhaps most important of all, small group teaching can provide feedback to students and tutors thereby assisting them to develop competencies effectively.

Personal growth

The goal of personal growth necessarily includes the development of communication skills and thinking. It also includes the notions of developing your self-confidence, managing your own learning, working with others, and insight into yourself and others. These affective goals are sometimes neglected yet they are important in the short term as well as the long term. In the short term attention to the affective goals may well encourage the group to talk and think. In the long term attention to these goals may assist a person to develop professionally as well as personally.

FACILITATING SMALL GROUP TEACHING

There are four simple, but effective, strategies which increase the chances of students talking and thinking while working in small groups. All of them are concerned with helping the group to feel safe enough to talk and share thoughts. These strategies are:

1 Seating arrangements
2 Expectations and ground rules
3 Safety
4 Making the small group smaller.

Seating arrangements

It is well known that seating affects interaction patterns (Argyle 1983) yet tutors often neglect this strategy. Perhaps this is because they think that their students are not affected by such minor matters as who sits where. Figure 4.5 shows three seating arrangements. (The position of the tutor is shown by a T.) Each is likely to produce different patterns of interaction. 'A' is likely to be tutor dominated with most interactions tutor–student, student–tutor. Most of the interaction is likely to come from the centre of the first two rows and least from the front and back corners. 'B' increases the probability of subgroups interacting and each subgroup interacting with the tutor but not necessarily with other subgroups. 'C' increases the probability of students talking to each other as well as the tutor. It is increased further if the tutor varies the seating pattern each session. Talkative students seated close to the tutor are, sometimes, inhibited, and shy students who sit opposite the tutor are more likely to make contributions if encouraged gently to do so. It is worth noting that distance between tutors and students and type of furniture can also influence interaction.

Expectations and ground rules

Students often do not know what is expected of them in a small group session, so it is worth while outlining and discussing your expectations and theirs so that you can arrive at an understanding or even an informal contract. One important feature of the contract is that students have permission to ask questions, no matter how trivial, and to try out ideas which may be wrong. In return the tutor should agree to tackle questions asked and to provide, in a matter of fact way, his or her view – rather than sniping. A 'contract' not only allays anxieties and clarifies goals but also provides a reference point for analysing later sessions.

Figure 4.5 Seating and interaction

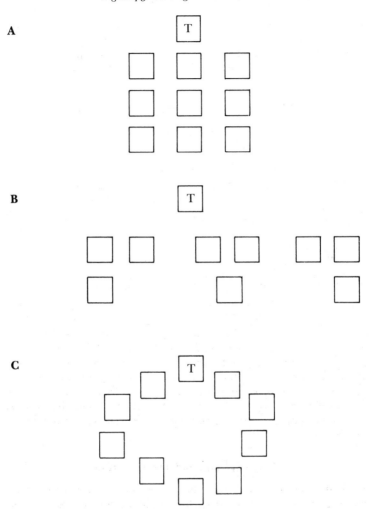

It might also be worth discussing with the group how groups tend to work together. There seem to be four phases – forming, storming, norming, and performing. The first phase is where the group are getting to appraise and know each other. The second phase is when the members of the group are struggling to establish their roles. In the third phase the group have arrived at an understanding of how to behave and in the fourth they are working together on the task.

It is sometimes observed that some seminars do not get beyond phase one, and some university committees beyond phase two. More seriously, the phases of forming, storming, norming, and performing have implications for the tutor. Clearly he or she may have to assist the group to move quickly through the first three phases.

Safety

Implicit in the ground rules is the notion that the group must feel safe enough to take risks rather than be too frightened to contribute. Indeed many small group sessions are plagued by fear. Some tutors fear they will be asked questions that they cannot answer or that they will lose control. Some students fear that they will be made to look stupid by their peers or the tutor so they avoid responding or even making eye contact.

Two basic tactics increase feelings of safety: 'rewards' and the reduction of risk. Both are related to expectations and ground rules.

Rewards are important. If a student makes a good point, or a valid inference, or adopts a creative approach to the problem, the tutor should tell him or her so. It shows that helpful contributions are valued and encourages more like it. Risk reduction can also be managed by the tutor. First, by making clear what is expected from the students (much fear stems from uncertainty). Second, by setting tasks or problems which are within the group's capabilities and resources. Third, by not 'putting down' students or allowing other students to do so. This does not mean that the tutor becomes 'soft'. Part of feeling safe is knowing the limits. So if students do or say something unacceptable or wrong the tutor must not only tell them, but also tell them why.

If tutors use facilitating methods skilfully the sessions can be rewarding both for them and for their students. Effective tutors can also prevent small group sessions from degenerating into covert, manipulative contests between the participants. Examples of these negative games are given in Figure 4.6 (see also Activity 4.4).

Making the small group smaller

The underlying principle of this strategy is to provide students with an opportunity to talk in groups of two or three without the tutor listening. This enables the students to check out their views and approaches without fear of being appraised by the tutor. Three variations on this theme are:

1 Buzz groups   Students are asked to discuss or solve a problem in twos or threes and then asked to

Figure 4.6 Games students play

Games, in small groups, are devices used by students to enable them to avoid making contributions. The ideal game is 'Grand Silence', but it is often difficult to sustain this for long, and alternatives have to be found. A very desirable game is 'Monologue'. This involves a lengthy lecture by the tutor, and if 'Grand Silence' fails to lead to 'Monologue' it can sometimes be induced by the simple game, 'What Do *You* Think?'. This is always worth a try. Certain tutors enjoy 'Monologue' and indicate a willingness to play it by arranging their seminar seating in lecture-room style. Such a layout is to be encouraged.

Some inexperienced Games Players confuse 'Monologue' with 'Hobby Horse'. 'Hobby Horse', once under way, is very similar to 'Monologue' and is therefore a Good Game. But it does require some astute observation of the tutor's interests, and this departure from passivity is clearly against the whole spirit of Game Playing.

A Game sometimes played by beginners is 'I Know But I'm Not Going To Tell You'. This Game should be avoided as it serves only to irritate the tutor, and in extreme cases it may lead to the unpleasantness of Uproar!

A much more subtle approach is 'How Can You Expect Little Ol' Me To Know When Clever People (Like You) Disagree?'. The 'Like You' is optional but this Game puts the tutor firmly in his place and may, with luck, even generate 'Monologue'.

If this fails then an acceptable alternative is often 'Martyrdom'. In this Game the group elects a martyr for the session and other members of the group are therefore liberated. Some groups have been particularly successful with this Game and have even persuaded tutors to institutionalize 'Martyrdom' by establishing the one-paper-a-session convention. That this method is so common is a testimony to the success of Game Playing everywhere.

give their views. A variation of this approach was also given in Chapter 3.

2 Brainstorming   Each student is invited to scribble down thoughts, ideas, or questions and then compare them with those of a few of his or her peers. This gives the students time to think as well as to check out their views.

3 Snowballing   Each student spends a little time noting and thinking, then compares his or her views with one other student. The pair compare their views with another pair. The quartet with another quartet. This rather formal method works well in problem-solving tasks as well as open discussion topics.

All these methods may be used in large group sessions as well as in problem-solving classes and other forms of small group teaching (see Activity 4.5). Bligh (1980, 1986) and Habeshaw, Habeshaw, and Gibbs (1986) provide further methods based on the notion of making the small group smaller. But like all strategies and tactics of small group teaching, overuse can be self-defeating. None the less the tactics are particularly useful during the early stages of teaching a small group and as occasional events during subsequent teaching. The tactics can be made more sophisticated by use of cross-overs in which one member of each subgroup moves to another subgroup for the second stage of comparison or discussion, and by 'fishbowls' where half the group observe the rest problem-solving, then discuss their observations of outcome and process. The roles are then reversed and the 'fish' become observers.

METHODS OF SMALL GROUP TEACHING

The range of small group teaching methods is enormous (see Bligh 1980; Jaques 1984). The methods may be characterized roughly in terms of two dimensions: structure and domination (see Figure 4.7). It is interesting to try to estimate where your habitual approach is on these dimensions and compare the results with the estimates that your students give. Given the range of methods available for small group teaching it is not possible to cover all the methods. So instead a sample of methods will be outlined and suggestions made for improving some of them.

Lecturing

This may seem an unusual method in small group teaching yet it is used frequently. Sometimes the tutor intends and plans a lecture, sometimes it may arise out of a set of students' questions and comments – and sometimes it may be the last refuge of a desperate tutor.

Lecturing for the whole of every tutorial is an ineffective use of learning time. So too, usually, are lectures which occupy the first half of a small group session. Such an approach encourages passivity. As indicated in Figure 4.6, students can sometimes manipulate the tutor into lecturing thereby avoiding talking and thinking. However, brief lectures or explanations of particular points are valuable. A brief lecture, of say twenty minutes, *after* the students have been actively involved in discussion or problem-solving can be very valuable – particularly if the lecture draws together the main points of the small group session.

Figure 4.7 Two important dimensions of small group teaching

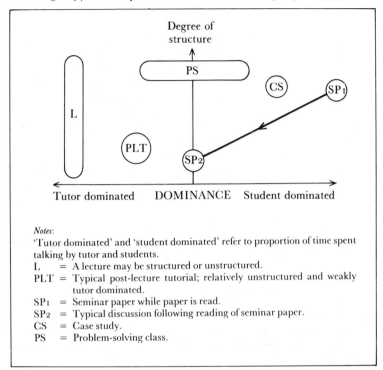

Degree of structure

Tutor dominated   DOMINANCE   Student dominated

Notes:
'Tutor dominated' and 'student dominated' refer to proportion of time spent talking by tutor and students.

L   = A lecture may be structured or unstructured.
PLT = Typical post-lecture tutorial; relatively unstructured and weakly tutor dominated.
SP₁ = Seminar paper while paper is read.
SP₂ = Typical discussion following reading of seminar paper.
CS = Case study.
PS = Problem-solving class.

The post-lecture tutorial

This method may be characterized as 'Any questions? You must have, please'. Ostensibly this session is to clarify any problems of understanding or issues raised by a lecture. In practice the post-lecture tutorial may have three handicaps. First, the tutor may not know what the lecturer actually did. Second, some (or all) the students may not have attended the lecture. Third, the vagaries of the timetable may have made the post-lecture tutorial into a pre-lecture tutorial.

There are a few ways of improving this method. You can invite the students who attended the lecture to bring their notes and to compare, in groups of two or three, what they noted. You can invite a student in some sessions to prepare a single transparency summarizing the key points of the lecture. Discussion questions can be set so that the students work on them in subgroups as well as the whole group. Problems can be set which are based on the lecture materials.

Sometimes it is better to begin with problems that are simple and build up to the type given in the lecture. It is also useful to provide some of the rationale and background information on the problems. Finally, you can plan a series of activities, questions, and problems based on the lecture course but not totally dependent upon the content of each lecture.

Step by step discussion

This method follows the sequence: brief introduction → problem/ activity → tutor input → problem/activity → tutor input. The method has several advantages. It provides a well-defined structure and also gives students an opportunity to discuss freely within the bounds of the sub-task. It varies the activity and pace of learning of students, it helps students to feel secure, and it can develop their problem-solving and discussion skills. It is particularly appropriate for complex topics. However it is important for the students to know the goals of the session – it can be very irritating to be required to jump through a series of hoops without knowing why.

The seminar paper

This method may be characterized as 'the paper chase'. In theory a student reads aloud from a written paper and this is then discussed by the group who question vigorously the evidence, methods, underlying assumptions, and implicit values of the paper. In practice the student reads the paper at two speeds: rapid for ordinary material and very rapid for material he or she is unsure about. Often only the tutor knows what is being said and is the only one to ask meaningful questions. Gradually the seminar becomes a conversation between the tutor and student-presenter with an audience. Eventually the audience may be left behind.

The method can be improved by using brainstorming prior to the presentation and buzz groups to discuss set questions before the formal discussion of the paper. Students may be invited to prepare questions on the topic before the actual tutorial. The presenter may be asked to spare a few questions for discussion and to chair the discussion.

Mini-presentation

In this method the student is told he or she must *not* read an essay or paper. Instead the student has to use audio-visual aids, provide a framework for discussion, or, if appropriate, attempt to teach the topic. Other students in the group may be assigned tasks such as asking questions, summarizing key points, offering alternative interpretations (even as devil's advocate), and evaluating the approach. The method has significant advantages over the seminar paper. It can develop oral skills, the management of discussion, and critical thinking. However it is important to brief clearly both the presenter and participants on their tasks.

Springboard seminar

In this method the lecturer provides a stimulus for discussion. The stimulus may be a very brief lecture, a video- or audio-recording, or a demonstration. The students may be asked to bear in mind certain questions while listening to the lecture or recording. After the stimulus they are expected to discuss perceptively the question or points raised. In practice springboard seminars can become nosedives. These can be avoided by ensuring that the stimulus is stimulating and the task of the group is clear. The method can be enhanced by the use of brainstorming, buzz groups, or snowballing before the plenary discussion, and by giving questions for the students to bear in mind while listening to, or watching, the stimulus.

Problem-solving

Problem-solving is a central activity in science, engineering, and, to a lesser extent, in social science. Suggestions on helping students to solve problems are given in Chapter 8. Helping groups of students to solve problems is challenging and can be intellectually stimulating for the tutor as well as the students. But there are three prior conditions if the method is to be successful. First, you must know how you solve problems. Second, you must know the common problem-solving strategies available in your subject (Chapter 8 is also useful on this topic). Third, you must know how to get a group involved in problem-solving.

Given these pre-conditions there is then consideration of the particular problems which students are being invited to solve. Clearly the tutor must know how to solve the problems, what common errors and false loops are likely to occur, and what hints to give or questions to ask to move the students on.

There are several variations of this method. You can set the problems prior to the class or during the early stages of the class. The students work on them individually and then compare their approaches in twos or threes. A student, or a small group of students, may be asked to represent the solution to the whole class. Since this can expose incompetence in a threatening way, it is important to have ground rules which include the notion that being wrong is part of learning to be right. A simple device for taking the sting out of correction is to provide a coloured prism to each student. When they agree with the reasoning they show green, when they disagree, red, and when a person wishes to take over the presentation, yellow. Used occasionally, the device can be fun.

Another variant of the problem-solving method is to hand out problem sheets at the end of one session and have them returned and marked before the beginning of the next session. This enables the tutor to conduct an analysis of common erorrs, novel solutions, and so on. Alternatively an agenda of difficulties can be drawn up by the tutor and students at the beginning of the session. Finally, there is little point in marking or stating that a solution is wrong unless you also show why it is wrong and the correct path to take. In short, feedback is a crucial (but neglected) feature of the problem-solving method.

Case studies, simulations, and games

Yorke (1981) points out that sharp distinctions are difficult to draw between games, simulations, and case studies because their characteristic features overlap. Figure 4.8 shows a way of representing the relationships. An exhaustive list of similarities and differences is unlikely to be of practical value. But broadly speaking, case studies are based on actual practice so they may be complex, perhaps interdisciplinary, and provide opportunities for developing understanding of the issues involved and for complex problem-solving. Simulations are stripped down versions of real problems, and games are even more stripped down versions which involve precise rules and develop understanding of principles and relationships. In this section we concentrate on case studies although the suggestions offered apply also to simulations and games.

Four phases can be identified in case study methods (MacLennan 1974). In phase one the tutor sets the scene, the objectives of the case study, and clarifies any problems of procedure. In phase two, private study, students are given time to read, digest, and note any issues involved. In phase three the students, in groups of three to six, share views, knowledge, and skills. They may have to judge the adequacy of the information given, then develop various solutions and choose the best alternative. Phase four is the plenary session in which each subgroup might present its 'best' solution and the tutor draws out the underlying principles and problems.

A variation on this method is to invite each student to prepare and

Figure 4.8 Case studies, simulations, games

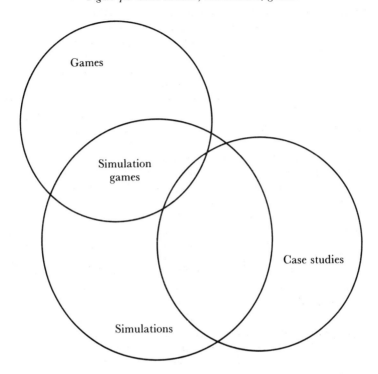

present a case study based on their own experience for discussion by
the group or subgroup. The approach is particularly useful for
professional training.

Case studies can be very effective. They can engage the students
actively, validate experiential learning, and offer relevant and realistic discussion of concrete issues and problems. But they are time-
consuming to prepare and the final phase, in which the principles
are highlighted, is crucial for their success.

Syndicate

In this method a topic is split into sections and the group divided
into teams. Each team works on a section of the topic and presents
its views. The tutor may act as a resource for each team and as co-
ordinator and summarizer in the plenary session. Good results can
be achieved by this method (Collier 1969, 1985) but it requires
careful organization and, in particular, the splitting of a complex

topic or issue may require prior analysis by the tutor. Alternatively the problem can be posed and the students invited to devise their own analysis of the factors involved and select their own teams and sub-topics.

THE SKILLS OF SMALL GROUP TEACHING

In most small group sessions the tutor talks, asks questions, listens, and responds to the students' answers and comments, and perhaps summarizes and closes the discussion. In the more lively small group sessions students also ask questions, listen and respond to each other, explain their ideas, and perhaps summarize each other's arguments.

It follows from the above description that the skills involved in small group teaching are *explaining, listening, questioning, responding, summarizing,* and *closure.* All of these skills are essential for students as well as tutors. Underpinning these skills is the skill of preparing for small group sessions which is discussed in a subsequent section in this chapter. Preparing for small group sessions is also important for students and this theme is discussed in Chapter 8.

Explaining

This skill has already been discussed in Chapter 3. But in small group sessions knowing *when* to explain is as important as knowing *how* to explain. Given that the objectives of small group teaching are to stimulate students to think and discuss, it is unwise to explain too much too early lest the group are induced into a passive mode. It is usually better to provide explanations *after* students have attempted the task of the session – even, perhaps, in the summary when you can draw together the responses of the group. Used in this way you can use explanations to correct any misconceptions that have been identified. More important you can use the students' own contributions in the explanation that is given. This strategy rewards students for their efforts, builds up their confidence, and increases group cohesiveness. In so doing it is likely to encourage students to think and contribute again in subsequent sessions.

Questions and questioning

The question 'What is a question?' is intriguing and not as simple as might appear (Brown and Edmondson 1984). However for most everyday purposes a question may be regarded as a request for information. The request may be for observations, facts, thoughts, opinions, and feelings. The information supplied enables the questioner to diagnose, appraise, and respond. The responses of the questioner may be to supply missing facts, correct misconceptions, explore thoughts and opinions, and, where appropriate, feelings. The questioner may use a sequence of questions to draw out contributions or build on them to develop new insights and conjectures. Clearly effective questioning depends upon listening and responding as well as upon asking the right questions. However it is convenient to consider questioning as a separate entity and to bear in mind Hamilton's (1928) observation that 'the whole of teaching and learning is shot through with the art of questioning'.

Classifying questions

Given the range and frequency of questions that we ask of students, it is curious that few of us attempt to classify the kinds of questions we ask in our academic subjects – or indeed even to check occasionally how many questions we ask in seminars and tutorials.

There are several ways of classifying questions (see, for example, Bloom 1956; Gall 1970; Kerry 1982; Jaques 1984; Hargie 1986). Many of the methods of classification are more useful for research purposes than for enabling effective teaching. So in this section we concentrate on a broad classification of questions and some dimensions of questions which colleagues who attended workshops on 'Questions and Questioning' have found useful and which are also related to research on questioning. It should be noted that more important than the particular classification of questions is an awareness of the range and kind of questions we ask with a group of students. It is also important to note that classifications of questions are context-bound. What may require thought by one student may simply be a matter of recall for another.

Conceptual, empirical, and value questions

The broad classification of conceptual, empirical, and value questions is a useful starting-point for considering questions within an academic discipline. All three types may be found in each discipline but with varying degrees of emphasis. Complex questions may involve sub-questions concerned with all three types.

Identifying which type of question (or sub-question) is under consideration often clarifies discussion, returns it on track, and may lead more quickly to a solution to the problem posed. For example take the question 'Are there more grandfathers in the world than fathers?' . . . (You might like to tackle this question before reading on.)

Those who take an empirical approach based on the notion that each of us has one father and two grandfathers are likely to become involved with the reliability of statistics of mortality and with probability estimates, thereby concluding that the question cannot be answered precisely. Those who consider the question conceptually will note that every grandfather is a father but not vice versa so there are more fathers in the world than grandfathers. (See notes and comments on p. 206 for a further discussion of this problem and the related [sic] problem 'Are there more male cousins in the world than nephews?' – p. 186).

You can invent a series of questions for discussion within your own subject which is based on the classification of conceptual, empirical, and value questions. This is a particularly useful exercise to carry out with first-year students. The classification may also be subdivided further in ways which are relevant to a particular subject and questions considered which are centred within a classification and on the boundaries. For example in zoology and botany empirical questions can be subdivided into those requiring field as opposed to laboratory investigations; in history, into different types of primary and secondary evidence.

The narrow–broad 'dimension'

Questions may be framed to require a relatively brief specific answer (for example 'Where is Ulan Bator?') or to require a relatively wide-ranging answer (for example 'What is your philosophy of life?'). These questions may be represented as points on a dimension although we should bear in mind that a narrow question in one context may be a broad question in another. Narrow–broad questions are sometimes described as closed–open questions or convergent–divergent questions. Not surprisingly, narrow questions yield short answers and when used too frequently they inhibit discussion (Andrews 1980). Sometimes the form of a broad question is used yet the tutor is searching for a narrow specific answer. Such pseudo-broad questions can evoke frustration or bewilderment rather than information. In one study over 50 per cent of this type of question failed to receive answers from students – so the tutor answered his or her own question (Barnes 1980).

The recall–thought 'dimension'

This dimension owes much to the work of Bloom (1956) who produced a taxonomy of questions from recall of simple facts to speculative and evaluative questions. This dimension is sometimes confused with the narrow–broad dimension. Yet it is clear that some questions may be narrow–thought questions (for example 'When is a right a duty?') or narrow–recall (for example 'What date was the Congress of Vienna?'). Some may be broad–recall questions (for example 'What did you do yesterday?') and some may be broad–thought questions (for example 'How can unemployment be reduced?').

Recall questions are often used in the initial stages of a discussion to assess knowledge and to start the students' thinking processes. However one danger of this approach is that students may be puzzled because the questions seem *too* simple. Rather than be caught out they remain silent. Hence it is useful to signpost the recall questions with a remark such as 'Let's begin with some fairly straightforward questions . . .'.

As indicated in the review section, higher-order questions are not asked as frequently as we might expect in tutorials and seminars (Andrews 1980; Barnes 1980). This may be because tutors do not prepare thought questions but expect them to arise spontaneously. However, it may be that if we want to ask questions which get students thinking then we have to think about the questions we are going to ask.

When higher-order questions are asked they yield a greater number of responses particularly when the higher-order questions are broad (Andrews 1980). Higher-order questions also yield greater gains in understanding and more positive evaluations of teaching (Merlino 1977). However we should bear in mind that the recall–thought dimension must be considered in relation to a particular group of students. What may require first-year students to think may only require final-year students to recall.

The confused–clear 'dimension'

Clear questions are usually brief, direct, and firmly anchored in context. Confusion may be generated by questions embedded in a set of ancillary statements (or, even worse, other questions) or when the context is not discernible and the listener has first to establish it. An example of the first type of confusion-inducing question is:

'I thought your paper was interesting but I wasn't at all sure whether you regarded Johnson's views and those of Wilson Knight's as more or less consonant or whether on the other hand you detected some sort of dissonance or indeed some unresolved dilemmas in both of their views. What do you think?'

An example of the second type is:

'So what do you think about it?'

A distinction may be made between questions which are unintentionally confused and leave the listener floundering and questions which are deliberately ambiguous to ensure a variety of responses such as:

'Is "Stimulating seminars" a good topic for discussion?'

The encouraging–threatening 'dimension'

The same question may be asked in a variety of styles which encourage or inhibit student responses. Given that you want students to think and contribute, you should usually adopt encouraging modes of questioning and responding. This is not to say that questions should not confront or challenge intellectually. But the right turn of phrase and tone of voice can change a perceived threat into an accepted challenge.

Tactics of questioning

Six useful tactics of questioning are pitching and pausing, prompting and probing, directing and distributing.

Pitching questions is related to the recall–thought and narrow–broad dimensions. Sometimes it may be necessary to pitch a variety of broad questions at the same level of recall, then summarize and lift the level of questioning. At other times you may wish to begin with a broad thought question and gradually move towards more specific questions involving recall of facts.

Pauses, sometimes known as wait-times, are necessary immediately after a question demanding thought and also helpful before you ask a thought question or switch level or type of question.

Prompts and probes are supplementary questions which ask a student to clarify the answer or provide more information. Prompts usually contain hints, probes contain challenges. Some examples of probing questions are given in Figure 4.9.

A tactic of questioning related to prompting which is sometimes used unknowingly is the implicit question. The tutor does not ask a question directly; instead he or she makes a comment which students are expected to connect with what is being discussed. For example in a discussion of a paper on the Elizabethan Era, the tutor said:

'Hmm, that's interesting. I wonder if there are any parallels with life in Germany in the 1930s.'

Figure 4.9 Examples of probing questions

- Does that always apply?
- How is that relevant?
- Can you give me an example?
- Is there an alternative viewpoint?
- How reliable is the evidence?
- How accurate is your description?
- You say it is x, which particular kind of x?
- What's the underlying principle then?
- In what situation would this rule break down?
- What distinguishes the two cases?

What he wanted the student to do was to

1 Identify the changing role of the police in Germany in the 1930s.
2 Note that she had omitted from her paper any mention of the methods of policing in Elizabethan times.

Implicit questioning is both a common and subtle tactic of questioning. Unfortunately its ubiquity is no measure of its success. Paradoxically if you want implicit questioning to work you have to make explicit to students this tactic of questioning.

Directing questions at specific students and distributing questions around the group are obvious (but not always used) tactics for monitoring and involving students in thinking and discussion. A common error is to ask questions of only one or two students – usually the students whose answers are worth while. Other common errors in questioning are given in Figure 4.10.

Figure 4.10 Some common errors in questioning

- Asking too many questions at once.
- Asking a question and answering it yourself.
- Asking questions only of the brightest or most likeable.
- Asking a difficult question too early.
- Asking irrelevant questions.
- Always asking the same types of questions.
- Asking questions in a threatening way.
- Not indicating a change in the type of question.
- Not using probing questions.
- Not giving time to think.
- Not correcting wrong answers.
- Ignoring answers.
- Failing to see the implications of answers.
- Failing to build on answers.

Figure 4.11 Sequences of questions

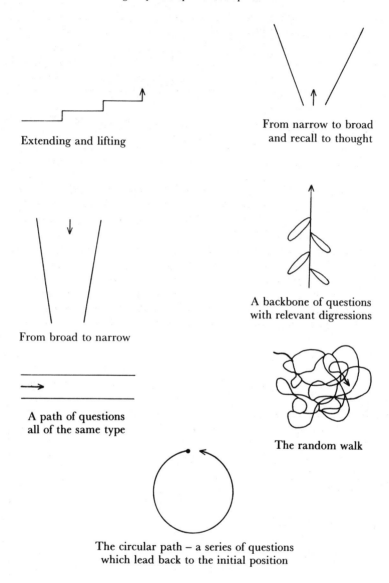

Extending and lifting

From narrow to broad
and recall to thought

From broad to narrow

A backbone of questions
with relevant digressions

A path of questions
all of the same type

The random walk

The circular path – a series of questions
which lead back to the initial position

Sequencing questions

There appear to have been no research studies of effective ways of sequencing questions in small group teaching but there are certain patterns of questioning which we have observed in seminars and tutorials which may help you to explore your own sequence of questioning. The sequences are shown in diagrammatic form in Figure 4.11. For an activity on questioning see Activity 4.8.

Responding

Responses to answers and comments are the linchpin of sequences of questions and discussion. They are the mechanism whereby new information is introduced, the topic is changed, or discussion is moved on. Both tutors and students report difficulty with the skill of responding (Luker 1987). Typical responses by tutors in discussion are shown in Figure 4.12.

Students sometimes ignore each other's contribution and so the seminar becomes a collective monologue with a co-ordinating tutor. One suggestion for helping students to build on and use each other's responses is given in Chapter 8 and further suggestions may be found in Bligh (1986). The tactics of responding in Figure 4.12 may also be used, in modified form, to help students to develop their discussion skills.

Figure 4.12 Responses to answers and comments

Answer/comment ignored	tutor asks someone else tutor changes question tutor changes topic
Answer/comment acknowledged	tutor asks someone else tutor changes question tutor changes topic
Answer/comment repeated verbatim	tutor merely states it tutor inflects voice to convert into question
Part of answer/comment echoed	tutor merely states it tutor inflects voice to convert into question
Paraphrased	tutor paraphrases directly tutor expresses paraphrase in the form of question

Praised	tutor praises contribution tutor praises contribution and elaborates tutor praises contribution and uses it to build on explanation and question.
Corrected	tutor corrects wrong part of answer tutor asks others to correct wrong part of answer
Prompted	tutor asks prompting questions or supplies direct hint to contributor
Probe	tutor asks probing question of contributor tutor asks probing question of other participants

Listening

Studies of listening focus almost exclusively upon responses after listening (Hargie 1986). No study has been discovered which tackles the central problem: 'How do we listen?' However in discussion with psychiatrists and counsellors four levels of listening were identified through introspection and reflection (Brown 1986).

Skim listening

This is little more than awareness that someone is talking. The message is unlikely to get beyond the listener's sensory memory unless a word such as 'fuck' or the listener's name is said. When this occurs the listener may switch to a deeper level of listening. Skim listening is more likely to occur when you are tired, anxious, bored, or thinking of more pressing matters.

Surveying listening

In this form of listening the listener is trying to build a mental map of what is being said. The listener filters out extraneous material and identifies key points or the main steps in the argument or descriptions.

Search listening

Search listening is active searching for specific information. For example a tutor or student may be waiting for a particular point to be made so that he or she can use it to further the discussion. One side effect of search listening is that it may filter out important but unanticipated ideas, facts, or suggestions.

Study listening

This is the deepest level of listening. It goes beyond the information given to the implications and hidden meanings of the content and to the patterns of thinking of the speaker. Study listening is a subtle challenging skill. It enables the listener to arrive at hypotheses about the speaker's thinking as well as developing the ideas and points made by the speaker further than the speaker has realized he or she can go.

A knowledge of levels of listening helps you to monitor your own listening skills. But there still remain some barriers to active listening. First, there is a 'gap' between the rate at which the brain processes information and the rate at which someone speaks. The brain may therefore be underused during a small group session especially if there is an oral presentation. Consequently it switches off; we microsleep. The result is *intermittent* listening. Second, the listener may attend only to information which fits his or her existing viewpoint. *Selective* listening is the result. Third, there may be a conflict between the words and body language of the speaker. *Confused* listening can be the result, although in such cases you are more likely to believe the body language than the words. Further, in a small group session students and tutors may be mentally rehearsing a point. During this period they may not be attending to what is being said by others. The result is *backtracking* and *discontinuities* in the discussion.

Summarizing and closing

Summarizing may be used at the end of a sub-topic as well as at the end of a small group session to draw together the key points, the unresolved questions, and the important links. Summaries not only provide brief answers to questions but also show the decisions and priorities in a subject. As such, summaries are vital for developing understanding and they require judgement about what to highlight and omit.

Closing a session involves summarizing and leave-taking. Thanking a group for its contributions and pointing out what has been achieved is good for group morale and the individual's sense of worth. These in their turn are good for developing the thinking and discussion skills of the group.

PREPARING FOR SMALL GROUP TEACHING

Preparing for small group teaching is usually less time-consuming but more challenging than preparing for lectures. In lectures the material, the setting, and to a large extent the responses of the student are controlled by the lecturer. In lecture preparation you have to take account of what the students know. In small group preparation you also have to take account of what they might say.

Figure 4.13 shows an overall approach to preparation for small group teaching which is based upon the content of this chapter. You can start anywhere in the diagram and take any path. If the material is unfamiliar then it is better to begin with content, work through strategy, method, setting, reflect on what goals you are likely to achieve, and recheck and refine. If you have very clearly defined goals then a useful approach is goals → setting → method → strategy.

Figure 4.13 Small group preparation

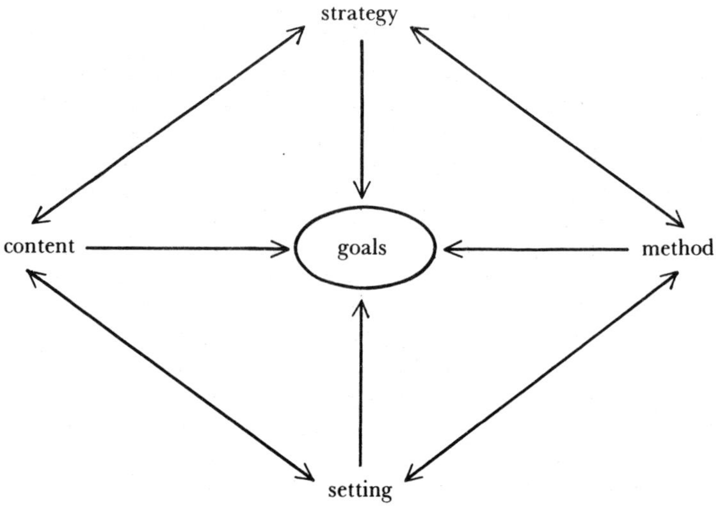

Goals

The overall goals of small group teaching are to develop discussion skills and to get students to think. These goals should be subdivided further into specific problems or issues related to content and the aims of the course. For example in a first-year course on electronics a goal of one small group session might be to get students to use second order differential equations to solve some basic problems of integrated circuits. In economic history the goal of the seminar may be to get students to appraise the impact of the railways on the economic and social structure of Britain. In psychology the goal of a session might be to get students to compare and contrast two theories of perception.

Content

The content of the sessions may be laid down by the syllabus, lecture programme, or course designer. None the less it may be possible to modify the order and time of the content. For example it is sometimes assumed that a small group session should follow a lecture. It may be that for some topics the small group session should precede the lecture so that the students have already grappled with the problems that the lecturer is addressing. The lecture may then be a more meaningful experience.

Strategy

The essence of the strategy is to prepare a strategy map of the topic or problem. Write the topic or problem of the session in the centre of a blank sheet of paper and write down whatever ideas, concepts, procedures, facts, questions come to you.Cluster the ideas as you go. Now take another blank sheet and group the ideas, facts, questions, and so on around the core topic. Figure 4.14 shows two examples which were the basis for seminars for colleagues on staff development.

When the second sheet is complete decide on the approximate order in which the topics might be tackled. Note down a few recall (narrow and broad) and thought questions (narrow and broad if possible) for each sub-topic.

The map of the topic may be used in the session to start discussion, to keep on track, to move the discussion to a related sub-topic, and as a summary of what the group has discussed. As students make new or unanticipated links and points, these can be added. In the final summary the tutor can use the map to state which issues have been tackled and omitted and what new suggestions have been made. This mode of summarizing gives the group a sense of achievement and lays the foundation for good future sessions.

The strategy may also be used as a joint exercise with students. Either students can prepare and compare their own maps of a topic, or tutor and students can together prepare the map for use in the session. The joint exercises are a useful basis for revision seminars and trouble-shooting sessions. The exercise can be used to help the students to see new connections within a topic. A tutor can also delegate to students the jobs of keeping on track and summarizing,

Figure 4.14 Strategy maps for discussions

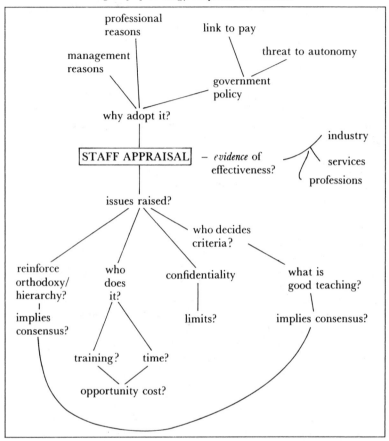

thereby developing the students' understanding and discussion skills.

Setting

The number of students in the session, the length of session, and the layout of the room all have an effect upon the patterns of interaction of the students. There is little point in choosing a method of free-flowing open discussion if you have a group of fifty students in a lecture theatre. Generally speaking you have to fit the methods selected to the setting and the goals of the session – or change the setting or goals. However if at all possible you should vary the

Figure 4.14 (cont.) Strategy maps for discussions

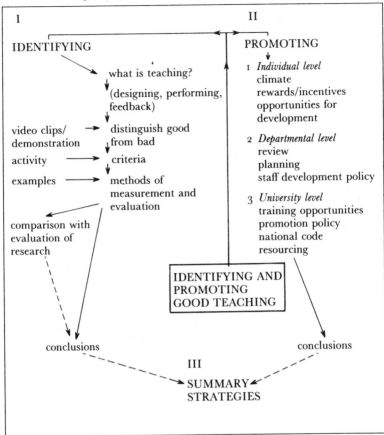

methods of small group teaching used within a course. Variety is not only the spice of life. It is the essence of effective teaching.

Method

This chapter has provided a list of methods of small group teaching. Choose a method which feels right for the group setting and tasks. If you want a fairly tight structure for the session then step by step teaching is probably the best method. If you want a more open discussion use the facilitating methods as a starting-point. The strategy map will help you to plan any method of small group teaching that you adopt. Having chosen the method think about

Figure 4.15 Rating schedule for small group sessions

This questionnaire has been devised to inform a tutor of your opinions concerning the small group sessions given by *this particular tutor*. Your responses are anonymous. They will be useful to the tutor when future courses are being prepared.

Please indicate your present thoughts by means of a tick on the five-point scale below. For example if you have found the course as a whole quite interesting you would show this as follows:

interesting _ ✓ _ _ _ boring

Any parts of the questionnaire which are not relevant should be left blank.

Name of tutor ....

Course ....

Please comment on each of the following:

A THE TUTOR

1 good group leader	_ _ _ _ _	poor group leader
2 fits into the group	_ _ _ _ _	too forceful
3 likes his or her opinions questioned	_ _ _ _ _	discourages the questioning of his or her opinions
4 patient	_ _ _ _ _	impatient
5 sarcastic	_ _ _ _ _	never sarcastic
6 lively	_ _ _ _ _	monotonous
7 pleasant manner	_ _ _ _ _	unpleasant manner
8 interested in students	_ _ _ _ _	not interested in students
9 interested in my ideas	_ _ _ _ _	not interested in my ideas
10 interested in me as an individual	_ _ _ _ _	does not know me
11 treats me with respect	_ _ _ _ _	does not treat me with respect
12 encourages me to discuss problems	_ _ _ _ _	unable to discuss problems
13 clearly audible	_ _ _ _ _	mumbles
14 interprets theories and ideas clearly	_ _ _ _ _	leaves me confused
15 gets me interested in his or her subject	_ _ _ _ _	bores me
16 stresses important material	_ _ _ _ _	all material seems the same
17 makes good use of examples and illustrations	_ _ _ _ _	never gives examples
18 inspires confidence in his or her knowledge of the subject	_ _ _ _ _	ill at ease with the subject
19 is up-to-date with knowledge	_ _ _ _ _	not aware of latest developments

20 is clear and understandable _ _ _ _ _ quite incomprehensible
in explanations
21 appears confident   _ _ _ _ _ not confident

B THE TUTORIALS

22 well organized   _ _ _ _ _ muddled
23 good progression   _ _ _ _ _ poor progression
24 tutorials are well prepared _ _ _ _ _ tutorials are not well
prepared
25 the group enjoys meeting _ _ _ _ _ the group does not enjoy
together   meeting together
26 time is well spent   _ _ _ _ _ they are a waste of time
27 new material covered   _ _ _ _ _ merely repeat lecture
material
28 have thrown new light on _ _ _ _ _ irrelevant to an under-
lecture course   standing of lecture course
29 too much time spent on   _ _ _ _ _ not enough time spent on
tutorial papers   tutorial papers
30 blackboard: easy to read _ _ _ _ _ blackboard: illegible
31 overcome difficulties   _ _ _ _ _ difficulties not dealt with
encountered in lectures

C THE STUDENT'S RESPONSE

32 I am fully aware of my   _ _ _ _ _ I seem to be 'working in
progress   the dark'
33 I enjoy contributing   _ _ _ _ _ I try to say nothing
34 I look forward to the   _ _ _ _ _ I would prefer not to attend
tutorials
35 I have learnt a lot   _ _ _ _ _ I have learnt nothing
36 My comments and opinions _ _ _ _ _ My comments and opinions
have been welcomed   have not been sought
37 I am more inclined to   _ _ _ _ _ I have developed an
continue with the subject   aversion to the subject

D THE WHOLE COURSE

38 difficult   _ _ _ _ _ easy
39 too much material   _ _ _ _ _ nothing much in it
40 vocationally useful to me   _ _ _ _ _ waste of time
41 interesting   _ _ _ _ _ boring
42 I will do further study   _ _ _ _ _ I will not pursue it

ADVICE OR SUGGESTIONS FOR THE FUTURE

Thank you for answering this questionnaire.

ways of opening the session, the likely stages of the session, and the closing of the session.

If the method is unfamiliar to you, try it a few times with different groups before deciding whether you wish to continue using it. Remember, the first few times you use a new method you are learning to use it as well as teaching so you should not be surprised if it feels strange.

EVALUATING SMALL GROUP TEACHING

Analysing small group teaching sessions can help to improve techniques (Brown 1981; Jaques 1984). Two major approaches are possible. You can obtain measures of products, such as students' reactions, by means of questionnaire, interview, and their examination results (see the section in Chapter 3 on Evaluating lectures, pp. 39–40), or you can study the processes of small group teaching, such as the pattern of questions or the types of student contributions. Figure 4.15 (pp. 82–3) shows a rating schedule that students could complete anonymously – but it is worth remembering that you can't please all of the students all of the time. The rest of this section is devoted to some simple methods of analysing processes in small groups.

Direct observation

During small groups you can observe and analyse the patterns of interaction – indeed this is part of leading the group. You can look for signals of boredom such as wriggling, sighs, clenched hands, tapping feet, and bodies oriented away from the tutor. You can look too for signs of interest such as eye contact, alertness, leaning forward, nodding, and other movement. You may find it interesting to keep a mental count of student contributions; they may be much rarer than you expect.

Interaction analysis

There are a number of methods of analysing the frequency and types of contributions in groups (Flanders 1970; Brown 1981; Galton 1983). Many of the systems are too complex other than for research purposes. One simple useful method is BIAS (Brown's Interaction Analysis Sytem), and the system presented here is a simplified version of this, known as Contracted BIAS. This can be learned in about 15 minutes and it can be used to analyse live or recorded discussion. Figure 4.16 shows the simple matrix that is used.

Every 3 seconds the observer codes what is going on in the group.

Figure 4.16 Contracted BIAS

CONTRACTED BIAS RECORDING SHEET

Use 3-second intervals

		Total
LT	///Q Q Q/////////// ////Q Q//Q Q /////Q /	35
ST	// / Q // ///Q / /Q	13
S	/ / /	3

LT = lecturer talk
ST = student talk
S   = silence
Q   = question

NOTES

Only questioning and talk were focused on.
The lecturer talked for approximately 70 per cent of the time, the students for 26 per cent.
The lecturer asked eight questions, the students three.
Extract from middle of seminar (time about 2½ minutes).

INTERPRETATION

Reviewing the sample you might want to question whether this small group session was becoming too tutor-dominated.

In its simplest form a stroke (/) is placed in the appropriate box. Codes such as Q for question, E for explaining, C for correction, and S for summarizing may be used. Thus if the lecturer were correcting a student's response there would be a C in one of the boxes on the LT (Lecturer Talk) line. If this correction continued for 3 seconds there would be another C in the next box. Silence at the code-time would produce a stroke in the S (Silence) line. A student question would then appear as a Q in the ST (Student Talk) line, perhaps with a subscript to indicate the identity of the student if it's only a small group. A worked example is given in Figure 4.16, though for clarity the box lines have not been reproduced here.

Quite complex processes can be identified even with this simple approach and the results can be useful in comparing different methods, different tutors, and different groups. Rogers (1986) has developed a microcomputer-based system for analysing BIAS which enables the user to analyse segments of the session and to explore visually the patterns and chains of interaction.

A method for analysing questions is shown in Figure 4.17. This requires an observer to code questions according to the dichotomies listed along the top of the sheet: narrow–broad, recall–thought, and so on. Again this very simple technique can produce very revealing profiles of a tutor's typical questioning style.

Figure 4.17 Analysing questions

	Type		Level		Quality		Target		Style		
	Narrow	Broad	Recall	Thought	Clear	Confused	Directed	Undirected	Encouraging	Neutral	Threatening
1											
2											
3											
4											
5											
6											
7											
8											
9											
10											

1 Note question briefly.
2 Tick relevant column appropriate to the question noted.
3 Use L for lecturer question, S for student question.
4 Don't attempt to note every question if the discussion is lively.

Leadership discussion

Figure 4.18 shows a system for analysing leadership style developed by Heron (1975). It highlights the use of authoritative and facilitative strategies by indicating whether a particular category of behaviour occurs at least once during a 30-second period.

Figure 4.18 Leadership style

Tick the appropriate category the first time the person you are observing uses it in each 30-second interval.

Seconds	30	60	90	120	150	180...	Totals
Authoritative 1 *Prescriptive* giving advice/direction, being critical, evaluative, offering judgements							
2 *Informative* giving information/ interpretation, being didactic							
3 *Confronting* directly challenging attitudes/beliefs/actions							
Total							
Facilitative 4 *Cathartic* releasing tension, encouraging laughter/ other emotions							
5 *Catalytic* eliciting information, encouraging self-directed problem-solving, being reflective							
6 *Supportive* being approving/ confirming/validating							
Total							

Authoritative/facilitative ratio A/F =

SUMMARY

This chapter has explored various approaches to the problems of getting students to talk and think. A review of studies of small group teaching methods indicates that they are valuable ways of developing thinking and discussion skills, but that many small group sessions do not achieve their full potential. Various facilitating methods were outlined which promote discussion and thinking. These were then used to enhance the more common method of small group teaching.

Underlying the methods of small group teaching are the skills of explaining, questioning, responding, listening, summarizing, and closing. Of these skills, questioning and listening were considered in detail since they are the basis of discussion and of developing thinking.

The penultimate section of the chapter provided an approach to preparing for small group teaching which is based on the strategy of developing a mental map of a topic or problem. The chapter ended with a brief description of some ways of analysing and evaluating your own small group teaching.

ACTIVITIES

4.1 What do you like and dislike most about small group sessions? You can put the question to your students, too, and compare the answers.

4.2 Work with two or three colleagues who are giving small group sessions on the same or similar topics. Describe to each other a tutorial or seminar which you gave recently. Analyse and compare your goals. What were the students' goals? How do you know?

4.3 What do you do in the first 10 minutes of your *first meeting* with a group of students? What do the students do? Is there any rationale behind your opening moves in terms of safety, expectations, and so on?

4.4 Students are not the only participants who play manipulative games in small group sessions. Tutors do too. Spend a few minutes thinking about 'games' which you have observed tutors play (or, be honest, have used yourself). You might like to give them an appropriate name. Here are some suggestions:
Battleships ....
Squash ....
Give-a-man-a-rope .....
Charades ....

4.5 You have been introduced in the chapter to three facilitating methods: buzz group, brainstorming, and snowballing. Spend a few minutes considering where each of these might be incorporated into some actual small group sessions which you run. Remember that the methods can be useful at different stages of a group session, and not just the beginning.

4.6 In spite of careful attention to facilitating the small group, things can still go wrong. Below are three common 'problems' which tutors have to deal with. Choose two and compare with a colleague how you would handle the incidents.

The silent student

For the past four weeks you have had a student in your tutorial group who has never spoken. Even when you have asked her a simple, direct question you have received only a monosyllabic answer, a grunt, or silence.

Today you tried again. You asked a question. The student answered your question at length. Unfortunately the answer was wrong.

What do you do next?

The know-it-all expert

In your seminar there is one person who answers every question and likes to dominate the discussion. One or two in the group are getting annoyed, but most are simply switching off and ceasing to participate once he starts speaking.

What can you do to retrieve the situation?

The aggressive student

You have just begun an important session with a relatively new group of students. Suddenly one of them leans forward and says angrily: 'I'm sick of these bloody sessions. In fact I'm pissed off with the whole course. When are we going to get down to something useful?'

What do you do and say in the next few minutes?

4.7 The key skills of effective small group work are explaining, listening, questioning, and responding. Which of these would you say you were best at? Worst at? What about your students?

4.8 For this activity you need access to a video-recording of a small group session. View 5 to 10 minutes of the session with a colleague or colleagues. While viewing, and immediately afterwards, jot down some notes on the *questioning technique* used by the lecturer. For example:
Note an example of a 'recall' question.
Note an example of a 'thought' question.
Note an example of a 'probe' or 'prompt'.
Try to identify a sequence of questions.
Discuss with your colleague(s) whether the tutor succeeded in getting the students to think. What did you think of the use of questions?

4.9 Think of a topic in your own subject and of a group of students whom you teach it to. Invent four or five questions you might ask of them in the teaching session. Classify them as narrow v. broad, recall v. thought, and clear v. confusing. Keep the classifications separate. Ask a colleague also to classify the questions on the same dimensions. Compare and discuss classification.

4.10 Working with a colleague, decide who will be the 'listener' and who the 'explainer'. The explainer explains a tiny segment of his or her subject for 3 minutes. The listener may ask questions but may not take notes. Then reverse roles. When both have been listener and explainer the first listener should report back what he or she was told. The explainer should correct any major errors or omissions. Then reverse the procedure.
What difficulties did you encounter in listening? Did the level of listening change? Did the exercise affect the way you explained?

4.11 Work with a colleague who teaches the same subject as yourself. Choose a topic from a common course and then design a tutorial using the 'mapping' procedure given in the chapter. Include key questions. After 8 minutes compare your approaches.
If possible, run the session and note what happened in relation to the map. Compare experiences with your colleague afterwards.

5
Effective laboratory teaching

> It is universally accepted that practical work is essential
> for the students in subjects where it is appropriate. [Think
> about it!]
>
> (Hale Report on University Teaching 1964)

INTRODUCTION

Practical work has a time-honoured place in the education of scientists
and engineers. Most practical work occurs in laboratories but field-
work, placements, and sandwich courses are also important features
of some courses. In this chapter we will be looking primarily at the
uses, skills, and methods of laboratory work, although many of the
activities, hints, and suggestions that we offer also apply to the
organization of field-work, placements, and sandwich courses.

The practical work is the most expensive part of an engineer's or
scientist's education. So, at a time when departmental grants are
being cut and demonstrator time is being reduced, it is particularly
appropriate to consider ways of making practical work more efficient
and more effective in your own courses.

The major goals of practical work are:

1 Teaching manual and observational skills relevant to the subject.
2 Improving understanding of methods of scientific enquiry.
3 Developing problem-solving skills.
4 Nurturing professional attitudes.

The first three of these goals are self-explanatory. The fourth is more
subtle and is probably the most important long-term goal. It is also
the most elusive. Most of us hope that our students will develop a
commitment to the subject that we teach and that they will incorporate its values into their thinking and actions. Practical work can, and
should, provide the opportunity for such attitudes to grow.

LABORATORY TEACHING IN PERSPECTIVE

In Britain the use of laboratories in undergraduate teaching dates back only to the mid- and late nineteenth century (Brock and Meadows 1977; Phillips 1981). Neither Oxford nor Cambridge had undergraduate science laboratories before 1870. There was considerable resistance to the notion of practicals in the nineteenth century – just as today there is some resistance to the notion of changing the underlying approach to practicals. Most of the early practicals were essentially demonstrations of important principles. They were also used to train students to build equipment and make accurate measurements. Later, practicals became exercises which led students to the 'right' answers. These traditions of laboratory teaching still persist – and, some would say, rightly so. During the past twenty years, however, there has been increased interest in the use of laboratories as a training ground for independent scientific enquiry. This interest has led to a spate of new methods and to reappraisals of the uses and methods of laboratory teaching. The recent studies of laboratory teaching may conveniently be divided into three groups: surveys of practices, studies comparing laboratory work with other methods of teaching, and reports of new approaches to laboratory teaching.

Surveys

Most science and engineering students in Britain spend between 50 and 70 per cent of their contact time in laboratory work. Chemists spend over 500 hours per year, biologists about 400 hours, and physicists about 300 hours per year in laboratories (Aspden and Eardley 1974). These differences may, in part, be accounted for by differences in manipulative skills required by different subjects. Chemical separation and distillation, dissection, and microscopy involve highly complex motor skills which may require intensive practice.

Time spent in practicals seems to be matched by private time spent on practicals. Fifteen years ago science and engineering students reported that they spent most of their private study on writing up practicals and that each major practical took up to seven hours to write up (Entwistle, Percy, and Nisbet 1971). These findings may still hold today, although many departments no longer insist that all practicals are written up fully. Even so some departments do not mark practicals and in others laboratory work may count for as little as 5 per cent of the degree assessment. The importance of practical work is not always reflected in course marks (Thompson 1979) (see Activity 5.1). One reason for this may be that marking of laboratory notebooks is often unreliable. Wilson et al. (1969) in their study of laboratory assessment discovered a 25 per cent variation in marks between sets of demonstrators who marked the same laboratory notebooks. Such variations can, of course, be reduced considerably by the use of double marking, explicit criteria, and by training demonstrators to mark consistently.

Perhaps the most important survey of teaching work in recent years is the Higher Education Learning Project (HELP) in physics. Bliss and Ogborn (1977) report the results of their survey and of discussions with lecturers, demonstrators, technicians, and students on the place of practical work in several university courses. Many students disliked practical work until they were doing their project or long experiment in the final year. Demonstrators sometimes were uncertain of their role and students reported wide variation in the quality of help from demonstrators. Daines (1986) in a subsequent study explored students' expectations of demonstrators. Most students valued the characteristics of fair marking, constructive criticism, clear explanation of errors, written comments on the students' work, and listening to students' questions.

Comparative studies

The findings from comparative studies of conventional laboratory classes and other forms of teaching also suggest that laboratory work is not as effective as one might wish (see the reviews by Shulman and Tamir 1973; Hegarty-Hazel 1986). Laboratory work does appear to be better than lectures, demonstrations *per se*, or small group discussions at improving manual and observational skills but, not surprisingly, less effective than lectures at teaching factual knowledge or concepts. However many of these studies used examination results rather than specially devised tests as the criterion, and so factors other than laboratory work could have influenced the results. Conventional laboratory methods do not appear to be any better than other methods at teaching the understanding of methods of scientific enquiry or problem-solving skills (see the discussion by Hegarty 1982).

Reports of new approaches

It is, perhaps, this disquieting finding that prompted some lecturers to develop alternative methods of laboratory teaching such as the use of single concept experiments (O'Connell, Penton, and Boud 1977). There have also been reports on the unit physics laboratory (Black and Whitworth 1974; Davies 1977) and the physiology course at Nottingham (Short and Tomlinson 1979). The Nuffield Foundation (1974) report on *Studies in Laboratory Innovation*, Bliss and Ogborn (1977), and Boud, Dunn, and Hegarty-Hazel (1986) provide details of new approaches in laboratory teaching in science, medicine, and engineering. Boud *et al.* (1978) also review reports on the new methods which include:

- Integrated laboratories
- Project work
- Participation in research
- Case study approach
- Computer assisted laboratory instruction
- Audio-tutorial laboratory method
- Keller plan.

Not all of these mthods have been evaluated systematically. Even if they had been, you would still have to evaluate them in the context of the goals of your own laboratory course.

The studies of laboratory teaching to date have yielded useful approaches and information which could be incorporated into courses. But, a century after the introduction of laboratory work, there have been no attempts to study systematically the *processes* of learning in laboratories and few attempts to evaluate rigorously the contribution of practical work to the education of scientists and engineers.

USES OF LABORATORY WORK

Most of the uses of laboratory work may be subsumed under the goals given in the introduction:

- Teaching manual and observational skills relevant to the subject.
- Improving understanding of methods of scientific enquiry.
- Developing problem-solving skills.
- Nurturing professional attitudes.

The main principle underlying laboratory work is that students learn effectively through doing practical tasks. Certainly even the most sophisticated learners benefit from concrete experiences particularly in new topics. But the principle of 'learning through doing' needs two qualifications. First, the tasks have to be perceived as relevant and meaningful by the students – otherwise interest may be minimal. Second, students (and lecturers too) have to receive constructive feedback on their performance – otherwise learning may be minimal. Practice does not itself make perfect but practice with feedback almost always improves performance. These points should be borne in mind when designing laboratory courses and marking laboratory work (see Activities 5.1 and 5.8).

SKILLS OF LABORATORY TEACHING

Laboratory teaching often involves giving brief explanations and instructions to the whole class and then dividing the class into pairs or small groups who work on a particular experiment. So, not surprisingly, some of the skills of laboratory teaching are similar to those of lecturing and small group teaching. We need to create interest, and to explain technical information; we need to ask students the right question, to know when to exercise control and when to let go, and how to judge the level of demand. Most important of all, we need to put ourselves in the place of the students who are doing the laboratory course so that we can choose appropriate experiments, give the right instructions, and make laboratory work into a challenging and rewarding experience.

Laboratory teaching also involves skills concerned with giving directions, with helping demonstrators and technicians, and with designing, organizing, and implementing laboratory work. Figure 5.1 sets out a list of essential skills of laboratory teaching. In this section of the chapter only a few of these skills will be considered. The skills concerned with preparing laboratory courses are discussed in a later section.

Figure 5.1 The skills of laboratory teaching

- Explaining and presenting information.
- Questioning, listening, and responding.
- Giving directions.
- Teaching demonstrators.
- Helping technicians.
- Preparing a laboratory course.

Giving directions

The precept that directions should be clear, unambiguous, and in the correct order is easy to understand. Following the precept is less easy. Flow charts, decision trees, and written statements supported by clear diagrams may be necessary for complex directions.

Activity 5.2 describes a simple but useful activity on giving directions which the authors have used in workshops on laboratory teaching and which participants found valuable for developing their general skill of giving directions.

Teaching demonstrators

Broadly speaking the role of the demonstrators is to help students to carry out their activities. The student activities may consist of following instructions, solving a design problem, setting up apparatus, checking the apparatus works, obtaining, observing, and recording results, calculating results, noting any peculiarities in methods or results and, perhaps, linking the results to theoretical principles or other results.

So clearly the demonstrator must understand the experiments, be familiar with the equipment and procedures, and know how to write good laboratory reports. This is necessary but not sufficient knowledge. Knowing how to do the experiment is one thing. Knowing when and how to help someone else carry out the experiment is quite another.

As a lecturer in charge of a laboratory course you can help demonstrators – and technicians and students – by providing a laboratory manual for the course (see the section 'Design the laboratory manual', pp. 105–7) and by providing the demonstrators with guidelines on what to do in laboratory sessions. You could also spend half a day on training the demonstrators. Indeed, given the emphasis placed on laboratory work, it is curious that there are few reported attempts to train demonstrators (Davies 1978).

To train demonstrators you need to identify the important skills of demonstrators and provide a series of brief, well-structured activities which would help them to develop their skills as demonstrators. Figure 5.2 lists skills required by demonstrators that our colleagues at Nottingham, Loughborough, and Newcastle found useful.

Figure 5.2 Demonstrator skills

Know how to do, and write up, the experiment AND:

- Observe students at work.
- Anticipate major difficulties of understanding.
- Recognize major difficulties of understanding.
- Give brief, clear explanations of processes and procedures.
- Give directions.
- Ask questions which clarify difficulties of understanding.
- Ask questions which guide students.
- Answer questions in a simple, direct, and non-critical way.
- Offer supportive and encouraging remarks.
- Know when to help and not help a student.

(See also Activity 5.3)

Helping technicians

One of the important jobs of technicians is to maintain and prepare appropriate equipment and materials for the teaching experiments. Another is to help demonstrators and students who are unfamiliar with a particular procedure or apparatus. It follows that technicians can best be helped by knowing what is expected of them. Here again a good laboratory manual, which sets out the timetable and sequence of experiments, is an invaluable aid in their work. But technicians, unlike students, have considerable expertise. The laboratory is their permanent work-place whereas students and demonstrators are, in a sense, visitors. You can help technicians by valuing their expertise, discussing minor changes, and collaborating with them on major changes in laboratory organization.

In short, the best way of helping technicians is to be a good manager.

SOME LABORATORY TEACHING METHODS

The essential principle underlying all laboratory teaching methods is that, as far as possible, students teach themselves and each other. The experiments, tasks, and guidelines are provided by the course organizers and the students learn through their own efforts.

In this section we do not propose to discuss in detail every known method of laboratory teaching. Instead we provide a range of methods which may help you to think about your own laboratory course and ways of achieving its goals. Some of the methods that we suggest are concerned with facilitating existing practices and some may be used to replace existing practices. The division is not a sharp one for some facilitating methods may be used also as full methods in their own right.

FACILITATING METHODS

Lecturers and demonstrators often have to repeat the same instructions or demonstrations several times in a year. Sometimes only a few students at a time can see an intricate demonstration and sometimes students need time to absorb the procedures and check their understanding. Many of the routine demonstrations and instructions can be tackled by using facilitating methods. All of them have the added merit of allowing students to work at their own pace.

Written instructions

These are the most common facilitating method. These may be handouts or, preferably, a laboratory manual. They should contain the explicit goals of the experiment, clear instructions, and well-labelled diagrams. They might also contain questions on the experiment or its implications. The written instructions may be used with a set of slides, a video-recorder and/or an audio cassette.

1 SLIDE BOOKLETS are particularly useful for showing a process, a complex procedure, or complicated apparatus.
2 TAPE/BOOKLETS can be used to provide instructions, descriptions, and methods of calculation.
3 TAPE/SLIDE PROGRAMMES can also be used to provide instructions, demonstrations, and descriptions of apparatus.
4 WALL CHARTS are useful for displaying instructions, graphs, and key features of equipment.
5 VIDEO-RECORDINGS AND FILM LOOPS may be used to provide instructions, the workings of the equipment, and demonstrations of techniques or procedures.
6 MICROCOMPUTER PROGRAMS may be used to describe the experiment, to provide instructions, to plot or calculate results, or to show the student how to carry out the calculations, and to ask questions which alert the students to possible interpretations of results.
7 INTERACTIVE VIDEO combining a video-recorder or video-disc with a microcomputer may eventually be feasible as a facilitating method or as a laboratory simulation.

All of the facilitating methods may be used to improve the efficiency and effectiveness of laboratory teaching. For example many of the routine instructions and directions can be set out on a videotape or tape/slide programme which students can study. This practice saves time and energy of demonstrators. But there is a cost factor. Preparing good-quality presentations is time-consuming so you may want to use the more sophisticated methods only for experiments which are done frequently. A simple 10-minute demonstration of first-class quality may take 4 hours to video-record; a complex one may take 20 hours.

SOME CONVENTIONAL METHODS OF LABORATORY
TEACHING

The most common methods of laboratory teaching are demonstrations,
exercises, enquiries, and projects. These vary in the degree of open-
ness of the task and in time spent on the task (see Figure 5.3).

Figure 5.3 Levels of experiments

	Level	Aim	Materials	Method	Answer
Demonstration	0	Given	Given	Given	Given
Exercise	1	Given	Given	Given	Open
Structured enquiry	2	Given	Given part or whole	Open or part given	Open
Open enquiry	3	Given	Open	Open	Open
Project	4	Open	Open	Open	Open

Demonstrations

These are designed to illustrate theoretical principles which are
outlined in lectures. They may be carried out by a demonstrator or
the students themselves. A common weakness is that the experimental demonstration may occur long after the lecture so the principle is
no longer uppermost in the student's mind, or it may occur before
the lecture so the principle is not known. A facilitating method may
be used to provide the necessary information, or you could use one of
the alternative methods given below.

Exercises

These are tightly structured experiments which are designed to yield
well-known experimental results. Students follow precise instructions
and in so doing learn specific techniques of observation and manipu-
lation. Careful reading of the instructions of such experiments can
often reveal the answers required.

Structured enquiries

These are lightly structured experiments which may require students
to develop their own procedures and/or provide their own interpretations of the results. Structured enquiries involve problem-solving

skills and interpretative skills as well as manual and observational skills.

Open-ended enquiries

These may require students to identify a problem, formulate the problem clearly, develop experimental procedures, interpret results, and consider their implications. The constraints on the students may be time and the range of equipment and materials available. Hegarty and Lee (1979) describe such an approach in microbiology which could be used in many subjects. They call their method the 'tutor's kit' method.The students are set a problem which simulates a real-life problem of diagnosis and treatment. The student may ask for any information or materials in the kit but he or she has to give reasons for the request. The demonstrator or lecturer can monitor the quality of requests. The students have to provide a report of diagnosis and recommended treatment.

All open-ended enquiries use, in miniaturized form, many of the skills of the research scientist (see section 'Helping students learn from laboratory sessions' on pp. 169–171). They are a useful preliminary to:

Projects

These are based upon long experiments, field studies, or a series of experiments. The end product may include design plans, a model, or a computer program. Project topics may be selected by a student or offered by his supervisor or by local industry (see Adderly *et al.* 1975; Dowdeswell and Harris 1979 for examples of projects in different subjects).

Projects are usually carried out in the final year of a first degree although it could be argued that a mini-project in the first year might be a useful introduction to this type of open learning. The final-year project is usually a miniaturized version of postgraduate research and may be a better predictor of research potential than conventional written papers. The advantages of projects are that they enable a student to explore a field deeply, they develop initiative and resourcefulness, and they stimulate a student's intellectual curiosity. Students enjoy them and value them highly. The disadvantages of projects are that they may be time-consuming for project supervisors to set up, monitor, and provide feedback on – and they may be difficult to assess fairly. None of these disadvantages is insurmountable, nor should they be used as a justification *per se* for not using projects.

Project supervisors are involved in the formulation of a problem, the conduct of the investigations, and the report on the project. Time and needless frustration can be saved by giving students guidelines which provide a light, flexible framework for the project but do not prescribe too closely the methods to be used (see Chapter 6 on 'Effective research and project supervision').

In the preparatory phase students can meet in groups to share, discuss, and formulate their problems. During the conduct of the investigation and the report stage it is useful for the students (and their supervisor) to hold brief, regular meetings so that they keep on target or, at least, let you know if they have changed their target. The role of the project supervisor changes subtly throughout the project. At first he or she may direct the student to look at particular problems and difficulties. Gradually the project supervisor may withdraw direction and encourage the students to anticipate their own particular problems and difficulties. By the end of the project the lecturer should have worked him- or herself out of the job of project supervisor. This gradual withdrawal from the role of supervisor may not be a linear process. Project students, like research students, go through periods of elation, uncertainty, and despair.

SOME ALTERNATIVES TO CONVENTIONAL METHODS

Not every laboratory session need be an experiment; not every experimental task need be a full experiment; and, of course, not every laboratory session need fulfil all the goals for a laboratory course. Instead you can use alternative approaches which fulfil some of the goals of the course. Here are a few approaches which a lecturer can use in laboratory courses:

1 Paper and pencil activities which require a student to solve an experimental problem or create an experimental design.
2 Provide the experimental data, such as the output of a mass spectrometer, and ask groups of students to interpret it.
3 Present a video-recording of an experiment which shows readings on various instruments. Ask the students to note, calculate, and interpret the results.
4 Set up a microcomputer so that students can enter the results and obtain immediate graphic displays or calculations of data.
5 Set up the apparatus for the students so all they have to do is to take readings.
6 Sidestep part of the experiment. Ask students to perform the parts of an experiment which can be done quickly and provide pre-prepared materials for the slow part of the experiment (as is done in some Open University courses).

7 Design a set of *brief, simple* experiments which exemplify fundamental principles.

8 Organize the laboratory work so that groups of students do sets of experiments and then each group receives an illustrated talk and discusses each of the experiments. The talks and discussions should be given by members of the group.

You can also use more radical alternatives to laboratory courses or parts of laboratory courses. These alternatives allow students to work at their own pace and give them some freedom of choice. Some examples are described below.

Keller Plan/personalized system of instruction (PSI)

A course based on do-it-yourself instructions and guidelines which students pursue at their own pace. Some courses use proctors – students who have already completed the course – as well as the self-instruction materials. Tests are given at frequent intervals and each test must be passed before proceeding to the next stage (see Kulik, Kulik, and Cohen 1979; Boud, Dunn, and Hegarty-Hazel 1986 for a description and review of the effectiveness of this method).

Audio-tutorial method (AT)

The AT method uses audio- and possibly video-cassettes, booklets, and simple apparatus. Theoretical and practical aspects of a topic are integrated within the programme. Lectures and tutorials may be optional extras. One such system has yielded highly significant improvements in problem-solving skills (Brewer 1985).

Computer assisted learning (CAL)

The use of computers as learning aids rather than as calculators. Often used to provide simulations which cannot be studied by direct experience because of cost, time, or complexity involved (Kahn 1986).

Learning aids laboratory

Basically a miniature resource centre of audio-visual aids such as slide/booklet, tape/slide programmes, or microcomputer programs which may be used to supplement laboratory experiments, lectures, or problem-solving classes. This can also be used as a revision aid in the form of multiple choice quiz (see Ramsay 1973; Cryer and Rider 1977).

Modular laboratory

A set of instructional packages which can be tackled in any order by students (Goldschmid and Goldschmid 1974).

Integrated laboratory

Different disciplines are integrated into a common laboratory course. For example physiology, pharmacology, and biochemistry, or physics and chemistry (Short and Tomlinson 1979; O'Connell, Penton, and Boud 1977).

Project work

This was discussed earlier since it is now a common feature of final-year courses (Adderly *et al.* 1975; Cornwall, Schmitals, and Jaques 1978). Mini-projects could also be used earlier in a course.

Participation in research

Undergraduates work as members of a research team alongside postgraduates and lecturers. Their contributions are assessed as part of their degree (S. A. Cohen and McVicar 1976; Mathias 1976; Smith 1980).

PREPARING A LABORATORY COURSE

Preparing a laboratory course has many features in common with preparing for small group teaching sessions and lecturing. You have to think about the course in the context of the overall programme and you have to consider constraints such as time available, equipment, materials, student numbers, and laboratory space. Within these constraints there are four major tasks:

1 Establishing or rethinking the aims of the course.
2 Choosing appropriate tasks for students.
3 Designing appropriate tasks.
4 Designing a laboratory manual.

Each will be considered in turn, although in practice you may find you zig-zag from task to task.

Establish or rethink aims

Activity 5.1 may be helpful here. Short and Tomlinson (1979) and Hofstein and Lunetta (1982) also provide lists of uses of laboratory work. You may want to add or subtract from these lists and specify more precisely certain goals such as 'how to use a mass spectrometer' or 'how to prepare a particular culture'. You should try to avoid producing a list of aims which are merely a hidden description of all the experiments on the existing course. Instead, look at some of the ideas given in this chapter, in Nuffield Foundation (1974) or Boud, Dunn, and Hegarty-Hazel (1986), and see if these would be useful in your laboratory course. Then ask yourself: 'Which tasks best fulfil some of the aims?'

When you think you have chosen an appropriate set of tasks you should prepare a matrix of aims and experiments (see Figure 5.4).

Figure 5.4 The laboratory course

Set up a matrix.

Write aims on the vertical axis and proposed laboratory experiences on the horizontal axis. Put a tick in the appropriate cell for each aim.

Aims	*Experiments*
	I 2 3 4 . . . . n
	I
	2
	3
	4
	.
	.
	.
	.
	.
	.
	n

Then, if necessary, go back to reshaping the aims or choosing different activities. Incidentally, the use of Figures 5.3 and 5.4 on an existing laboratory course can often reveal ways of improving its effectiveness and efficiency.

Design the tasks

Having chosen the tasks, you may need to think about each task in turn and, in particular, consider:

1 What do the students need to know to carry out the task?
2 What manual and observational skills will they use?
3 What equipment and materials are necessary?
4 What do you expect the students to know and be able to do when they have completed the task?

The questions are simple but the answers may have to be detailed. (To check how good your general skills of giving instructions are try Activity 5.2.)

Design the laboratory manual

The written instructions and background information of experiments are a crucial part of a laboratory course. A good manual can improve the overall effectiveness of a laboratory course, show links between the course and the lectures, and save time in the laboratory for students and demonstrators. A manual provides students with a model of design and layout. So, incidentally, do tatty, half-baked instructions.

When designing a manual it is probably best to begin with the experiments and tasks and then consider other features of the manual. Hartley and Burnhill (1977) and Hartley (1984) contain hints on the design of instructional texts.

For each experiment or task you need:

1 Explicit aims

So the students know what they are expected to know and do when they have completed the experiment. At the same time you might tell the students, briefly, how the experiment fits into their overall programme particularly if the experiment is a prerequisite for a future experiment. If the experiment assumes that they have done related experiments earlier in the course then remind them of these. These simple suggestions will help the students to see the relevance of the experiments. You can also use the explicit aims for designing assessment and for analysing student achievements.

2 Clear instructions

These should indicate where apparatus and materials are located and then describe the procedures. The instructions need not always be chunks of prose. Flow charts and algorithms are often easier to follow and they have the added merit of forcing you to think out carefully the order of procedures.

3 Illustrations of good quality

These should be designed so that students can see clearly the important features of apparatus or material. This principle applies to slides and transparencies as well as to illustrations and diagrams in the text. Cox and Ewan (1981) contain useful hints on illustrations and transparencies.

If written materials, tables, or graphs are essential for interpreting the data, you could include them in an appendix to the manual. This will save valuable time during the laboratory sessions and, if the students can use the material from the appendix in their own laboratory books, they will be able to save time when writing up.

4 Questions

Questions provide cues for essential points and they can motivate a student to think or to check that he or she has carried out the procedures correctly. Questions are best located immediately after a description of a task although questions which ask the students to observe processes during the experiments should be inserted in the procedures. Of course, students should be encouraged to read and think about all aspects of the experiment or task before embarking upon it and again afterwards so it is useful to build some of the questions into:

5 Self-evaluation check-lists

These can be used to direct students to assess how well they carried out the practical task, to reflect upon the implications of the experiment, and to consider how they might improve. If the students are working in small groups or teams, they can use check-lists to assess one another and to match the group's assessment and the self assessment. You can also use multiple choice questions or other test items. Answers could be provided – but not necessarily in the manual.

6 The layout of the manual

The first page of this should be devoted to 'How to use this manual'. In the first section of the manual spell out the overall aims of the course and the experiments. You could use the matrix from Figure 5.4, 'The laboratory course'. You might also comment briefly on the relationship between the laboratory course and the programme of lectures and tutorials. A common complaint of students is that laboratory classes bear no relationship to the lectures they are attending. Either the relevant lecture is several weeks before or several weeks after the experiment. If this is true of a course you are running, be honest and say so. (Better still, change the organization of the course.) Include in this section details of how the laboratory work is assessed and refer them to the section of the manual dealing with laboratory reports.

In the second section of the manual include any general points of laboratory organization, the layout of the laboratory, and the help which demonstrators can and cannot be expected to give. In the third section describe each experiment or task in turn – with objectives, instructions, questions, and self-evaluation check-lists. Follow this with a section on writing up laboratory reports. Include a few excerpts from 'good' and 'bad' reports. If you want the students to give illustrated talks on their experiments then provide them with a few specific hints and suggestions.

When these tasks have been completed compile a contents list, annotated bibliography, and index. You can use different coloured paper for different sections of the book or for different features of the experiments. When the manual is given to students, spend about 15 minutes showing them how to use it. The compilation of a laboratory manual is a major task but a good manual is probably the single most important resource of laboratory teaching. Indeed it could be regarded as part of the usable laboratory materials which students pay a contribution towards on most courses.

EVALUATING LABORATORY TEACHING

Laboratory teaching, like all other forms of teaching, may be evaluated by studying the products of teaching such as examination results or reactions to a course, or by studying the processes of teaching and learning in laboratories through direct observation or discussion with students, demonstrators and technicians. Boud, Dunn, and Hegarty-Hazel (1986) provide a useful chapter on these themes. Here we present just a few of the possible approaches.

Studying products

The most common products arising out of laboratory work are laboratory note-books, results of written examinations, and project reports. None of these products may be used directly to evaluate laboratory teaching but all of them can provide pointers to ways of improving laboratory work. For example you can:

- Identify experiments or tasks which seem unduly difficult.
- Set and analyse specific questions or multiple choice items on crucial procedures.
- Look for common strengths and weaknesses in a set of project reports.

In addition you could set and analyse miniaturized experimental tasks to assess practical skills and to evaluate the laboratory course. Harden and Cairncross (1980) have developed such an approach in medicine which could well be adapted to any laboratory course.

But perhaps the most useful direct method of evaluating a laboratory course is to ask the students a series of well-constructed questions on the experiments and laboratory organization. Include a few open-ended questions so that they can comment freely. You might also ask the demonstrators and technicians for their comments on the laboratory course and the performance of students.

Studying processes

You can study the processes of learning in a laboratory in two major ways:

1 Watch and note

Spend a couple of hours observing students at work in a laboratory class. Time a few activities, watch for points where time is wasted through queueing for a piece of equipment or because apparatus is faulty, and observe which students do what and in what order. For example, some students always do the experiment while their partners always note the results. Some students always interpret and explain the instructions while others always listen. Some students read only half of the instructions and then seek help from a demonstrator. To find out what students do in your laboratory you could observe them at work or, better still, ask colleagues to observe one of your laboratory classes and you observe one of theirs. Alternatively video-record one or two groups of students who are doing an experiment and analyse the recordings.

2 Use check lists

If you want to be more rigorous in your observations you can design a simple check-list for observing students at work (see Figure 5.5). You could also incorporate into the check-list some of the objectives of the experiments. Check-lists may also be used to observe what demonstrators do. The results can be matched against the instructions given to demonstrators.

Figure 5.5 Check-list for setting up apparatus

This check-list may be used for observing groups of students who are setting up apparatus. Tick each activity *the first time* it occurs in each of the minute segments.

Time in minutes:	1	2	3	4	5	6	7	8	9	10
Reads instructions										
Looks at apparatus										
Handles apparatus but does not set it up										
Ask each other questions										
Checks layout of apparatus										
Checks instructions in relation to apparatus										
Seeks advice of another group										
Seeks advice of demonstrator										
Attempts to set up apparatus										
Checks apparatus in relation to instructions										
Checks apparatus is working properly										

Estimate the proportion of time spent on each activity. If the group you are observing is small then use initials of each member of the group.

SUMMARY

This chapter has looked at some of the uses of laboratory teaching. It provided a brief survey of studies of laboratory teaching. It outlined some methods which may be used to augment conventional methods and some alternatives which may be used instead. The chapter offered some suggestions on preparing laboratory courses, writing a laboratory course manual, and evaluating laboratory work. The activities given at the end of this chapter may provide you with further ideas and suggestions for developing your laboratory courses.

ACTIVITIES

5.1 Set out below are eighteen possible uses of laboratory courses. Mark the five most important and the five least important. Then rank these 1–5 and 14–18. Then rank the remaining items in the order 6–13. Then decide which of these objectives can, in your view:

● be developed in the ways in which your present laboratory practical classes are conducted;
● be developed in other ways than laboratory practical classes;
● be developed in simpler, more efficient ways in laboratory classes than those used at present in your laboratory.

Note: the second and third objectives may apply to the same item.

1 to teach theoretical material not presented elsewhere
2 to illustrate and amplify lecture material
3 to develop manipulative skills
4 to develop ability to follow instructions
5 to familiarize students with instruments and apparatus
6 to familiarize students with the design and construction of experimental equipment
7 to develop observational skills
8 to develop skills in gathering and interpreting data
9 to develop a concern for accuracy
10 to develop skill in communicating experimental results
11 to develop the ability to write coherent and well-argued reports
12 to develop the capacity for self-directed learning
13 to encourage independent thinking
14 to stimulate thought through experimental interpretation
15 to develop the students' skill in problem-solving with a wide number of variables and many possible solutions

16 to encourage enterprise, initiative, resourcefulness
17 to develop personal responsibility and reliability for experimentation
18 to develop the ability to work effectively as a member of a team.

If possible compare your list of priorities with colleagues who teach the same subject as you and who teach other subjects.

5.2 Meet in a group of about five.
Choose a simple practical task which you can demonstrate how to do, can give directions on, and which the rest of the group can practise immediately. The task may be related to your own subject or to some everyday activity (for example how to set up a simple apparatus, how to read a section of a map, how to read a table, how to take a pulse reading). During each demonstration two people should act as observers and the remainder attempt to follow the directions. After the demonstration they should give their evaluation. The demonstrator and the 'learners' should then suggest ways, if any, in which the directions could be improved When everyone has carried out a demonstration, the group should summarize briefly what they have learnt about giving directions and consider the implications of their experience for designing laboratory instructions.

Note: If the activity is video-recorded the cameraman should focus on the attempts of some of the participants to carry out the task as well as on the demonstrator and his or her directions.

5.3 Think about the skills your demonstrators need. Design a half-day workshop of activities. You will find some of the activities in this book helpful. You could also use brief video-recordings of laboratory sessions and parts of your laboratory manual.
Give the workshop. Ask for comments from the demonstrators. Prepare a set of guidelines for your demonstrators. If possible, carry out this activity with the colleagues who contribute to your laboratory course or similar laboratory courses. How well do you consider that your demonstrators carry out their tasks? How could they be helped to improve further?

5.4 Select four experiments from your laboratory course. Use the grid on the next page to classify each of the experiments. If possible, check your classification with those of a few colleagues.
The grid provides a method of estimating the level of scientific enquiry involved in an experiment or project. The level is determined by the degree of student involvement in selecting a

problem and designing appropriate experiments (based upon Hegarty 1978).

Level	Aim	Materials	Method	Answer
0	Given	Given	Given	Given
1	Given	Given	Given	Open
2	Given	Given part or whole	Open or part given	Open
3	Given	Open	Open	Open
4	Open	Open	Open	Open

5.5 Now invent a couple of simple experimental tasks in your own subject which require a little ingenuity. Try the tasks with a group of colleagues or students and discuss with them which objectives of laboratory work are involved in the tasks. Modify the tasks if necessary and try them again.

5.6 Meet with a few colleagues who have used all or some of the alternatives we described in the section describing alternative methods, pp. 101–3, and discuss with them the advantages and disadvantages of the alternative approaches for some aspect of your laboratory course.

5.7 Read the following two extracts from different laboratory manuals. Decide what the differences are between the two approaches.

Physiology of the thyroid gland

Introduction

The purpose of the class is to study the normal functions of the thyroid and the effects of interference with normal function by various processes.

Background reading (abridged)

1 Normal function of the thyroid.

Antibiotic sensitivity testing

Introduction

First examine the demonstration cultures showing antibiotic sensitivity tests performed with heavy and light inoculations of bacteria. These show that the size of a zone of inhibition can vary depending on the techniques used.

For the rest of your career you will be relying on the results of antibiotic sensitivity tests, therefore it is important that

2 Interference with normal thyroid function and control, e.g. thyroid hormone injection. Inreased hormone levels cause a decrease in TSH production and thus a decrease in all the activities of the thyroid gland.

3 The use of radioactive iodine.

Experimental procedure

Each group of medical students will be allotted four rats of each type below:

1 Normal rats.
2 Rats which have been interfered wth, e.g. have received a thyroid hormone injection of thyroxine, 5mg/kg body weight, 48–96 hours before the class.

Each group should give every rat the radioactive iodine solution (131(I) as sodium iodide) by intraperitoneal injection as demonstrated. Keep rats in labelled cages. Allow two hours for 131(I) uptake. The rats should then be killed with ether and their thyroids examined as demonstrated and counts of radioactivity compared.

When you have the count, express it as a percentage of the injected count. Make appropriate allowance for background and for natural decay of the isotope.

Put your results on the blackboard. Be sure you understand the results.

These will be discussed at the end of the class.

you appreciate the need for strict control of testing procedures. In what other ways could the size of a zone be modified?

Material (per bench)

10 tubes of melted agar (in 52°C water bath)
10 sterile petri dishes
Standard inoculum of penicillin-sensitive Staphylococcus aureus
15 discs of penicillin G (2g)

Procedure

1 Students at each bench should plan a simple experiment to determine what variables could influence the size of a zone of inhibition around an antibiotic disc other than inoculum size. The material listed above is available for this experiment.

2 Carry out the experiment planned above and place the inoculated plates in the incubation box together with appropriate instructions for growth conditions.

Question

What could be done to minimize variability in the results of antibiotic sensitivity testing in microbiology laboratories?

(Examples reprinted from Hegarty and Lee 1979, by kind permission of Update Publications.)

5.8 How important is laboratory work in your subject? What proportion of a degree do you think should be assigned to practical work in your subject?
What proportion is assigned?
How are the marks obtained?
Discuss the above questions with a few colleagues.

5.9 Think about ways of evaluating your laboratory course and ways of improving it. Reread this chapter to check which suggestions will help you to redesign your course. Discuss your ideas with colleagues and try them out in a pilot experiment on your laboratory course.

6
Effective research and project supervision

The PhD . . . will include a full period of postgraduate
training. . . . It will be a real and very great departure in
English education.

(Rutherford 1918)

INTRODUCTION

Research and project supervision is probably the most complex and
subtle form of teaching in which we engage. It is not enough for us to
be competent researchers ourselves – though this is vital. We need to
be able to reflect on research practices and analyse the knowledge,
techniques, and methods which make them effective. But there is a
step beyond even this. We have to be skilled in enabling our research
students to acquire those techniques and methods themselves without stultifying or warping their own intellectual development. In
short, to be an effective research supervisor, you need to be an
effective researcher and an effective supervisor.

In this chapter the issues involved in supervising research students
are explored. Although the chapter is primarily concerned with the
supervision of postgraduate research, many of the suggestions and
guidelines are also relevant to the supervision of undergraduate
projects. The chapter provides an outline of official reports and
studies of research supervision and their implications. It provides a
model of the factors involved in research supervision. It considers
the role of the supervisor and the problems faced by research students. The management skills required for effective supervision are
discussed and some suggestions for examining dissertations and
theses are provided.

STUDIES OF RESEARCH SUPERVISION

Although universities have had a research function alongside their
teaching function from earliest times, the system of higher research
degrees is relatively new (Simpson 1983). The PhD did not come to

Britain until the 1920s. In part, the motive for its introduction was the desire to attract overseas students, at that time particularly Americans, to British universities, and at first the new degree encountered considerable suspicion and hostility. The manner of its introduction has left a number of anomalies to this day – not least a certain fuzziness about the dividing line between an MPhil. and a PhD.

Despite the obvious importance of research supervision there has been surprisingly little research on research supervision. But this has not prevented the practice of research supervision from coming under scrutiny. Indeed most of the writings on research supervision have been expressions of concern about its adequacy by government and funding agencies (e.g. SERC 1982; Swinnerton-Dyer 1982; ESRC 1985; CVCP 1985).

There have also been comments on research supervision from the academic community itself (Robinson 1957; Witton 1973, 1974; Chapman 1974; Gardner and Stanley 1974) and some criticisms of research supervision (e.g. Baum 1980; Baddeley 1983).

Unfortunately there has been little empirical research into the *process* of research supervision to substantiate the claims and counter-claims of writers. In Britain the work of Welsh (1978, 1979, 1980, 1981) and Rudd (1975, 1981, 1985) stand out as virtually the only sustained research in the area. Their work is based upon questionnaires and interviews of research students and research supervisors. It identifies problems that many students experience such as methodological difficulties, time-management, writing up, isolation, and inadequate supervision. Rudd's recent work was concerned with the question of why some research students fail to complete their degree. While it does not claim to provide complete answers to this problem it does provide pointers and suggestions. Walford (1980) and Delamont and Eggleston (1983) report their findings from surveys of research students which tend to confirm the work of Welsh and Rudd. Wright (1986) is analysing perceptions of the skills required by research students in different subjects and the particular problems faced by overseas students. Her work suggests that there are different modes of working in different subjects. For example arts students tend to spend longer on choosing a problem and are more likely to change topic than are science students (see Activities 6.1 and 6.2). Moses (1984) has also identified problem areas in research supervision including choice of topic, the role of the supervisor, and the responsibilities of students. She has produced a useful bibliography (Moses 1982) which details relevant work in Australasia and North America as well as Britain.

One aspect of research supervision which has been almost totally neglected is the research tutorial. Yet it is the research tutorial which is at the heart of the supervision process. For this reason Shaw (1987) has developed a system for analysing conversations in research tutorials and he is developing a training programme for research project supervisors.

ISSUES IN RESEARCH SUPERVISION

Criticisms of research supervision expressed in the literature seem to lie in four main areas: that it is inefficient, inappropriate, fallible, and abused.

The charge of inefficiency is levelled particularly at those subject ares where PhD completion rates are low, or where students seem to require considerably more than three years of full-time study to complete a PhD. The system is seen as inappropriate on two counts: it places more emphasis on the outdated workings of the individual scholar than on the relevant competencies of the team member; and it gives more importance to the end thesis than to the acquisition of research skills. Fallibility is alleged in the lack of agreed criteria or procedures for assessment including the absence of full appeal rights. Abuse is said to occur through negligent supervision and, more seriously, through the practice of using research students as unacknowledged assistants or as a cheap teaching force for the department.

Behind these criticisms lie some genuine divergences in perception of the nature and purpose of postgraduate research, especially research for a PhD. At least four basic tensions can be discerned. These are set out in Fig. 6.1.

Figure 6.1 Tensions in research supervision

Scholarship? .... Training?
Original? .... Collaborative?
Independent? .... Team member?
Apprenticeship? .... Employment?

On the one hand, there are those who believe that a PhD study should be a work of scholarship, making a valued contribution to a subject in terms of new knowledge or new conceptualizations. A thesis is entirely the student's work, the product of original and independent thought, the foundation for a lifetime's study. As such the research period is not unlike an apprenticeship during which the student acquires the skills of the craft and is socialized into the (academic) profession. It follows that the PhD is the proving ground for those seeking a lectureship.

On the other hand, the PhD can be seen as pre-eminently a period of training in which the student should acquire a wide repertoire of skills which can subsequently be used on other projects both within and without the academic world. The specific problem for the student to research is best defined as part of a larger collaborative project on which the student is a team member. The thesis will take the form of a report and may well make use of the work of other team members. The results (or product) obtained by the student are not seen as his or her exclusive property, but rather as a contribution to the team project. The student is likened to an employee on contract to the project rather than an apprentice to a 'master craftsman'. There is no assumption that the student will automatically proceed to a tenured post in higher education.

Depending on your position along these dimensions and their associated values (see Activity 6.2), it is likely that the experience of research students will differ quite significantly. The satisfactions and difficulties of the scholar may not be those of the team member.The former, for example, will probably be given a significant degree of choice over topic, methodology, and ideological context; the latter, little or none.The former may find difficulty in managing his or her own time effectively; the latter may find frustration in being tied to the timetable and priorities of the team project. The scholar can feel isolated; the trainee may find that daily contact is superficial.

FACTORS IN THE SUPERVISION PROCESS

You need to keep these divergences of perception, and their consequences for the student, in mind when considering the factors which interact to influence the process of research supervision. An attempt to model these factors is set out in Figure 6.2.

This model indicates the importance of context and of expectations of students and supervisors. In addition to the value positions discussed in the previous section, the system of postgraduate research supervision is influenced by other contextual factors. Among these are the arrangements made by departments and institutions for selection, training, and monitoring research students and research supervisors. Currently moves towards selectivity in research funding and a cut-back in the real level of research funding in some subjects is also influencing research supervision. There is, for example, more pressure on individuals and departments to show better completion rates and a higher research profile.

However the major factors affecting the supervision process are the academic experience and existing skills of both the supervisor and the student. The model indicates that an effective research

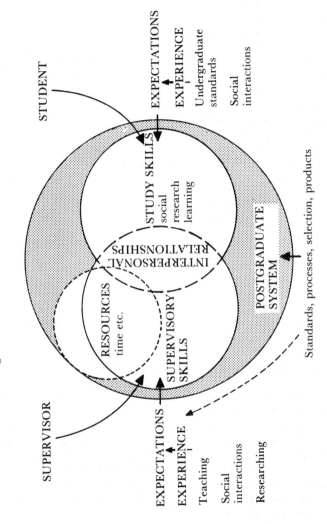

Figure 6.2 Factors in the supervision process

STUDENT

EXPECTATIONS
EXPERIENCE
Undergraduate
standards

Social
interactions

STUDY SKILLS
social
research
learning

INTERPERSONAL
RELATIONSHIPS

RESOURCES
time etc.

SUPERVISORY
SKILLS

POSTGRADUATE
SYSTEM

Standards, processes, selection, products

SUPERVISOR

EXPECTATIONS
EXPERIENCE
Teaching

Social
interactions

Researching

supervision requires professional and personal skills on both sides. Hence the importance of considering various roles, problems, and tasks of supervisors and students.

ROLES OF THE SUPERVISOR

It is possible to identify a variety of roles which you can take as supervisor. Some of these are set out in Figure 6.3.

Figure 6.3 The roles of the supervisor

- Director (determining topic and method, providing ideas).
- Facilitator (providing access to resources or expertise, arranging field-work).
- Adviser (helping to resolve technical problems, suggesting alternatives).
- Teacher (of research techniques).
- Guide (suggesting timetable for writing up, giving feedback on progress, identifying critical path for data collection).
- Critic (of design of enquiry, of draft chapters, of interpretations of data).
- Freedom giver (authorizes student to make decisions, supports student's decisions).
- Supporter (gives encouragement, shows interest, discusses student's ideas).
- Friend (extends interest and concern to non-academic aspects of student's life).
- Manager (checks progress regularly, monitors study, gives systematic feedback, plans work).
- Examiner (e.g. internal examiner, mock vivas, interim progress reports, supervisory board member).

Given the range of possible roles it is not, perhaps, surprising that differences in opinion can exist as to what the role of the supervisor *should* be (Welsh 1979; Rudd 1985). Areas of potential disagreement exist at every stage of a research study. For example there may initially be disagreement over the extent to which the selection of topic should be the supervisor's or the student's. Choice of theoretical framework can be similarly contested. Once under way, there may be differences in expectation over the frequency of meetings and over the amount of practical help offered. Finally, there can be a difference in view about responsibility for the standard of the work done, and over the extent of assistance which should be given in the writing-up stage. These differences in perception can exist between subject areas, between academic staff within a single department, and between an individual supervisor and his or her research student (see Activity 6.2).

What does seem likely, however, is that within a general orientation supervisors move from one role to another. These changes, conscious or unconscious, may be triggered by the personality of the individual research student or by the nature of a specific project. More commonly, the changes occur as different stages in the research project are reached (Welsh 1979). Thus during the initial stages a supervisor may be directive, but later allow the student more freedom and autonomy. He or she may revert to a directive stance once again during the writing-up stages when the pressure to see the student complete on time is strong.

The role that you adopt obviously has implications for the research student. A list of possible relationships between supervisor and student is shown in Figure 6.4.

Figure 6.4 Relationships between supervisor and student

Director	:	Follower
Master	:	Servant
Guru	:	Disciple
Teacher	:	Pupil
Expert	:	Novice
Guide	:	Explorer
Project manager	:	Team worker
Auditor	:	Client
Editor	:	Author
Counsellor	:	Client
Doctor	:	Patient
Senior partner	:	Junior professional
Colleague	:	Colleague
Friend	:	Friend

Supervisors in different subject areas may perceive these relationships differently. Thus what may seem perfectly acceptable to some (e.g. master–servant) may carry overtones of exploitation to others.

Styles of supervision

Welsh (1979) found that both supervisors and research students saw the relationship in terms of professional *and* personal characteristics. The supervisor was expected to offer expertise, skill, experience. But a good supervisor was also seen as one who shared friendship and showed a concern for the personal well-being of the student. If we take the complementary dimensions of structured direction and friendliness, it is possible to plot different styles of supervision on a grid (see Figure 6.5).

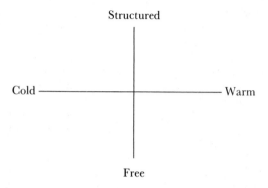

Figure 6.5 Dimensions of supervisor style

The evidence on student preference (Welsh 1979; Battersby and Battersby 1980; Wilson 1980; Rudd 1985) indicates that the *least* preferred style is the cold and free approach. However, too little structuring, even when combined with a warm, friendly manner, is not popular either. This style may be characterized as 'a really nice guy, but no bloody good as a supervisor'. Preferable to this is the supervisor who, while somewhat aloof, nevertheless provides direction and keeps the student on track. But the most popular style was the one which coupled personal warmth with professional guidance.

Students, like supervisors, may change their idea of what constitutes an ideal style of supervision during the course of their project. McAleese and Welsh (1983) found that in the first year of research good personal relationships were seen as important, but that 'expertise' and 'regular contact' were given increasingly greater importance in the second and third years. Second- and third-year research students tended to find the amount of supervisory contact they received inadequate.

The increasing importance which research students seem to attach to expert assistance helps to explain the findings on 'ideal' supervisor characteristics also reported by McAleese and Welsh (1983). From a pre-specified list of characteristics, the four items which received the greatest endorsement from the students were: knowledgeable, available, helpful, stimulating. These characteristics corresponded closely with the 'ideal' characteristics described by the supervisors in the same study. They emphasized: helpfulness, subject expertise, personal experience, and availability. The degree of congruence is illuminating though we should note that 'availability' had a higher priority for the students.

PROBLEMS AND DIFFICULTIES FACED BY RESEARCH STUDENTS

During a research project, the student undertakes many different types of task calling for different skills – skills which he or she may not *necessarily* have developed in undergraduate study (Wright 1986; Zuber-Skerritt 1985). In the early stages it is a matter of choosing, defining, and refining the topic until the nub of the problem is identified and its importance understood. The next stage in many subjects usually requires design skills and decisions over methodological techniques. The field-work, experimental periods, or document searches have their own practical competencies to be mastered. Once the data have been collected, analysis, synthesis, and interpretation of results come to dominate. Last but not least, the skills required for drafting and writing take over. Throughout many projects the student may have to cope with highly technical literature, complex statistical or mathematical techniques, and the use of the computer. In addition to these tasks, the research student has to learn to manage his or her own time effectively, to negotiate access to resources and expertise, and to handle materials and procedures correctly. Research life is likely to have a different rhythm from life as an undergraduate or employee, not least in the ambiguity of the position of the research student: neither member of staff nor undergraduate. Finally, if the student is on a short-term, temporary contract he or she will have to cope with the insecurity that such an appointment brings.

Postgraduate research students can encounter difficulties and problems in almost any of these aspects of their research. A recent study of postgradute failure (Rudd 1985) revealed that the reason for non-completion, or late completion, usually lay in a combination of difficulties rather than in a single factor. Figure 6.6 sets out the most common categories of problem.

Figure 6.6 Common problems for research students

---

1 Poor planning and management of project.
2 Methodological difficulties in the research.
3 Writing-up.
4 Isolation.
5 Personal problems outside the research.
6 Inadequate or negligent supervision.

1 Poor planning and management of project

Careful organization is generally regarded as indispensable to successful and timely completion of a research project (e.g. SERC 1982). Planning and management are needed at every stage and not just at the start. For example critical path analysis is needed for sequencing data collection; a timetable for writing-up. Nevertheless, a slow start to the study can be a particular problem in itself. It is possible for a student to spend too long refining the design, reading background literature, and building apparatus. Accordingly Rudd (1985) suggests that research students should have completed these preliminary tasks before registration for a research degree. Similarly the SERC recommends use of the long vacation prior to the start of the project for background reading, while the ESRC would like students to have completed any necessary training in research methods before they embark on a PhD study.

Associated with poor time management is the failure to plan carefully the relationship between the various aspects of the study. If the data collection has not been linked systematically to the definition of the problem, and if the analysis is not planned in relation to the data collection, the result can be a mass of uncollatable material. Students are then faced with the difficulty of deciding what are and what are not relevant data, and sometimes with the need to repeat experiments or search for yet more information. Gaps appear in the results, and relationships between results cannot be tested adequately. There is also the danger that one aspect of the work will come to dominate with consequent loss of direction. For example, without a clear structure it is possible for students to get 'hooked' on computing so that a methodological tool becomes an end in itself.

For research students on group projects a carefully elaborated programme is particularly important. Without such planning, a student may find him- or herself diverted on to aspects of the project which, while interesting, do not contribute to the student's own study. The project timetable may come to dominate, overriding the student's need to meet higher degree requirements, while daily, informal contact with project staff may be no substitute for properly planned supervisions (Rudd 1985). Finally, those on short-term contracts may be under pressure to move on to new projects before they have had the time to write up their part of the previous project as a thesis. This has led the SERC to recommend that post-doctoral salaries should not be paid to project researchers until the thesis has been successfully completed.

2 Methodological difficulties in the research

Rudd (1985) argues that the ideal topic for a research student has three characteristics: it is interesting to the student, it is manageable within the time constraints, and it contains scope for original work while yet being capable of solution. Unfortunately, as he himself points out, it is sometimes impossible to know in advance if the third characteristic will pertain. One of the most serious difficulties, therefore, which research students may have to face, is the need to change design or direction, or methods, if the original plan proves too difficult to execute in practice.

But technical problems can arise for other reasons too. Chief among these is the lack of appropriate methodological skill and technique, either in data collection or in data analysis. Inadequate skill emerged as the most common difficulty reported by the respondents to the Delamont and Eggleston survey (Delamont and Eggleston 1983). The problem is likely to be exacerbated where unfamiliar computer programs or advanced statistical techniques are required. Although lack of skill emerges as a serious problem for many students, it is a problem that can be resolved (Delamont and Eggleston 1983). Practical help and training can usually be obtained from service courses (though there may be difficulties in attendance for part-time students), and from supervisors.

3 Writing-up

Difficulties encountered in writing-up could be classified as lack of necessary skill. But it seems to be such a frequent problem that it is given separate treatment here. Rudd (1985) found two interrelated aspects to the problem: slowness in formulating what to write, and difficulty in bringing the material into coherent shape. Beard and Hartley (1984) report findings that show that academic writing is far from easy for lecturers themselves. Nor did they find much uniformity in the way academic staff approached their writing tasks. The same seems likely to apply to research students when writing their theses. Beard and Hartley do argue, however, that academic writing is a skill and as such can be broken down into sub-routines. These sub-routines can, in their turn, be learned separately and practised in combination until they become part of an automatic and integrated approach (see also Chapter 8). This argument lends weight to the recommendation of the SERC, among others, that research students should undertake regular written assignments during their study. The writing-up of the final thesis should not be the first occasion on which the student has had to express him- or herself in coherent English prose. It may also be necessary to offer students workshops on thesis/dissertation writing (Zuber-Skerritt 1986). Such workshops can function not only at the level of practical guidance but also as a useful source of group psychological support.

The second aspect of the problem – selection and ordering of material – usually arises from lack of systematic planning, or from inadequate record keeping. Good project management should avoid the 'shoe box syndrome' of non-related and unanalysable data. But for some research students there is the rather different problem of misplaced perfectionism. These students defer the writing up while further data are collected, or more literature is scanned, or yet more analysis is carried out. They find it hard to accept that no study is perfect, that not all variables can be controlled, that no instrument is totally free from bias, and that no interpretation of results can be completely exhaustive.

4 Isolation

After difficulties with methodological skills, isolation emerged as the most common problem for research students in education (Delamont and Eggleston 1983). Moreover, it was a problem for which there had been no preparation and for which there seemed to exist little by way of solution. Other authors have reported similar findings (Welsh 1979; Beard and Hartley 1984; Rudd 1985). The problem may be particularly acute for part-time and for overseas students. While a certain amount of isolation may be creative and even essential for independent or original thought, it is clear that too much isolation is debilitating. Absence of external 'push' factors, such as discussion of ideas, can lead to a general decline in motivation (Rudd 1985). Practical help with methodological problems may not occur, thus setting back the study. The student can then become increasingly insecure, and doubting of his or her ability. Equally serious, there may be too few sources of constructive criticism and feedback in the course of the study and this can lead to eventual failure which could have been avoided. Recognition of these dangers has led to recommendations for more opportunities for research students to share, test, and defend their ideas and work. Collaborative projects have been encouraged on similar grounds (Beard and Hartley 1984). However Rudd sounds a warning note: in times of scarce job opportunities research students may be less willing to risk disclosure of their tentative results to potential competitors or in front of potential employers (Rudd 1985).

5 Personal problems outside the research

Rudd (1985) identified several factors outside the research project which could contribute to late completion or to failure to complete. These factors included problems with personal relationships, family commitments, finance, employment, illness, and injury. The first four may pertain particularly to part-time students. Such difficulties, however, are not usually the sole cause of failure. Rather, they tend to travel in company with other problems more directly connected to the research such as loss of interest in the topic or a change in career plans. Indeed the picture given is one of complex and highly idiosyncratic causality.

6 Inadequate or negligent supervision

Poor supervision does not emerge as a major problem in the few studies of postgraduate research reported in Britain. However, for a minority of respondents in each survey it was a significant problem. Given the very high level of dependence on a single supervisor as the sole source of encouragement, support, advice, and criticism, the reported bitterness of students who have experienced poor supervision is understandable. The quality of supervision is, arguably, the single most important factor in successful undertaking of research. The criticisms of supervisors are set out in Figure 6.7.

Unfortunately when students have experienced poor supervision, they have not always been able to find alternative supervisors (Delamont and Eggleston 1983). However, current recommendations from the research councils in Britain may mean the introduction of formal procedures to uncover and remedy inadequate supervision on a departmental basis (SERC 1982; CVCP 1985). Such procedures do not obviate the need, however, for careful selection of supervisors

Figure 6.7 Common criticisms of supervisors

- Too few meetings with students.
- No interest in student.
- No interest in topic.
- Too little practical help given.
- Too little direction.
- Failure to return work promptly.
- Absence from department.
- Lack of research experience.
- Lack of relevant skills and/or knowledge.

and for careful matching of supervisor, student and topic. Training in supervision skills may also be needed (Moses 1984).

STUDENTS AT RISK

The discussion of the problems and difficulties faced by research students suggests that it should be possible to identify students at risk. A student who avoids encounters with his or her supervisor, or a student who seems unable to accept any responsibility for the conduct of the study, are two obvious examples. But as supervisors we may need to be alert for other signals. For example can the student state, clearly, the central problem being investigated? Does the study require techniques which the student has never used *in practice* before? Is the student personally well suited to the type of research that has been decided on? Are there major changes in the student's personal life? Is the student behind schedule? Is there evidence that the student can write adequate academic prose? Some of the more common behaviours which can be 'warning indicators' are set out in Figure 6.8.

Figure 6.8 Warning indicators

- Postponing supervisions.
- Making excuses for unfinished work.
- Focus on next stage, not current task.
- Frequent changes in topic or method.
- Filling time with other things.
- Resisting advice or criticism.
- Procrastinating on writing.
- Intellectualizing practical problems.
- Blaming others for shortcomings.
- Failing to integrate earlier work.

Overseas students

Students who have not been undergraduates in this country may face additional problems to those already identified. A survey conducted by UKCOSA (1982) shows that loneliness and difficulties in forming relationships were the two most frequent problems. But incorrect expectations were the next more serious source of difficulty. The style of teaching and learning experienced by some students prior to arrival can be a poor preparation for independent and original research. Such students may find it hard to assess evidence critically, or to question authoritative assumptions, or to engage in knowledge creation. Their undergraduate studies may also have afforded few opportunities for deep and critical reading, for practical laboratory work, or for computer use. Written English may not be of an acceptable standard, and the canons of academic writing poorly understood. At a deeper level, overseas students may have very different cultural traditions for the presentation of evidence and argument (Gassin 1982). This can affect the way they approach the design of a project and the structure of their final thesis. Teaching such students the 'correct' way for the host academic context may be a vital task for the supervisor. Paradoxically, where an overseas student is insecure it may be harder to get him or her to adopt western intellectual practice than if he or she is confident and able. Valuing the 'home' customs of the overseas students may be a precondition to effective transition to those of the 'host' country.

The UKCOSA research also revealed difficulties in making cultural adaptations. This could show itself both in the context of the research project (for example uneasy relationships with technicians) and, of course, in their personal lives. Finally, in addition to anxieties over finance and accommodation common to many research students, there was the added burden of liaison and negotiation with sponsoring government departments both in this and in their home country. It would seem therefore that in accepting an overseas research student you are often accepting greater responsibility for supervision. Put rather bluntly, supervising overseas students may require more time, effort, and skill than supervising home British students (see Activity 6.6).

Part-time students

The BERA study of part-time research students showed that not only do they tend to have greater commitments outside the research but also they experience the problem of isolation in a more acute form (Delamont and Eggleston 1983). The intermittent nature of their attendance can make it difficult for their supervisor to form a close academic relationship with them. It also makes it hard for them to meet other research students, to get to libraries, or to attend service courses. Departments may need, therefore, to think out ways of facilitating contact for these students. Evening or weekend seminars, distance learning arrangements, or the setting up of self-help groups can be appropriate.

More fundamentally supervisors may need to direct or advise part-time students towards certain kinds of research project and away from others. Given the length of time between start and completion there is a real danger of data becoming dated, of problems being overtaken by events, of findings being pre-empted by others. On the other hand, designs which include cohort studies, or evaluation over time, are particularly suitable for part-time study. Whatever the design chosen, however, you probably need to give as much, if not more, attention to the management and monitoring of the stages of the research as you do for full-time students.

Recommendations for departments

Although most of the responsibility for research students is seen as resting with the individual supervisor, in recent years some recommendations have been targeted on the department (e.g. SERC 1982; CVCP 1985). Departments should take responsibility for ensuring that the selection of supervisors is properly conducted bearing in mind the need to match student, topic, and supervisor as well as possible. 'Buggins' turn' is no longer regarded as an adequate criterion for allocation of supervisory duties. Nor is it taken for granted that any member of academic staff is capable of being a supervisor. Expertise and research experience are needed. Supervisors may need support and even training – and they should be responsible to their head of department or external sponsor for the adequacy of their supervision.

More careful selection of supervisors is matched by an increased insistence on clear procedures for the selection of research students and on systematic reviews of their progress. The use of regular written reports, of supervisory boards, of progress panels, and mock vivas have all been advocated. Once again it is possible to summarize the recommendations in the form of a check-list. Such a list is set out in Figure 6.9.

THE STRUCTURE AND SKILLS OF SUPERVISION

The first prerequisite for effective supervision is to be actively involved in research yourself and to be able to analyse and reflect on your own research experience. Without this foundation it is difficult to empathize with students' difficulties and problems, or to understand the different demands of the different stages of a research project. The supervisor must also have the research skills needed by the student such as choosing and refining designs, carrying out the field or laboratory work, analysing and interpreting data, and presenting results in an academic form. Where specialist techniques are needed, supervisors must, arguably, at least understand the principles on which they are based and the limits of confidence which they

Figure 6.9 Check-list for departments

1 Are there safeguards against over-enthusiastic headhunting of students?
2 Are courses provided in methodological skills?
3 Is there help available for students who lack advanced study skills?
4 Is there more than one source of advice and criticism for students?
5 Do students know how to gain access to specialist expertise when needed?
6 Is the supervisor also doubling as the internal examiner?
7 Is there supplementary support for overseas students?
8 What arrangements have been made to help part-time students?
9 Are there regular seminars or other meetings where research students can present their work?
10 Is there a procedure for students who are not satisfied with the supervision they are getting?
11 Do the students know this and other procedures?

carry. Good management requires more than just referral of the student to other sources of expertise.

But there is more to good supervision than applying the lessons of experience and of being aware of your characteristic approach. There are interpersonal and teaching skills involved in research supervision which come into play on first meeting the research student, continue to the viva, and even beyond to publication. Underpinning these skills are the equally important skills of planning and structuring the research project with and for the student.

Interpersonal skills

The importance of the personal element in the relationship between supervisor and supervisee has already been documented and discussed. The good supervisor is concerned for the general well-being and intellectual growth of the student, and not just with the mechanics of the project. But if a good relationship is to develop, supervisors have to lay the foundations for it in the first few meetings. A comfortable, safe, and relaxed atmosphere has to be created together with the expectation of regular, planned, and structured work. Accordingly, there are at least three objectives for the first meetings.

First, you need to check that the research student is settling in satisfactorily. Matters of accommodation, grant or pay, travel, access, registration, membership of appropriate associations or groups, and introductions to other staff or students may need to be sorted out before any work on the research project can begin. By showing concern for such problems, supervisors can indicate from the beginning that they are interested in the student's personal well-being while on the project or study.

Second, both supervisor and student need to establish, in the first meeting, respective expectations of the role of supervisor and supervisee. Delamont and Eggleston (1983) recommend that an informal 'contract' should be negotiated. Any mismatches in perception can then be revealed and openly discussed. You may also want to establish a regular pattern of meetings from the start. Even if at first these meetings are relatively brief, they ensure that supervision will not become a random and infrequent process.

The third objective should be the setting of a task which will get the student into the project and allow the supervisor to diagnose any likely shortfalls in skill. For this purpose, a short task requiring evidence of writing ability may be particularly appropriate. Suitable tasks might include: a short review of one aspect of the literature, an account of how the student became interested in the problem under investigation, or an interpretation of some statistical data. Feedback on this task can then include a discussion of attendance on any service courses being offered – for example in research methods, computing, or English (for overseas students). You may also need to check in these first meetings that an adequate record-keeping system has been established. A written task may enable you to check this; it also usefully establishes the expectation of regular written papers which will eventually form the basis for thesis chapters.

Relevant skills of teaching

If the maximum benefit is to be obtained from the meetings with your research students then such meetings require planning and structuring. You also need to use certain teaching skills such as questioning and explaining – and help your students to develop these skills as well. Figure 6.10 lists the essential teaching skills for research tutorials. Explaining, questioning, listening, and responding have been dealt with in earlier chapters so here we focus upon structuring the research tutorial and providing feedback. Planning is discussed in a separate section (see pp. 137–40).

Structuring a supervision

It is limiting to see the supervision merely in terms of an *ad hoc* discussion. As Moore said of the Oxford tutorial, it is essentially 'a meeting for work, which usually involves discussion . . . both sides should be at work, understanding, discovering, adjusting' (Moore 1968). Rudd (1985) also suggests that supervisors who gave no

Figure 6.10 Some essential skills in supervisory teaching

---

1 Structuring the research tutorial

- Questioning, e.g. about progress, problems, results, interpretation
- Listening, including going beyond the information given
- Responding, including decision-taking
- Explaining, including demonstration and presentation of argument.

2 Providing feedback.
3 Planning and monitoring the project.

---

advance thought to supervisions, preferring to play them 'by ear', were in part responsible for the failure of their students. Such supervisors failed to notice when their students were falling behind on work, or were wasting their time. Relying on the student to ask for help, or even to know which questions to ask, is risky, especially if the student feels reluctant to take up your time.

One way of ensuring that supervisions are purposeful working encounters is to consider the structure of an individual supervision. The model set out in Figure 6.11 below is based on the work of Shaw (1987).

Figure 6.11 Stages in a research supervision

---

1 Opening	Rapport established
2 Review	Current context established
3 Definition	Scope and purpose of present meeting
4 Exploration	Problem(s), results, and so on
5 Clarification	Decisions needed
6 Goal-setting	Decisions taken, next tasks identified
7 Conclusion	Evaluation, summary, disengagement
8 Recording	Notes on supervision made and filed

The opening of the supervision may contain enquiries as to the non-academic aspects of the student's life; so may the conclusion. Some such conversation from time to time is desirable to help maintain the personal aspect of the relationship. The review of the current context, aided by notes made from the previous supervision, allows you to check perceptions of decisions made, to recall previous discussions, and to enquire into progress towards the goals established. The definition of the purpose of the current supervision can include the identification of problems and difficulties which need to be sorted out. But there may be other purposes such as the giving of feedback on written work, the organization of field-work, or discussion and interpretation of results.

Following identification, the purposes and/or problems should be explored. This stage may contain analysis, reconstruction, explanations, demonstrations, discussion, extrapolation. Links may be made to other aspects of the project or to previous work. Some avenues may prove to be abortive and there will probably be a few digressions. At some point, however, the supervision should move into a clarification and decision-taking stage. Alternative routes and procedures will be evaluated and provisional solutions identified. Tasks will be established for the next period of work with suggested deadlines. At this stage the supervision may enter an iterative sequence if there was more than one purpose or problem to be covered.

The concluding stage should be marked by statements summarizing what has been achieved in the supervision and how well the student is progressing. The date of the next supervision should also be fixed. Ideally a brief record of the main decisions or solutions reached should be made both as a record and to provide the basis for review in the next meeting. This record-keeping can be done singly or jointly.

It is not suggested that every supervision should conform to this model. More important than this particular set of stages is the idea that there should be a purposeful structure behind supervisions of research students (see Activities 6.7 and 6.8).

Providing feedback

Providing feedback has long been recognized as an essential ingredient of effective learning (see for example Turney 1984). Included within the processes of giving feedback are summarizing, evaluating, advising, motivating, and facilitating understanding.

Research students need feedback from their supervisors for at least four interrelated reasons: for criteria of performance, for assistance in improving methods of research, for a sense of achievement, and for deepening understanding.

Criteria of performance Feedback gives the student, who may be working in semi-isolation, a feeling for the criteria against which his or her work will be judged. Students may be unsure of the standard they are expected to attain or may be cue-deaf to indirect sources of information (Delamont and Eggleston 1983). Even completed theses in his or her area may not be much help to a student needing a yardstick to measure achievement on interim stages of a project. The long-term aim here is usually to help the student to become skilled in self-assessment. But this is a skill that can take time and practice to acquire. Initial attempts at self-assessment can be very unreliable (Daines 1986). You may find, therefore, that at first you have to make precise comments on submitted work, explaining both the criteria behind the assessment and the way in which they have been applied. Gradually, and particularly through the use of subtle 'Socratic' questioning, you should be able to help the student examine his or her own work critically. By the end of the research period, you should be needed only as an external check or second professional opinion on the assessment already arrived at by the student. One way a supervisor can help students to internalize the criteria of assessment is to offer them the opportunity to write reviews jointly, and to present critiques of new articles at informal team meetings (Smith 1980). Later, you may need to find ways for your students to submit their work to others for critical comment and observation. Regular seminars, and presentation and defence of work to supervisory boards, have both been recommended frequently (e.g. CVCP 1985).

Improving methods of research   The second reason for giving feedback is to improve students' methodological skills. For although students may be able to identify weaknesses in competency, without help they may not know how to improve their performance to reach the level they desire. Here, once again, the underlying purpose will be to help students to develop their own strategies for identifying and remedying shortfalls in skills. But this too may not occur automatically. For example a student may have 'learnt' some new techniques for multivariate analysis on a research methods service course. He may suspect that such techniques might solve a problem in his own data analysis. But now that the problem is real and meaningful he finds that in practice he does not know how to go about it. At this point, the supervisor may need to teach the student how to select and apply the appropriate test. The student is likely to need a concentrated period of tuition followed by regular refresher sessions before the new technique is firmly established in his or her repertoire. If the technique is new, or the application is unusual, the supervisor may wish to conduct a final check with the student before the viva.

Supervisors may need to adopt a similar approach when helping students to improve their study skills, especially writing. Here, in the early stages, you may decide to make detailed corrections of style and presentation, once again explaining carefully the reasons for the suggested improvements. Later, the student can be invited to make his or her own corrections under guidance, as a joint activity. Ultimately you hope that the student can take full responsibility for this aspect of the work since constant correction by the supervisor not only detracts from more important feedback tasks, but also becomes demoralizing for the student. In some universities, however, there is provision for extra tutorial help with writing for overseas students – a service which can be useful right up to the final draft of the thesis.

A sense of achievement   Regular, constructive assessment provides the student with a cumulative sense of achievement. This is the third and sometimes neglected reason for giving students feedback. A feeling of achievement is motivating. So is a sense of progress. Students need to know that their work is valued and that their supervisors are genuinely interested in it. Supervisors probably need to give this kind of feedback at every stage of the research project. There may also be times when sympathetic support is needed – for example when experiments go wrong or access to sources is denied. If there is a long period of routine field or laboratory work before the student obtains any results, this can become demotivating too. Simple encouragement may be the most appropriate feedback until the experience of success becomes an internal source of motivation for the student. There is one danger, however, with feedback designed to motivate. It can be meaningful only if the overall process of supervision is sound. A glib reassurance ('yes, that's fine') after a cursory glance at the work will at best leave the student with unresolved anxieties, and at worst can seriously mislead. Spurious support from an over-busy supervisor can pave the way to a catastrophe.

Deepening understanding   The fourth reason for giving feedback is to help students to deepen and extend their understanding of the problem or topic they are researching. But helping students to think is not always the easiest of tasks. There are probably four things a supervisor has to do: engage, enquire, share, explicate. It is difficult for you to help students to advance their understanding unless you have engaged with their work to some extent. You also need to find out how a student has approached the particular problem or stage. (For this in itself can sometimes be a source of limited thinking.) Thus prepared, you can then share in exploration of the topic or problem through discussion. This can include time spent interpreting the data, or speculating from the data, or forming new links and attempting to build theories. If possible, the student should be helped to relate any new conceptualization or insight that emerges to his or her own pre-existing cognitive framework. In so doing the student should be helped to challenge, test, and evaluate the supervisor's contributions in the discussion. Over time, the strategies which the supervisor has used to develop understanding should be made explicit. These may include: worst case–best case analysis; hypothesis–test–hypothesis–test chains; search for negative cases; establishment of (null) hypotheses; testing of alternative interpretations; brainstorming; systematic distinguishing of cases on key variables or characteristics; deductive reasoning followed by tests for necessary implications. By making such strategies explicit, you can help the student to own them and, eventually, to transfer them to other contexts. This kind of feedback is probably the hardest of all to get right. Yet without it, a student's thesis can be disappointing, never daring to develop beyond a safe but limited presentation of results.

PLANNING IN RESEARCH SUPERVISION

It goes without saying that planning and organization are essential features of research supervision. However, management of the research is not solely the responsibility of the research student. The balance of responsibility within the relationship is dependent not only upon the values of the supervisor, but also on the expectations and abilities of the student and the nature of the project. One possible approach to helping a student organize a project, and to monitor progress, is set out below. It is based on the authors' own experience and you may need to adapt it for your own subject – or indeed to develop your own approach. Two notions are implicit in our approach. First, that the order of chapters in the final thesis is *not* the order in which the research should be tackled. Second, that writing should take place *throughout* the research and should not be left to the final stage.

1 Preparation and refinement

There are six parts to this first stage:

1 Reading, visiting, discussion of topic area.
2 Attendance on research skills service courses if appropriate.
3 Setting up adequate record-keeping systems.
4 Narrowing down of topic until central question(s) or problem for investigation identified.
5 Investigation designed; methods piloted.
6 Rough draft of chapter on design of study.

2 Field-work or experimental work

This is the stage of practical activity. The procedure for collecting data needs to be preplanned and carefully sequenced. Data should be collected in the form needed for analysis (e.g. ready for computer analysis). The student should still, if possible, continue to read round the subject.

3 Writing-up

At this stage the student is ready to write the second draft of the chapter describing the design of the study. The chapter should include a statement of the hypotheses investigated, the sample selected, methods used for data collection and analysis. It should read like a recipe which other researchers could follow if replicating the work.

4 Analysis of results

As the analysis is conducted decisions should be made about the form in which the results will be presented. Rough notes should be made on each set of results. The process of analysis should also begin to suggest points for interpretation and, possibly, for further testing. The points should be noted down separately to be used later in the chapter on discussion of results. If the student is engaged in a 'hypothesis–test–hypothesis–test' study, a further cycle of design, data collection, and analysis may now occur.

5 Writing-up

The chapter presenting the results should now be written using the notes made during analysis and following the order of hypotheses already set out in the chapter on design of the study.

6 Review of the literature

By this stage the student should be able to see what literature is, and what is not, relevant to the results obtained. On the basis of this criterion the chapter giving the review of the literature should now be written from the notes made while reading in the early stage of the study and from any further reading now required. Each section of the review chapter should mirror the hypotheses as set out in the chapter on design. Forward linking statements should be incorporated as appropriate.

7 Writing-up

The student is now in a position to write the chapter on the discussion of the results. This chapter interprets and discusses the results in the light of the literature pertaining to the problem (and just written up). Use should be made of the notes recorded during the analysis of the data. The limitations of the field-work and methodology should be pointed out and suggestions made for future research. The student should not be afraid to offer new theoretical models, nor to make informed speculations grounded in the results obtained.

8 The introduction

This is the final and often most difficult stage. The student has to write an introduction which sets out the background to the study, states the problem investigated, and describes succinctly the design of the rest of the thesis. The best preparation for this task is to read through all the chapters completed so far, arranged now in the order in which they will appear in the final thesis, and note the central focus of the investigation.

9 Bibliography and appendices

We suggest that students should put together the appendices (if any) as they go along. However a final arrangement of material may now be needed. Similarly, students should sort out the cards giving the references for each chapter as it is written up. The cards can now be checked, arranged in alphabetical author order, and handed to the typist as one batch ready for typing.

10 Mock viva

It is suggested by SERC (1982) among others that students should experience a mock viva in preparation for the defence of the thesis before the external examiner. Some suggestions on preparing for and giving a viva are given later in the chapter.

If this approach to sequencing the stages of a research project is adopted, it will be possible to make the comparison between final thesis and actual order of writing shown in Figure 6.12.

Figure 6.12 Comparison of project and thesis

STAGES OF PROJECT	ORDER OF THESIS
1 Design of study	1 Introduction
2 Data collection	2 Review of literature
3 Analysis and presentation of results	3 Design of study
4 Review of literature	4 Presentation of results
5 Discussion of results	5 Discussion of results
6 Conclusions and suggestions	6 Conclusions and suggestions
7 Introduction	7 Bibliography and appendices
8 Final check of bibliography and appendices	

Note: The figure provides a broad overview of the approach. When different sets of experiments or case studies are being reported it may be better to have a chapter for each set which provides details of design, presentation of results, and discussion. A chapter discussing the complete set of results may also be necessary. Clearly the suggestions given here are for research based on data collection. Other forms of research will require different stages and thesis structure. The important point is to distinguish the stages and the likely structure in the first stage of the research.

Many students will need guidance and encouragement by the supervisor throughout all the stages of the project. It is also useful to provide occasional seminars for research students on doing research. The tips for research students given in Figure 6.13 are a product of such workshops.

Figure 6.13 Tips for research students

Think about these and adapt them to your needs.
1 Don't panic too often.
2 Only write on one side of paper.
3 Be nice to librarians (especially in inter-library loan).
4 Remember that your supervisor is a busy person; if he or she isn't, change your supervisor.
5 Find out how *you* work best.
6 Read your degree regulations.
7 Always have a couple of areas you can work on at any time.
8 Read a few dissertations or theses from this university in your area.
9 Budget for typing and binding.
10 Plan ahead.
11 Don't think that photocopying is the same as reading.
12 Put your external examiner's book on the bibliography.
13 Get a good typist or use a good word-processing package.
14 Don't think it will be absolutely perfect . . .
15 . . . read your supervisor's thesis.

16 Remember that ideas change – what you wrote at the outset may need changing.
17 Write the introduction last.
18 Put typing conventions on cards for your typist.
19 Don't be afraid to point to your strengths and to the weaknesses of others.
10 Keep *full* bibliographical details.
21 Have someone comment on your written style at an early stage.
22 Set yourself short-term goals . . .
23 . . . and if you aren't meeting them, work out why.
24 Allow *plenty* of time for writing up.
25 Step back from time to time.
26 With each piece of work ask if it is worth doing.
27 Don't begrudge *some* time spent reading very widely.
28 Find out early on about: length; presentation conventions; submission dates.
29 Talk to people about it.
30 Don't begrudge time spent thinking.
31 Only write on every other line.
32 Think of it as a meal ticket.
33 Keep writing.
34 Don't think that reading just one more book will solve all your problems.
35 . . . and don't use that as an excuse for not starting writing.
36 Criticize, evaluate, analyse; don't just describe.
37 Find a typist who has done your sort of work before.
38 Use your research to make contacts.
39 Use quotations selectively . . .
40 Use a card index for references, ideas, etc.
41 Don't be afraid to be imaginative.
42 Make sure your bibliography is comprehensive.
43 Label your diagrams, graphs, and tables properly.
44 If you set something aside for a while, make some notes about your ideas for its continuation.
45 Organize an efficient filing system.

(From Wilson (1980) 'Group sessions for postgraduate students', *British Journal of Guidance and Counselling* 8(2): 237–41.)

EXAMINING THESES

It is normal practice for departments to issue guidelines to their internal and external examiners. Nevertheless, it can be helpful to have your own set of tactics for reading theses and for preparing to conduct a viva. Once again, the strategy which is offered below is based on the authors' own experience and you will probably need to adapt it.

1 Getting a global impression

Start by reading the full title and the abstract in order to get hold of the central idea, or question, or topic that is being researched. Then turn to the final chapter(s) to see how far the student seems to have got in developing the idea, solving the problem, and so on. Make a note of any methodological weaknesses raised. A scan of the contents page and appendices (if any) should indicate whether there is likely to be sufficient, appropriate evidence to support the conclusions reached. Return to the introduction and re-read for a closer definition of the problem in its context.

2 Reflection and formulation of questions

Stop reading and reflect on the overall impression obtained. Formulate a number of questions which, on the basis of what has been read so far, you would hope to see discussed or answered, for example questions on congruency of methods and problem, on likely sources of bias.

3 Systematic reading with questions in mind

Read each chapter in turn. Make notes on points to be raised in the viva.

Review of the literature
To what extent is the review relevant to the research study?
Has the candidate slipped into 'here is all I know about x'?
Is there evidence of critical appraisal of other work, or is the review just descriptive?
How well has the candidate mastered the technical or theoretical literature?
Does the candidate make the links between the review and his or her design of the study explicit?
Is there a summary of the essential features of other work as it relates to this study?

Design of the study
What precautions were taken against likely sources of bias?
What are the limitations in the design? Is the candidate aware of them?
Is the methodology for data collection appropriate?
Are the techniques used for analysis appropriate?
In the circumstances, has the best design been chosen?

Has the candidate given an adequate justification for the design used?

Presentation of results
Does the design/apparatus appear to have worked satisfactorily?
Have the hypotheses in fact been tested? '
Do the solutions obtained relate to the questions posed?
Is the level and form of analysis appropriate for the data?
Could the presentation of the results have been made clearer?
Are patterns and trends in the results accurately identified and summarized?
Is a picture built up?

Discussion and conclusions
Is the candidate aware of possible limits to confidence/reliability/validity in the study?
Have the main points to emerge from the results been picked up for discussion?
Are there links made to the literature?
Is there evidence of attempts at theory building or reconceptualization of problems?
Are there speculations? Are they well grounded in the results?

4 Reflection

Put the thesis down and look through the notes. Return to the original questions posed in Stage 2 and see whether they have been satisfactorily answered. Consider also at this stage the more fundamental questions:

Is the standard of literary presentation adequate?
Is the thesis (substantially) the candidate's own work?
Does the candidate have a general understanding of the relevant field and how this thesis relates to it?
Has the candidate thought through the implications of the findings?
Is there evidence of originality?
Does the study add to existing knowledge of the subject?
Is there evidence that the candidate has developed skills in research at this level?
Is it worth publishing, albeit in modified form?

Where you find yourself in disagreement with the candidate it is worth asking whether the disagreement is the result of differences in ideology (or values) between yourself and the candidate or whether it is due to something else.

5 Prepare for the viva

By this stage you should have identified some key questions to put to the candidate in the viva. You will also have formed an opinion on the strengths and weaknesses of different parts of the thesis and may have considered whether you will advise publication of all or part of it. There are some approaches to the viva, however, which are best avoided:

- The proof reader
- The committee man
- The hobby horse rider
- The kite flyer
- The reminiscer.

One of the least productive ways of using the viva is to go through the thesis making detailed corrections of spelling, punctuation, and grammar ('Shouldn't there be a comma on page 67, third line up in the fourth paragraph?'). If the standard of presentation is poor it is more sensible either to ask the candidate to get the thesis retyped or hand the candidate a list of corrections to be made after the viva is concluded. Nearly as bad is the examiner who takes up points, page by page, in the order in which they occur in the thesis, rather than synthesizing them into key questions about the design, results, and interpretations. The application of highly personal preferences and prejudices is also to be avoided ('I see you haven't quoted my friend/ enemy Lovejoy?') providing the candidate is aware of the main work relevant to the study. Targeting questions on items tenuously related to the study as defined by the candidate is also unfair. Finally, the temptation to use the viva as a vehicle for your own memories or indulgences should be resisted ('Ah, I see you're from Liverpool, did you by chance know Professor Smith in the Psychology Department?').

THE VIVA VOCE

It is sometimes forgotten that viva is an abbreviation of viva voce and viva voce may be roughly translated as lively discussion. The good viva, like the good research tutorial, has structure and purpose. So even if examiners are presenting independent reports, it is advisable at least to agree in advance the form that the viva will take and some of the questions that will be asked.

The first stage is usually to establish rapport and make the candidate feel comfortable and relaxed so that he or she can present and defend the work to best advantage. A friendly but detached stance on the part of the examiners is helpful here. Thereafter, the examiners will wish to raise the major questions they have identified and engage with the candidate in discussion of them. The questions may be directed, in turn, to the ideas and assumptions in the research, to the experimental work, to the results and their interpretations, and to which parts of the thesis might be published.

Examiners differ in their practice as to when to tell the candidate of the decision reached. With a nervous candidate, an early reassurance that he or she has passed may enhance discussion. With a confident candidate the reverse may be true. If a candidate is to be failed, it may be better to lead him or her to a realization of that likelihood through careful questioning rather than shatter abruptly.

It would be wrong to leave this discussion of vivas and examining without pointing out that there are difficult issues involved. For example where you suspect that a poor thesis is the result of negligent supervision, how much account can be taken of this? Similarly where flaws in design are the result of problems in the larger project of which the student is a junior team member, can allowance be made for this? If the experimental work on which the thesis is based turns out to be a total failure is it still possible to assess whether the candidate did do three years' work at PhD level? If you are interested primarily in the research skills acquired by the candidate, how can these best be tested? When is a PhD worth only an MPhil? If the final result is a product (e.g. a suite of software programs) should different criteria apply to the evaluation of design? There are no pat answers to these issues, but as the debate over the appropriateness of postgraduate research continues, it is likely that examiners will have to come to terms with them more openly in the future (Nightingale 1984).

SUMMARY

This chapter has provided an overview of studies of research supervision and highlighted some value questions and conflicts in research supervision.

It has provided a discussion of the role of the supervisor, tasks of research students, and of the special problems of overseas and part-time students. The interpersonal teaching skills necessary for effective research supervision have been highlighted and some suggestions given on ways of identifying students at risk, and helping students to organize their research. An approach to reading a thesis and conducting a viva has been outlined and some issues in examining theses have been raised.

ACTIVITIES

6.1 How do you supervise a research student? Spend a few minutes jotting down your usual approach from the time you first meet the research student to the submission of the thesis. Compare your approach with those of a few colleagues either from your own department or other department.

6.2   **Values and roles**

Set out below you will find eleven pairs of conflicting statements. (You may not agree fully with either of the statements.) Estimate your position for each item and mark it on the scale. Then average your rating for the three sections of the schedule and compare them. If possible, ask a colleague or small group of colleagues to complete the schedule also, and discuss any differences in your ratings.

You can also use the rating schedule with research student(s) and compare their perceptions with your own and those of your colleagues.

If you wish to explore the question of supervision styles and role further, you can turn Figure 6.4 into a similar rating profile exercise. Alternatively, you can use Figure 6.3 to plot changes in your supervisory role during an actual research project.

Role perception rating scale

Read the pairs of conflicting statements listed on this sheet. You may not agree fully with either of the statements. Therefore, please estimate your position and mark it on the scale.

Topic/course of study

1 It is the supervisor's responsibility to select a promising topic	1 2 3 4 5	It is the student's responsibility to select a promising topic
2 In the end, it is up to the supervisor to decide which theoretical frame of reference is most appropriate	1 2 3 4 5	The student has a right to choose his/her own theoretical standpoint even if it conflicts with the supervisor's
3 The supervisor should direct the student in the development of an appropriate programme of research and study	1 2 3 4 5	The supervisor should act mainly as a sounding board for the student's ideas and give advice

Average ☐ for 1–3

Contact/involvement

4 Staff–student relationships are purely professional and personal matters should not intrude 1 2 3 4 5 Close personal relationships are essential for successful supervision

5 The supervisor should initiate frequent meetings with the student 1 2 3 4 5 It is up to the student to decide when he/she wants meetings with the supervisor

6 The supervisor should know at all times at which problems the student is working 1 2 3 4 5 The student should have the opportunity to find his/her own way without having to account for how he/she spends his/her time

7 The supervisor should terminate his/her supervision if he/she thinks the project is beyond the student 1 2 3 4 5 The supervisor should support the student right through until the thesis has been submitted regardless of his/her opinion of the work

Average ⊞ for 4–7

The thesis

8 The supervisor should ensure that the thesis is finished not much later than the minimum period 1 2 3 4 5 As long as the student works steadily he/she can take as long as he/she needs to finish the work

9 The supervisor has direct responsibility for the standard of the thesis 1 2 3 4 5 The supervisor advises only and leaves all decisions concerning content, format, and standards to the student

10 The supervisor should insist on seeing drafts of every section of the thesis in order to review them 1 2 3 4 5 It is up to the student to ask for constructive criticism from the supervisor

11 The supervisor should assist in the actual writing of the thesis if the student has difficulties 1 2 3 4 5 The supervisor should be very wary of contributing too much to the thesis

Average ⊞ for 8–11

6.3 Draft a list of tips for research students. Each tip should be a one-line statement. Figure 6.13 (pp. 140–1) provides an example of such a list. Alternatively draw up a set of guidelines.

6.4 Use Figure 6.13 for the basis of a discussion on hints for research students. Put a tick by those you think would be helpful, a question mark by those you are uncertain about, and a cross by those you think would not be helpful. Compare your markings with those of a few colleagues and discuss any disagreements. Then compile a list of hints.

6.5 The tasks of research students may include: choosing a research problem; refining it; design; data collection; analysis; interpretation; writing up; and the general task of time-management. Which task is your forte? At which task are you least good? What are the usual weaknesses of your students?

6.6 Here are three brief 'cases' based on problems of overseas students. Spend a few minutes thinking about how you would deal with the problem and what advice, if any, you would offer the student. Discuss your comments and suggestions with a few colleagues.

  1 A bright, hard-working research student who has already obtained a lectureship in Britain comes to you to say that her parents in India have requested her to return home to marry and settle in India. Her PhD requires a further six months' work but her parents want her to go home in three months' time.

  2 A male Saudi Arabian student who is charming, fluent in spoken English, and apparently capable has, after considerable pressure from you, submitted a first draft of his thesis. It is appalling. It is ungrammatical, florid in style, omits much of the data analysis, and its conclusions are wrong.

  3 A hard-working, rather serious, but not very able male Tanzanian student has come to you to say he does not understand how to analyse his data – even though you taught him and he has been working on it for two months while you have been away in Canada. He is distressed because his family, at some sacrifice, has paid for him to come to Britain. Without a PhD he dare not return home because of the shame to his family.

6.7 Audio-record or video-record a supervision with one of your research students. Listen to it and try to analyse it into separate stages. Figure 6.11 may be used to identify possible stages. In what ways could the research tutorial have been improved? What kind of feedback did you provide to your student?

6.8 Audio-record or video-record a supervision and discuss it with the research student. Explore with him or her the stages of the tutorial and whether the tutorial could be improved from the student's point of view.

6.9 Work out your approach to reading a thesis and giving a viva. Compare your approach with those of a few colleagues.

6.10 Design a short (lunch-hour) seminar on some aspect of research supervision for your department or research unit. The seminar could be for supervisors, students, or both. Some possible topics for discussion and analysis are: Expectations of supervisors and students; What's a PhD?; Planning a project; Problems in writing; Problems and issues in marking a PhD; Assessing student progress; Students at risk.

7

Studies of student learning

The most important single factor influencing learning is
what the learner already knows. Ascertain this and teach
him accordingly.

(Ausubel 1968)

INTRODUCTION

The first chapter raised the question 'What is teaching?', and presented a model of teaching as an intentional, interactive process.
Using this perspective, succeeding chapters have explored teaching
in the main modes encountered in higher education: lecturing, small
group sessions, laboratory work, and individual research or project
supervision. It is now time to pose two complementary questions:
'How do students learn?' and 'How can we help students to learn
more effectively?'. This chapter considers the first of these questions;
Chapter 8 gives some suggestions in answer to the second.

HISTORICAL SKETCH

For much of this century, the question 'How do students learn?'
would have been perceived in behaviourist terms of stimulus and
response (S–R) (McKeachie 1974). The answer would have suggested
that students learn through conditioning, or by associating certain
actions with certain consequences. Repeated practice and the use of
rewards would help appropriate responses to be retained (Skinner
1954; Hilgard 1963).

The last twenty years, however, have seen a dramatic shift in the
conception of learning. The S–R approach, with its analogy of the
mechanical telephone exchange, has been replaced by theories which
see the learner as an active processor of information. The dominant
analogy is now the computer. This new cognitive psychology has
benefited from several sources, both conceptual and empirical.

CONCEPTUAL DEVELOPMENTS

A key figure in the emergence of the new cognitive psychology was

Ausubel (quoted at the start of the chapter). He drew attention to the importance of learners' pre-existing knowledge in determining what new information would be assimilated, and how. He highlighted the need for 'anchoring' concepts, 'advance' organizers, and clear structuring of material (Ausubel 1968). Norman (1977) focused attention on the need to analyse learning tasks. He suggested that different types of learning tasks could be distinguished which made different demands on the learner. Three such tasks were: *accretion* – those that simply required the student to add to existing knowledge; *fine-tuning* – those that required the student to refine knowledge or skill so that it can be used more effectively; and *restructuring* – those tasks which require the student to extend or alter previously acquired conceptions, or to make new links between existing patterns of knowledge. Of these three types of task, restructuring is the hardest to achieve.

RECENT EMPIRICAL WORK

The new cognitive psychology has also drawn on clinical, experimental, and survey-type research. One strand of this research has been directed to the effects of personality and motivation on learning (see Wittrock 1986 for a recent review). For example interviews and personality measurements of students have shown that the way students perceive themselves, and the way they account for their academic successes and failures, have a strong bearing on their motivation and their performance. Students are likely to initiate learning, sustain it, direct it, and actively involve themselves in it when they believe that success or failure is caused by their own *effort* or lack of it, rather than by factors outside their control such as ability, luck, or the quality of teaching. Similarly praise, reward, or other positive (teacher) reinforcements are likely to enhance motivation only if students perceive them to be related to factors over which they have control. Thus building up students' sense of control over their own work, giving them opportunities to exercise responsibility for their own learning, and helping them to develop self-management skills can all help to make them more successful and effective learners.

A second strand of empirical work has been focused on individual skills, strategies, styles, and approaches to learning. The results from these studies are pertinent to lecturers since most of the subjects have been undergraduate students engaged on academic tasks. Three sets of studies have been particularly influential: the 'clinical' studies by Marton in Sweden; the experimental work undertaken by Pask;

and the surveys and interviews conducted by Entwistle and his colleagues in Britain.

The clinical studies of Marton

The seminal work on student learning is undoubtedly that of Marton and his co-workers at the University of Gothenburg, Sweden (Marton 1975; Marton, Hounsell, and Entwistle 1984; Marton and Saljo 1976). In one set of studies students were asked to read a 1,500-word article. They could take notes on it if they wished, and they were informed that they would be asked questions on it by the interviewer. In the interviews the students were encouraged to reveal what they remembered about the content of the article and the process of reading it, how they felt about the task, and their normal approach to studying a text. The interviews were transcribed and analysed.

These studies yielded two distinctive approaches to study, which Marton described as 'deep-level' and 'surface-level' processing. The 'deep' approach may be characterized as an active search for meaning. Users of this approach start wih the intention of understanding the article, they question the author's arguments and conclusions, and they try to relate them to previous knowledge and to personal experience to enable them to appraise the validity of the author's conclusions. In contrast the users of the 'surface' approach try to memorize those parts of the article which they think they might be questioned on. They tend to focus on specific facts which may not be connected and they seem anxious about the conditions of the learning experiment.

The deep approach was almost always associated with deeper understanding, and even after a five-week interval the users of this approach had a better recall of detail than those who used the surface approach.

In later work by Fransson (1977) the categories were divided into deep active, deep passive, surface active, and surface passive according to the degree of activity and involvement displayed. Fransson also showed that students who felt threatened tended to adopt a surface approach. Other researchers (Svensson 1977; Dahlgren 1978) have shown that an excessive number of factual questions and, perhaps, an overwhelming curriculum appear to induce a surface approach. Svensson argues that a deep approach to studying is doubly important, for it affects the level of understanding reached and the number of hours of study. Habitual surface learners tend to find learning difficult and only a few seem willing to put in long hours of study.

Marton and his co-workers emphasize the context dependence of learning, the use of 'real' learning tasks, and the methods of intro-spection. The development of universal laws of learning is not their concern although their work has been replicated with similar results in other countries (e.g. Rossum and Schenk 1984). Within their own paradigm there is but one major limitation: the ability of the student to articulate accurately the process whereby he or she studies.

The experimental studies of Pask

The clinical work at Gothenburg is in large measure corroborated by the carefully controlled laboratory experiments of Pask (1976; Pask and Scott 1972). Pask has been particularly concerned with two strategies of learning: the 'serialist' and the 'holist'. These have affinities with surface and deep approaches. Serialists look closely at details and the steps in the argument. They tend to make little use of analogies, metaphors, or illustrations. Serialist strategies appear to be a sophisticated surface approach. Holists begin with a broad focus, they try to see the task globally, to relate it to previous knowledge, and to use analogies, illustrations, and other explanatory devices. Pask describes the habitual use of the serialist strategy as the style of 'operational learning' and habitual use of the holist strategy as the style of 'comprehension learning'. He also identifies a third style, 'versatile learning', which indicates that the user has readily available either of the other styles of learning.

The styles of operation learning (serialist) and comprehension learning (holist) also have associated pathologies. Comprehension learning, in its search for interconnections, carries with it the ten-dency to reach conclusions from insufficient evidence and to generalize too readily. Pask describes this error as 'globe-trotting'. The errors associated with operation learning he describes as 'improvidence' – the tendency to be overcautious, to be too concerned with detail, and thereby miss important links between ideas, facts, and conclusions.

Pask has also explored the effects of matching and mismatching extreme holists and serialists to tasks which require only holist or only serialist strategies. The matched groups were significantly better than the mismatched group. He has shown in some of his experi-ments that serialists, when teaching what they have learnt, tend to use a serialist approach whereas holists are more able to vary their approaches. He has also shown that students may select inappropri-ate approaches for the task in hand.

Pask's method of study is essentially the independent and depen-dent variable approach of experimental psychology. The materials used are unfamiliar, the tasks are extreme examples, and in some experiments only students with very distinctive styles of learning were used. It would, therefore, be rash to infer directly from his experiments that tasks or students may be divided neatly into holists or serialists.

The Lancaster studies

The works of Marton and Pask have been brought together and refined considerably by Entwistle and his research team at the University of Lancaster and more recently at the University of Edinburgh (Entwistle, Hanley, and Hounsell 1979; Entwistle, Hanley,and Ratcliffe 1979; Ramsden and Entwistle 1981; Marton, Hounsell, and Entwistle 1984; Richardson 1986). Entwistle also drew on the surveys of study methods carried out by Biggs (1978a, 1978b) in Australia. Entwistle and his team have developed study inventories, they have carried out carefully designed surveys of study methods and of perceptions of academic environments, and they have conducted in-depth interviews of students on study methods. Their findings show clearly that deep and surface approaches are distinctive processes. Comprehension learning (holism) is closely related to deep processing, and operational learning (serialism) is a form of surface processing, but both strategies may be necessary to achieve understanding.

Entwistle has also identified three stable orientations or styles of learning which he describes as 'personal meaning', 'reproducing', and 'achieving'. Personal meaning is associated with intrinsic motivation, a preference for autonomy, and a deep or versatile approach to learning. Reproducing is associated with extrinsic motivation, fear of failure, anxiety, syllabus-boundedness, and surface approaches. Achieving is associated with hope for success, a calculative approach to study, a willingness to adopt any method which leads to high grades. Low scores on achieving are associated with dilatoriness, personal disorganization, and random study methods.

Ramsden and Entwistle (1981) have related these orientations to students' perceptions of their academic departments. They used a sample of 2,200 students drawn from departments in arts, social science, science, and engineering. The findings indicate that the departments where 'good' teaching was reported were strongly oriented towards personal meaning. In departments reported as having 'poor' teaching the orientation towards reproducing was strong. 'Good' teaching included such variables as effective lecturing, help with specific difficulties, and perceived freedom to learn. Poor teaching included such variables as 'ineffective lecturing', heavy workload, inappropriate assessment, and lack of freedom to learn.These results held for all departments and took account of differences in the pre-university qualifications of the sample. Ramsden and Entwistle's results are in line with the studies of Fransson (1977). The work of Becker (1961; Becker, Geer, and Hughes 1968) on medical students and of Miller and Parlett (1974) also show how a heavy workload can induce reproductive strategies and that perceptive students ('cue-seekers') appraise the system of assessment of a department and match their learning strategies accordingly. Laurillard (1979) shows how students can and do vary their approach to study according to their interest in the task. It seems, too, that relatively small changes in an assessment task can produce quite dramatic changes in learning behaviour.

Reports on the in-depth interviews on study methods conducted at the University of Lancaster reveal deep and surface approaches and these were further subdivided into distinctive categories of 'personal experience', 'relationships', 'meaning', 'unrelatedness', 'memorization', and 'unreflectiveness'. The analysis of interviews provides further confirmation of the existence of stable orientations to study which are relatively independent of subject areas (Entwistle and Ramsden 1983).

IMPLICATIONS OF RECENT RESEARCH

The research reviewed in the previous section suggests strongly that students have relatively stable orientations to study, but that some, at least, are able to select from a repertoire of learning strategies the ones most appropriate to achieving the outcome they desire, or that the context induces. However, there is no universal way of learning. Different students will use different strategies on different tasks. Students may have only a limited range of strategies available and may select inappropriately. Nevertheless two dominant orientations can be identified:

● knowledge seeking
● understanding seeking.

Both orientations have their respective strategies and both can probably be pursued in either an active or a passive manner. Figure 7.1 sets out a characterization of the two orientations.

There has been a tendency in the discussion of recent research results to infer that the knowledge seekers produce shallow or superficial learning, while the understanding seekers engage in deep processing. The concomitant implication is that the first orientation is inferior to the second. For some subjects and some tasks, this may be true. But not necessarily for all. The knowledge-seeking dimension

Figure 7.1 Orientations to learning

KNOWLEDGE SEEKER

Adds to store of facts, concepts, and so on
Collects skills, procedures
Breaks down problems and tasks into separate sub-units
Makes links within units of knowledge
Uses memorization skills
Works methodically through logical order of task or problem
Analyses
Uses systematic trial and error
Evaluates data

UNDERSTANDING SEEKER

Tries to relate information or task to own experience
Makes links to other bodies of knowledge
Restructures for personal meaning
Synthesizes
Likes to work from 'whole' picture
Searches for underlying structure, purpose, and meaning
Intuitive use of evidence
Uses analogies, metaphors

---

should not be dismissed out of hand. 'Knowing that' and 'Knowing how' are important. For example an engineer may have to know Lagrange equations before she can solve a particular problem in fluid mechanics. Similarly a neurologist needs to know the specific neurological function of the optic nerve before he can make a diagnosis, or a prognosis of a particular patient. An historian needs to know the terms of the Treaty of Versailles before attempting an analysis of Germany's problems in the 1920s.

It seems more helpful, therefore, to consider both the learning-for-knowledge orientation and the learning-for-understanding orientation as necessary and useful. Learning can then be conceived as a continuous process of development backwards and forwards between the two orientations. Many first-degree subjects such as law and medicine make considerable initial demands on the knowledge dimension with students having to acquire a basic working knowledge of several new subject areas quite rapidly. Other subjects, particularly those in the arts, may require students to develop first in the understanding orientation. But it is likely that students in all subjects will need to be competent on both orientations at some point in their course, and for the orientations to become interrelated. A change in the depth of understanding of a topic is likely to result in an expansion of knowledge of that subject. Expansion of knowledge may lead to a reconceptualization of a topic or field and thus deepen understanding. Similarly procedures and techniques, before they become automated skills or 'knowledge how', may have consciously to be understood at a deep level – 'knowing why'. Concepts and ideas may also be subject to deep processing before they become part of the habitual way of approaching problems in a subject area.

TEACHING STUDY SKILLS

The research on student learning has led to increased interest in evaluating the effectiveness of the teaching of study skills. Summaries of this research can be found in Hartley (1986), Weinstein and Mayer (1986), and Tabberer (1987). On balance there is evidence for short-term benefits accruing from study skills courses including favourable student perceptions. However there is less evidence of tangible long-term benefits such as improved examination performance.

Traditional study skills courses, taught to groups of students, have been criticized on various grounds. For example it has been said that they are too broad or too generalized to be meaningful (Gibbs 1981), that they are based on a naive conception of the psychology of learning (that there is one 'correct' method) (Wells 1986), and that they encourage students to have problems – but not to solve them for themselves. They also tend to avoid difficult areas such as motivation, values, and attitudes. Similar criticisms are made of some books on study skills which are evangelical in tone, or assume that all students are similar in their approach to learning (Wells 1986). Recent developments of the traditional approach, especially in the USA, have therefore tended to focus on more specific information-processing strategies (Bransford 1979) or on executive and operative strategies (Dansereau et al. 1979), the latter designed to help students cope with anxieties, organize their environment for effective study, and maintain a positive attitude to study (Hartley 1986).

More favoured, currently, in Britain is an approach to study skills teaching which is congruent with the findings of Marton and Entwistle. This approach stresses the individual, personalized nature of learning and adopts more of a counselling than a lecturing stance (Gibbs 1981; Marshall and Rowland 1983; Hounsell 1984a; Martin and Ramsden 1987; Main 1984; 1986). The aim is to enable students to become aware of their own learning style and to monitor and evaluate their effectiveness as learners. It is believed that students must understand something about the psychology of learning, and be able to interrogate their own learning, before they can expand or develop their repetoire of study skills (McKeachie 1986). More attention is paid to the purpose of study than to techniques of study *per se* (Hounsell 1984a), and the student remains centrally responsible for choosing the most appropriate methods of learning for him- or herself on real tasks.

STUDY SKILLS AND METACOGNITION

Awareness and conscious, selective use of your own cognitive processes as a learner have also been advocated by Nisbet (Nisbet and Shucksmith 1984). He uses the term 'metacognition' (the seventh sense) to describe such a capability. Nisbet sees the process of learning to learn as one of movement from specific to more generalizable, and therefore transferable, skills. As a first step specific *skills* learned in the context of a particular topic or task need to be put together in different sequences as *strategies* such as planning, monitoring, checking, and self-testing. At the next stage use of strategies should lead the learner consciously to analyse what is required in a new task, what strategies and skills he or she has available, and how best the two can be matched.

Nisbet draws particular attention to the need for learners to develop the capability of transferring learning strategies from one situation or context to another. For this to happen the learner has to be able to articulate the strategies consciously, and also must have the opportunity to practise them so that eventually they become part of his or her habitual repertoire.

The lecturer can facilitate metacognition in three ways: as direct teacher of the skills and strategies initially; as a model who makes explicit the mental processes going on in his or her own mind as he or she demonstrates a skill, solves a problem, composes creative writing or criticism, and so on; lastly the lecturer can act as a provider of opportunities for practice. Gradually, it is suggested, as students acquire more awareness of their own mental processes and become skilled and able to monitor their own performance, control can be passed from the teacher to the learner, and the learner given more responsibility for his or her own learning effectiveness.

SUMMARY

It is possible to put together the various strands in the new approach to cognition as a model of student learning. Such a synthesis is shown in Figure 7.2.

The model can then be interpreted as a set of general guidelines

Figure 7.2 A model of student learning

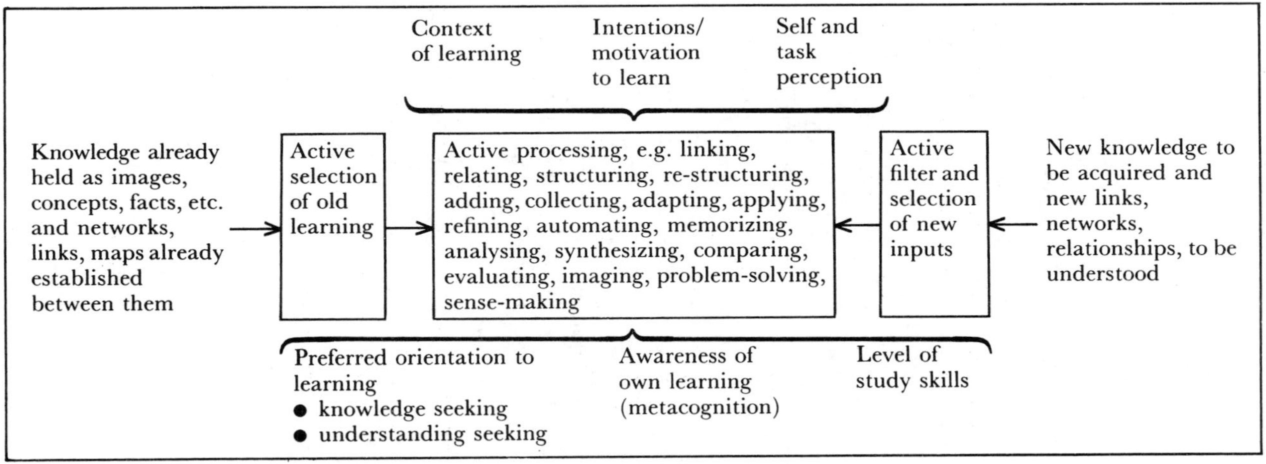

Context of learning   Intentions/ motivation to learn   Self and task perception

Knowledge already held as images, concepts, facts, etc. and networks, links, maps already established between them

Active selection of old learning

Active processing, e.g. linking, relating, structuring, re-structuring, adding, collecting, adapting, applying, refining, automating, memorizing, analysing, synthesizing, comparing, evaluating, imaging, problem-solving, sense-making

Active filter and selection of new inputs

New knowledge to be acquired and new links, networks, relationships, to be understood

Preferred orientation to learning
• knowledge seeking
• understanding seeking

Awareness of own learning (metacognition)

Level of study skills

160 Effective Teaching in Higher Education

for lecturers who wish to improve the effectiveness of their students' learning. Such a set is given in the next section. However, it probably remains more valuable for you to reflect on and analyse your own learning so that you can make more explicit to your students those strategies and skills which are particularly effective in the context of your subject.

Guidelines

Learning is essentially an active process of relating new material to old, and of establishing networks and connections within and between units of knowledge. It follows that effective learning is more likely to occur when:

1 The lecturer accurately diagnoses what the students already know and how that knowledge is organized.
2 The lecturer consciously designs learning tasks that build from the students' existing cognitive structures *towards* the new knowledge or understanding that is to be acquired.
3 New knowledge and understanding is made meaningful to the student(s) by links to personal experience or prior knowledge.
4 Students are cued in advance to select and retrieve the existing knowledge they will need to make sense of new inputs.
5 There is a match between students' preferred orientation to learning and the nature of the learning task. Or any one of a number of learning methods can be used to perform the task.
6 Students are aware of their own learning strategies and alternatives.
7 Students develop a repertoire of learning skills and strategies from direct teaching, explicit modelling by the lecturers, practice, and feedback.

8
Helping students learn

It is strange that we expect students to learn yet seldom
teach them about learning. We expect students to solve
problems yet seldom teach them about problem solving.
And, similarly, we sometimes require students to remember a considerable body of material yet seldom teach
them the art of memory.

(Norman 1980)

INTRODUCTION

This chapter presents a series of suggestions and examples of activities which you can use to help your students learn more effectively.
These suggestions are based upon the work in the earlier chapters of
the book. The chapter is divided into two main sections: helping
students learn in formal sessions (lectures, small group sessions,
laboratories) and helping students learn from private study (reading,
writing, and problem-solving). Examples of activities which are
integral to the text are provided throughout the chapter. Additional
activities are given at the end of the chapter.

Throughout the chapter emphasis is laid on three things:

1 The need to diagnose students' existing knowledge and understanding.
2 Different orientations and strategies of learning.
3 The need to develop the 'learning to learn' or 'metacognitive'
skills of students.

The examples provided are drawn from a variety of subjects; obviously you must decide whether a particular approach is appropriate
and how to modify it for use in your own subject.

HELPING STUDENTS LEARN FROM LECTURES

Many lecturers, and especially those in science and engineering, are
concerned with the clear transmission and useful recording of knowledge (coverage). If you asked your students 'Why do you take notes
in lectures?' it is likely that the answer would contain the idea of
accurate recall of definitions, facts, formulae, procedures – perhaps

assisted by worked examples. Learning in such lectures, then, falls primarily in the knowledge-seeking dimension. Understanding comes later, often in private study or problem classes, when the student is required to apply and extend the knowledge.

On the other hand, many lecturers in the arts and social sciences would say that their purpose in lecturing was to provide understanding. Students in their subjects may also feel that they go to lectures in order to obtain new insights or interpretations of subject matter that is already familiar to them, or works that they have already read.

A first step therefore in helping students learn from lectures is for both lecturer and students to discover how the other perceives the purpose of the lecture, or lecture course. If discrepancies emerge, they can be made explicit, and a common perspective reached on the balance between the 'knowledge' and 'understanding' purposes of lectures.

The second type of activity suggested for the start of a new course is for the lecturer (and students) to discover what the students already do know – and what they don't. It is a common complaint among students that lecturers assume too much, and among lecturers that students don't understand the basic facts and concepts when they have already taken a 'foundation' course the year or term before. There are a number of possibilities here:

1 Give questions to the whole group who work privately on the questions, then compare answers before you provide the 'correct' answers. A show of hands can be used to estimate common strengths and weaknesses.
2 Give multiple choice or true/false items. These may be marked in pairs, the answers given on a transparency or handout. A show of hands can be used to estimate the common strengths and weaknesses of the group.
3 Give the students a short passage to read and ask them to mark the sections that they don't understand.
4 Give the students a short passage to read in which they have to spot deliberate errors.
5 Give the students problems to solve at increasing levels of difficulty. Students working in pairs can compare their approach and solutions and indicate each level that they got correct.

If this type of diagnosis is undertaken in the introductory lecture, there can be time to adapt the level and content of subsequent lectures. The remainder of the time in the first lecture(s) can, if necessary, usefully be given over to remedial teaching and problem-solving on those formulae, concepts, or procedures which are basic to the course.

Even if it proves difficult to diagnose in fine detail what a large group of students knows, there is every reason to suggest to students that they rehearse mentally what they know about the subject before the lecture begins. This will make it easier for them to absorb and make sense of new information. This can be done by students reading through previous lecture notes in the first few minutes. Students can also be given the topic and asked to spend a few minutes identifying for themselves key questions about the topic before the lecture begins. These questions can then act as 'advance organizers' for the students' listening and note-taking. Students can be made aware of the structure of lectures, and also be made more sensitive to the different processes of lecturer talk. They can be taught the basic structuring tactics used in delivering lectures.

Cued to listen for signposts, frames, foci, and links (see p. 22) students will find it easier to make clear notes. Similarly if the underlying method is explained – classical, problem-centred, sequential (see pp. 32–4) – it is easier for students to follow the line of development of a lecture.

At a more elaborate level, students can be sensitized to categories of lecturer talk and thereby improve their listening skills. They can, for example, be taught to discriminate aurally between:

- Preamble   to the lecture
- Orientation   what the lecture is about and how it is organized
- Key points   (which should probably be noted)
- Extensions   to the keypoints or main argument
- Examples   these may be positive or negative
- Asides   these may be relevant or irrelevant, interesting or uninteresting
- Reservations   to the keypoints or main argument
- Summary/ies   these may occur during a lecture as well as at the end of a lecture.

A listening activity incorporating these categories is given as Example 8.1. It can be used live or with video-recordings of brief lectures. (Some transcripts of brief lectures are given in Appendix 2.) Students usually find it helpful to use the schedule more than once – initially it is not easy to listen, think, categorize, and tick. There are bound to be disagreements, especially on what was, or was not, a key point. More important, however, than whether a particular coding was 'right' or 'wrong' is the increased sensitivity in listening which the exercise engenders. It seems to be easier, after such an activity, for students to make more effective notes in lectures (Brown and Daines 1981a).

EXAMPLE 8.1

Listen to a brief extract from a lecture. Try to classify the lecturer talk using POKE EARS. Compare and discuss classifications with those of a few others. Now listen to a brief extract and use the time line display. Code on every third second the category of talk the lecturer is using. Use 'X' – unclassifiable – if you are not sure. Compare and discuss your time line display with those of a few others. Repeat the activity a couple of times. (Some transcripts of brief explanations are given in Appendix 2 which may also be used in a variety of ways for helping students learn from lectures.)

Seconds		3	6	9	12	15	Totals
Preamble	P						
Orientation	O						
Key points	K						
Extensions	E						
Examples	E						
Asides	A						
Reservation	R						
Summaries	S						

Source: Brown 1979
Note: The categories are not intended for direct use in note-taking. Their main use is to sharpen your perceptions of lecturer talk in lectures.

Students' metacognition is helped if you make explicit the processes you are using when lecturing. But students also need to become more aware of their own learning strategies in lectures especially in the matter of taking notes. It is possible for a lecturer to help students to improve their note-taking by giving them opportunities to discuss their notes, and try out and evaluate new techniques. A simple, awareness-raising activity is to ask students to compare their notes, in pairs or fours, on a small portion of the lecture, paying particular attention to style of layout, ways of highlighting key points, and so on. They might also like to draw up a list of 'dos and don'ts of note-taking' which can later be collated and turned into a hand-out for the class. Examples of advice from students are given in Figure 8.1 (Brown 1979).

Figure 8.1 Advice on note-taking in different subjects

Research students were asked what advice they would give to first-year students on note-taking from lectures. Here is a sample of their views.

BIOLOGY

Important in science not to miss vital piece of information. Difficult to keep up with pace. Make headings and side-headings in different colours. Underline or write in capitals important words. Gaps left to copy up missing parts later. Tell lecturer if we couldn't read what he'd written on the board. Tapes of lecture in library in third year where you could listen again. Lecturers willing to explain again if asked. Headings and important facts written on board are a great help. Interesting examples and jokes help you to remember things.
Disliked characteristics: Lecturers who talk too fast. Lecturers who cannot explain clearly.

ECONOMICS

Wait for really basic points – don't try to write it all down, don't try to copy out jargonistic definitions. In time important points become recognizable – if they don't, lecturer is at fault and his talk is probably useless. Develop your own shorthand plus skill of writing and listening at the same time. Use headings and numbered points if possible.
Disliked characteristics: First of all tell them if you dared and boycott them if there was no improvement.

GEOGRAPHY

At start of first year had no method – tried to write everything said – all notes incomplete so began using only major headings plus a few words detail underneath. Sometimes unable to recognize new section because lecture was so poorly presented. This resulted in frantic note-taking from reference list prior to exams. Prefer use of blackboard to clarify points made, also found a brief summary to conclude lectures gives one chance to fill in any points missed. Quality of notes varied with quality of lecturing. Best notes were taken from audible, well-presented, well-prepared lecturers, who did not try to cover too much subject matter yet kept pace moving.
Disliked characteristics: Is unprepared, cannot be heard.

PHYSICS

In science less words, more maths. Copied from board maths with
notes of explanation inserted. With mumbling lecturers (Profs) picked
out 'keywords' from monologue. Often half a page of notes was a list of
disjointed words, usually headings which had to be followed up later.
Usually months later. Own shorthand developed. With very poor
lecturers gave up. Took down intro. and watched the rest without
taking notes. Usually found that anything, however trivial, written on
the board I copied down. Often led to confusion later. References given
also blindly noted. Proved useful later.

Disliked characteristics: Main problem disorganized lecturers who
ramble on. They appear to have no structure throughout and leap from
point to point. General reaction to this is I give up and look at the
ceiling.

Source: Brown 1979.

You might wish, following such an activity, to talk to the class
about note-taking in relation to your own subject. You might, for
example, want to draw a distinction between notes for accurate
recall and notes to give an overview of a topic. It is worth remarking
here that lecturers whose purpose is to illuminate need to allow
students time to make notes in *their own words* of insights, thoughts,
and new lines of approach. This takes longer than is commonly
realized and students then miss or block out the next section of the
lecture because they are still trying to assimilate and actively process
the preceding point. It may also be useful to demonstrate to students
the uses of simple diagrams, flow charts, and 'mind maps' (see
Chapter 4 and Buzan 1982) as alternatives to longhand notes.

Often the least effective part of students' learning from lectures is
what they do with their notes after the lecture. Even if their notes
need little tidying up or rewriting, students still have to learn and
think about them. This final, crucial stage is frequently omitted.
You can, at least, suggest that students spend 10–15 minutes actively
recalling and restructuring the lecture material in their minds or on
paper with some 'organizing questions such as:

● What were the main points?
● What were the advantages and disadvantages of . . . ?
● What is the evidence for and against . . . ?
● What extra information do I need to insert?

Alternatively you can give your students a problem to solve which
will require them to apply the knowledge in their notes. Approximately 60 per cent of a lecture is likely to be forgotten within 24

hours unless reinforced in some way (McCleish 1976), so it is important for students to do a follow-up activity, preferably on the same day.

LEARNING FROM SMALL GROUP SESSIONS

Sometimes the purpose of a small group session is specifically to clarify difficulties of understanding or correct misperceptions of knowledge. Problem-solving classes and essay tutorials can take this form, as can the post-lecture seminar (see Chapter 4). If a diagnosis of difficulties has not been obtained from marking students' work, it may be necessary to devise some simple activities for the purpose.

Students can be asked to 'brainstorm', 'buzz', and then list the points they find hard to understand. These can then form the agenda or 'map' for the session. Alternatively the tutor can ask students to produce a 'map' of the topic, which shows connections between different parts of a topic. The tutor can use the 'maps' to identify relationships that do not seem to have been fully grasped. Alternatively a problem can be set or a case explored with the tutor 'tuned' to pick up lack of knowledge and lack of understanding.

If the topic for the session is complex, and the tutor wishes to check that learning has occurred, then a sequence of input → discussion → applied activity → feedback → input, and so on, may help the students to learn more easily especially if they like step-by-step (serialist) learning strategies.

If the aim is development of sophisticated skills, say of criticism or diagnosis, then the sequence practice → feedback → input → practice, and so on may be better. In the early stages practice should be on relatively brief tasks. The inputs should be concerned with underlying principles and rationale so the students' understanding is developed.

In theory, small group sessions are designed to deepen students' understanding. In practice, they frequently degenerate into knowledge-giving monologues by the tutor or into fragmented collections of points generated by *ad hoc* discussion among the students. Facilitating methods for avoiding monologues are suggested in Chapter 4.

It is also possible for the tutor to help students learn in small group sessions by making them more aware of the purpose and strategies of good discussion. A new group can be asked to 'brainstorm' the purpose of discussion for a few minutes and then to compare their perceptions. The tutor can then ask the group for ideas on how to translate their purposes into a reality for the current sessions. This activity raises awareness and also starts students thinking about the nature of discussion or joint problem-solving activities. It can lead to the informal 'contract' between tutor and group suggested in Chapter 4. A similar 'brainstorm' on the purpose of discussion towards the end of a course can also be used to show the students how their perceptions of group discussion have changed. The quality of contribution and response in discussion can also be enhanced by simple activities, as illustrated in Example 8.2

EXAMPLE 8.2

Introduce a contentious subject as the topic for discussion. Each member of the group must make a contribution in turn. The only rule is that each contribution must use, or build on, the previous contribution. The group judges whether this has been achieved.The game can be scored, or more simply, a student who fails to use the previous point can be 'out'. The discussion of this activity can help students to become more aware of the skills of active listening and of the difference between a collection of points and the development of an idea or argument.

Examples of topics which can generate controversy amongst different groups of students are:

1 Engineering is merely applied physics.
2 Should girls aged under 16 be prescribed the 'pill' without parental consent?
3 History tells us nothing useful about the present.
4 The law is an ass.
5 Literary criticism is a parasitic subject.
6 Most surgery is an admission of failure.
7 Biology is more like stamp-collecting than it is like physics.

Activities can be used to help students become more aware of the *type* of discussion in which they are engaged. The group can be asked to categorize a list of topics or problems within the subject, for example as to whether they are primarily:

1 Conceptual requiring logical analysis of ideas, definitions.
2 Empirical   requiring attention to the quality and nature of evidence.
3 Value   requiring analysis of values, attitudes, beliefs.

Alternatively the tutor can contrive to introduce discussions on a topic or problem in each of the three categories. Following the discussions the group can be asked to reflect on the differences in the nature of questions posed by the topic and in the cognitive responses required to deal with the issue.

Since questioning is an essential skill of small group work, there is no reason why a tutor should not teach students how to use questions tactically to deepen their own understanding and move the development of the discussion or activity along. Students should, for example, be able to select and use appropriate probing questions such as:

- Is there an alternative view?
- How accurate is that?
- What is the evidence for saying that?
- Can you give me an example?

Finally, a tutor might give some thought to the question of whether students should take notes in small group sessions. There are at least three potential uses of notes:

- An *aide-mémoire* of points raised.
- A means of recording key questions.
- A way of mapping networks between ideas, points, theories, and so on.

If notes are to be used to help deepen understanding, it is probably necessary to give students 'time out' during the session to think about the points which have been made, restructure them in their own minds, and put their thoughts down on paper in their own words. This also helps to make notes coherent. Maps and networks can be made as a summary group activity, and in relation to the 'map' drawn up in advance by the tutor (see the section in Chapter 4 on 'Preparing for small group teaching').

HELPING STUDENTS LEARN FROM LABORATORY SESSIONS

The need to diagnose what students know and understand is as important in laboratory work as elsewhere. There is evidence to support lecturers' suspicions that:

1 Often undergraduate students hold an 'incorrect' belief about phenomena, forces, processes, and their interrelationships.
2 Even when presented with evidence from experiments of a 'gap' between their own belief and the 'correct' explanation, they do not necessarily abandon their pre-existing frameworks.
3 When lack of understanding exists students may

   - ignore the 'correct' explanation,
   - hold their own and the 'correct' explanation at the same time despite logical contradictions,

- revert to their own explanation outside the lab or course.

(For a review of the evidence, see White and Tisher 1986.)

The amount of learning for understanding that occurs in such circumstances can be limited. Some students are likely to resort to superficial rote-learning techniques and store the knowledge gained in the lab as an isolated unit, unconnected to their other learning and, perhaps, personally meaningless.

Where experiments depend for their full learning potential on mastery of key concepts, it may be worth designing a prior mini-experiment or activity that tests the basic understanding needed. This could take the form of questions on a set of findings, or an alteration in the design of an experiment to produce a different given result. Short, multiple-choice, self-test and revision programs on a microcomputer could also be used.

Much laboratory work falls along the knowledge dimension. Students are required to follow predetermined procedures on set experiments. The learning engendered by this tradition tends, unfortunately, to be surface learning. Students may extend their 'knowledge how', but there is little evidence that they acquire any deep understanding of scientific method. It is, however, likely that enquiry-based laboratory practicals, where students are required to design and operate their own experiments, will lead to gains in such understanding (Hegarty-Hazel 1986). There is also some evidence that incorporating self-assessment techniques in laboratory work can lead students to have a better grasp of what they are doing and why (Daines 1986).

If students are to be helped to learn effectively from laboratory work, lecturers and demonstrators may need to pay more attention to science as a process rather than as a body of knowledge.They may need to make explicit to students not just the procedures to be followed in a particular experiment, but the rationale behind the procedures and, at a deeper level, how this rationale relates to other scientific 'methods' and processes. In this way, for example, students may come to understand that the use of randomized control groups in an experimental design is related to the notion of confidence in one's results. They can be encouraged to think about whether this form of design is appropriate for different phenomena and different situations and what alternatives may have to be used. Similar examples may be identified in all branches of science and engineering.

Direct teaching may be needed to move the student from a passive recording of the results of a particular set of experiments, to seeing connections with other hypotheses, or to understanding the relationship of this practical to larger units of knowledge. An example of a simple experiment designed to encourage students to think about processes and to make new connections is given below.

EXAMPLE 8.3

Reacting to sight and touch: which is faster?

Spend a few minutes discussing this problem:
Given a metre rule and a flat wall determine the reaction time of your subject to a visual signal.
Try to control and standardize as many variables as you can.
Now try to determine the reaction time of your experimental subject to a tactile signal (touch). Again standardize as many variables as possible.
Carry out the experiment. Give your subject some practice and then carry out ten trials under each experimental condition. Without calculating the reaction times for each condition, can you decide whether your subject's reaction times to sight and touch were different?

Discussion of task

1 What variables did you control?
2 What assumptions did you make?
3 What can you infer from the results about the transmission of nerve impulses?
4 Was this an experiment?
5 What type of scientific method, if any, were you using?

HELPING STUDENTS LEARN FROM PRIVATE STUDY

There are three parts to this section: reading, writing, and problem-solving. The section on reading and writing may be supplemented by reference to several texts such as Maddox (1967), Rowntree (1977), Open University (1979), Palmer and Pope (1984). These texts contain useful tips and activities for students on self-management including the organization of time and tasks, getting down to work and thinking positively about studying. Overseas students may find the text by Ellis and Hopkins (1985) particularly helpful. Those interested primarily in reading should consult Harri-Augstein, Smith, and Thomas (1982), those interested primarily in essay writing might consult Clanchy and Ballard (1982) and those concerned with scientific writing might consult Barrass (1984).

The section on problem-solving draws on research in artificial intelligence and other aspects of cognitive psychology, practical suggestions, and the recent studies of student learning described in Chapter 7. Indeed it is curious that various approaches to problem-solving have not hitherto been brought together and that there has been little research on effective ways of teaching problem-solving.

IMPROVING READING

It is obvious that reading is an interaction of reader and text. It follows that to help students to improve their reading you must be able to identify various types of texts which a student will encounter when studying your subject and various strategies of reading which he or she might adopt. Thus the questions 'How should you read?' needs to be broken down into specific questions such as 'How do you read a pure maths text, a poem, a seventeenth-century diary, a legal document, or a biochemical journal?'. Underlying each of these specific questions is the question of the goals of the reader. Reading to get the feel of a topic is a very different process from reading for specific information.

This combination of goals, reading strategies, and types of texts in a subject should inform any approach to helping students to improve their reading. Clearly therefore a first task in helping your students to improve their reading in your own subject is to identify the different types of text and to reflect upon your own reading strategies. Here, however, we must enter a caveat. Expert readers are likely to have developed sophisticated strategies of reading which a novice may not possess (see Harri-Augstein, Smith, and Thomas 1982; Calfee and Drum 1986). Thus it is also important to discuss with students their approach to reading and perhaps to provide them with brief specific reading tasks. The first of these tasks might be incorporated into exercises requiring students to use an academic library.

Studies of reading in various contexts suggest strongly that the factor which accounts most for what is learned and recalled is what the student already knows. Put more technically, learning from reading is dependent upon the prior existence of relevant structures of knowledge in the mind of the reader (Calfee and Drum 1986). These findings corroborate the model of student learning (Figure 7.2) in Chapter 7.

As that model indicates, all texts rely on readers to make links and inferences or extrapolation as they are reading. It is this active processing which makes the text meaningful. If readers know a lot about the subject of the text it is likely that they will make many relational links between the content and what they already know, even to the extent that new representations are created which go beyond the text itself. On the other hand, readers with no prior relevant mental schemata may be quite unable to fill in the implicit, inferential gaps in the text and consequently will find it 'hard to understand'. It follows that lecturers who wish to help their students learn more effectively from their reading need to:

1 Check that the students already have adequate relevant knowledge and understanding to make sense of the text. And if not . . .
2 Provide a conceptual scaffolding or framework which will help students to organize and relate the new material, or . . .
3 Design a few preliminary activities on easier texts that will provide 'anchors' or 'organizers' in advance of the more difficult reading.

READING STRATEGIES

Although different texts and tasks may require different reading strategies it is possible to offer some general strategies for reading which can be adapted for use in most subjects.

The first of these may be labelled as 'awareness of purpose'. The self-directed questions 'Why am I reading this?' and 'How should I read this?' can prompt a reader to vary level and speed of reading. The classification of levels given in Figure 8.2 is a useful starting-point for discussions of reading activities with students and with lecturers.

Figure 8.2 Approaches to reading

Scanning	when you want to find a particular item of information
Skimming	when you want to gain a quick impression of a text or article
Surveying	when you want to uncover the structure and 'topography' of a text or article
Light study reading	reading passively for factual information, general background, and/or with no specific purpose
Directed reading	reading actively for specific knowledge acquisition or for grasp of pre-determined concepts, procedures, theories
Deep study reading	reading actively to make connections, meaning, consider implications, and to evaluate argument

READING DEEPLY

Many reading tasks in higher education require a directed or deep approach. It can therefore be useful to suggest strategies that may help students to achieve these deep, active levels. Palinscar and Brown (1984) have developed a six-point strategy for this purpose.

1 Understand the purpose of the reading task.
2 Activate relevant prior knowledge of the subject.
3 Identify important content and focus on that. Do not give equal concentration to content of less or trivial importance.
4 Make a conspicuous attempt to evaluate the content for internal consistency, compatibility with prior knowledge, and with common sense.
5 Monitor your own reading. Review your understanding of the text periodically.
6 Make and test inferences deliberately including interpretations, predictions and conclusions.

Similar strategies can be found in books on study skills (see for example Maddox 1967; Harri-Augstein, Smith, and Thomas 1982; Palmer and Pope 1984). Helping students to become aware of the existence of such strategies is probably not enough, however. They will also need opportunities to develop and analyse their own reading skills. It is possible to design short, structured activities or exercises which provide these opportunities. Some suggestions are given below together with some sample pieces of text which have been used in workshops with students and lecturers.

1 Underline key sentences which carry the argument or make the main points.
2 Draw a diagram or flow chart to show the main points in the procedure/argument.
3 Draw a diagram to show the main ideas in the article and show the relationships made between them by the author.
4 Put subheadings into a piece of extended text.
5 Write a summary sentence in your own words for each paragraph.
6 Restructure your notes in your own words so that similar points are grouped together under an appropriate subheading.
7 As you read, think up, and note down, questions to ask of the next section of text (inference, likely conclusion, extrapolation).
8 Write down some questions to ask yourself as a way of monitoring your own reading, for example:

   • What is the main point being made?

● Are there any exceptions to this rule?
● What evidence is being used?
● Am I reading at an appropriate level?
● Does this agree with what I know?

9 Delete all redundant or trivial points in a text.
10 Delete the least important 25 per cent of the text; then the next least important 25 per cent, then the next. What constituted the most important 25 per cent of the text?
11 Go through an extended argument. Put a cross for any sentence containing an incongruity; put a tick for any sentence that follows logically. (Cross out sentences that are irrelevant. Put an E for sentences that are just examples.)

EXAMPLE 8.4

Read the following extract and draw a diagram, flow chart, sketch, or model of the main features of the extract. Compare your diagram with those of a few other students/colleagues. Identify the ambiguities and unresolved issues in the extract.

Roughly speaking minerals may be classified as metals or stones. The metals may occur in relatively poor form in geological deposits or in conjunction with other non-metallic elements. The metals may be further subdivided into noble metals such as gold, platinum, or silver, rare metals such as lithium or uranium or common metals such as iron, copper, and aluminium. In addition there are various alloys of combinations of metals such as brass, bronze, or steel. A common classification of stones is 'precious' and masonry but not all stones fit these categories. Diamonds, emeralds, and sapphires are examples of precious stones. In addition there are various semi-precious stones and stones used in masonry such as granite, marble, limestone, and slate.

EXAMPLE 8.5

Read the extract below. Draw a diagram to illustrate the relationship between the concepts described.

Mechanics

There are three main theories of mechanics in current use:
NEWTONIAN mechanics is valid for systems which are large in comparison with atoms, moving slowly in comparison with

light, and not subjected to very strong gravitational field (such as those near black holes).

RELATIVITY mechanics includes Newtonian mechanics as a special case, and is also valid near the speed of light and for objects strongly attracted by gravity; it breaks down on the atomic scale.

QUANTUM MECHANICS also includes Newtonian mechanics, but remains valid for atomic and nuclear systems. A completely satisfactory fusion of relativity and quantum mechanics has not yet been achieved.

EXAMPLE 8.6

There are sixteen sentences in this passage. Cross out the eight which are the least important. Which of the remaining eight would you say were crucial to the author's conception of 'scientific method'?

We tend to think of science as a 'body of knowledge' which began to be accumulated when men hit upon 'scientific method'. This is a superstition. It is more in keeping with the history of thought to describe science as the myths about the world which have not yet been found to be wrong. Science had its roots partly in primitive pictures of the world and partly in primitive technology. There has been a great deal of discussion about the primacy of disinterested speculation or practical inventiveness in the early stages of science. Some maintain that those who said that the earth was made of air, or had an underlying mathematical structure, or was composed of atoms, were the originators of science; others uphold the claims of those who started measuring for irrigation schemes, or mixed tin with copper in order to make bronze, or guided their ships by the stars. Both parties are surely right; yet both fail to bring out the core of what we now call 'scientific method'. This began when men began consciously to challenge the stories that they were told and to produce counter-examples to support their contentions. Men may inherit stories from their parents; they may think them up on a cold winter's night in order to pass away the time; they may evolve them while trying to make better weapons or heal their wounds. This is a matter of history – often of personal biography – and is of little methodological interest. The crucial stage for the methodologist comes when conscious attempts are made to *test* the stories provided by tradition, speculative curiosity, or practical necessity. Showing a man that his story is wrong usually involves producing a better story oneself. In argumentation, discussion, and the production of counter-examples drawn from memory, observation, and testimony, we have the core of what we now call science. Experimentation, measurement, and all the paraphernalia of the laboratory are but more precise ways of confirmations or counter-examples. Science consists in conscious attempts to refute other people's stories and in the production of better stories to supplant them. The history of science is the history of stories which have been shown to be false or only partially correct.

IMPROVING WRITING

Writing, like reading, involves goals, tasks, and approaches. So an important first step for lecturers interested in helping their students to write is to analyse (not merely state) the tasks of writing in their subject and to reflect upon their own approaches to writing.

In addition, you might explore the recent studies of writing which have, in part, been influenced by the advent of the word-processor. An interesting, modest survey of how a sample of academics tackle writing is desribed by Hartley and Knapper (1984). Reviews of research may be found in Young (1976), Hounsell (1984b), Beaugrande (1984), and Scardamalia and Bereiter (1986). This research is beginning to explore the inner processes of writing, problems such as writer's 'block', and various ways we can help others to write. The research suggests that the usual advice – plan, gather material, organize it, write it, revise it – is useful but does not go far enough. The reviews cited suggest that writers rarely follow these steps sequentially. Instead they zig-zag across the steps, sometimes changing intentions and strategies so that the finished product is not necessarily what the writer anticipated. Indeed through the process of writing you become more aware of what you want to say and how to say it. Thus it is important to distinguish, for students, the task of writing to clarify your thinking and the task of writing to communicate your thoughts.

The process of writing

Three interrelated processes are involved in writing: searching, writing, and revising what has been written. These processes are central to the model of Hayes and Flower (1980) (Figure 8.3) which accords well with recent research findings. The model emphasizes the twin approach of metacognition (knowing what you are doing and why) and developing your skills. A useful preliminary activity is to ask the students to think about and discuss, in groups of three or four, how they set about writing an essay (or other writing task).

Figure 8.3 Structure of a model of the composing process

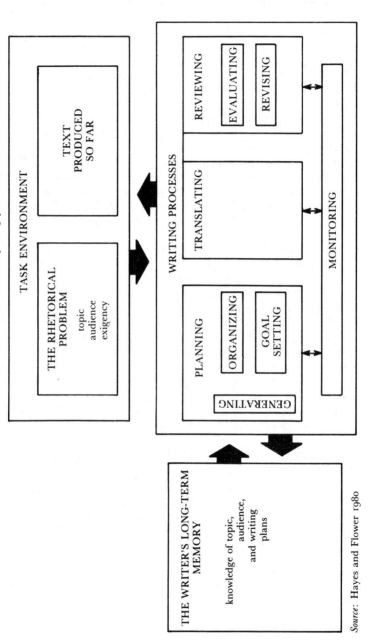

Source: Hayes and Flower 1980

Searching involves analysing the task in hand, thinking of what you already know – from your prior reading and thinking – and how that information may be restructured. It also involves thinking about different forms of writing style and text and selecting the approach that seems most appropriate.

Various activities may be devised on searching. Topics or essay titles may be given to students to unpack. They may be invited to brainstorm ideas, facts, words, images, writers' names, and to produce maps which show links and possible connections. Examples of different types of writing on a topic can be given to students to analyse and evaluate. Students can be asked to take an account written in one style, and rewrite it in a different style for a different audience. They may be asked to analyse how writers present convincing argument or cover their tracks.

The act of writing itself involves a hierarchy of skills from the more routine aspects of spelling, punctuation, and sentence construction to the subtle use of rhetorical devices in narrative and expository prose. Obviously the more automated the routine skills become, the easier it is to focus upon the task of conveying meaning.

The act of writing can be painful so it is not surprising that students develop tactics to postpone writing. A useful activity is to ask students to think about and discuss what tactics they use to avoid getting down to writing such as 'I'll just read a little more', 'I'd better check that reference', 'I'll start tomorrow', 'I'd better ring Mum'. This activity leads naturally into a discussion of how you can settle down to write and the process of writing itself. When students ask us how they should start writing we might ask them what they think they should do and try to build on their suggestions. Then lead them gently to the notion that they should search, think, and then write. One of our colleagues is more direct. He said at a writing workshop for students:

> If your writing is lumpy, unstructured, etc., keep writing. If you can't think exactly what to say, keep writing. If your sentences are ungrammatical or too long, keep writing. If you can't think of the phrase you want, leave a gap but keep writing.

While his advice may seem extreme it does underline the importance of getting words down on paper which can then be reshaped and polished.

Revising what you are writing may occur during the process of writing. It should always occur after you have written a draft but, preferably, not immediately after you have written a draft. During this part of the process metacognition, or knowing what you are doing and why, has a crucial role. Articulating your goals and subgoals can provide direction and structure. Here, for example, is an extract from an audio-recording of a student thinking aloud as she read the first draft of her essay.

'Mmm I ought to argue this [interpretation] more strongly. So these points ought to go first. Then I'll need an example. What? Yes, that's a good one and it leads on . . . Mmm that'd be better as a punch line so I'll move it to the end here. That sentence is awful. I'll change it. Ah! I didn't need to go into that at all. I'll cross it out. I could do with a quote here to back that up. That one from Heaney might do.

Constructive self-talk, including asking questions of yourself, is an important part of developing writing and revising skills. Some useful questions to ask yourself are 'Who is this for?', 'Why am I writing this paragraph?', 'Do I need to say this?', 'Should I tell them what this is about?', 'Would this be better at the beginning or the end?'.

Students can be invited to try out constructive self-talk activities with an audio-recorder. It may be interesting too for lecturers to listen to students' recordings and, of course, their own. Students might also be invited to generate questions to ask themselves when writing. Figure 8.4 provides some suggestions which students made at one of our workshops. Interestingly they are not dissimilar from the suggestions used by Scardamalia and Bereiter (1986) in one of their experiments on improving writing.

Figure 8.4 Asking yourself about your writing

```
 1 Why am I writing this paragraph?
 2 Why is this important?
 3 Am I going into too much detail?
 4 Will this bit be understood?
 5 Is this true?
 6 Could this be said more directly?
 7 What is the main point? Where is it?
 8 Should I change the order?
 9 Should this sentence be the other way round?
10 What is the structure? Will the reader know?
```

Finally it is worth reminding students of the interrelatedness of the processes of searching, writing, and revising. As Humes (1983) puts it:

Writers move back and forth among subprocesses. All of the planning is not done before words are put on paper; all of the words are not put on paper before writers review and revise.

Helping students write

Direct teaching of skills and strategies of writing in the ways suggested
in previous sections is a powerful way of helping students to improve
their writing. In addition, there are two major ways of influencing
students' writing: the assignments set and the feedback given.
There is evidence from various studies that when a task has an
audience or purpose beyond assessment then writing often improves
(Scardamalia and Bereiter 1986). This finding implies that writing
tasks for specific audiences may well be of value. Some possible
examples are 'Provide a test report for consumers', 'Review a text for
the journal of . . .', 'Prepare a talk for Radio 3 on . . .'.
At least as important as writing tasks for specific audiences are
writing tasks that require students to think as well as to expound
knowledge. Analysis of the assignments set in a course may well
reveal an *undue* emphasis upon knowledge rather than understanding.
Changing the type of assignment set may well change the level of
student thinking exhibited.
Feedback by tutors is, potentially, one of the most influential ways
of improving writing. Unfortunately feedback is not always provided
or used effectively. Traditionally students submit a final version of
writing. This is returned, perhaps long afterwards, with comments
on style and content. Given that an assignment feels to most students
like a single creative act there is likely to be little transfer of tutor
advice from the margins of one essay to the active process of writing
the next.
For this reason an alternative form of feedback known as 'conferencing' has been advocated (Graves 1978). Conferences are brief
consultations during the writing of an assignment. They provide a
student with an opportunity to talk through what he or she is
currently writing. The tutor asks questions about, and comments
on, the current draft. The amount of active tutor involvement may
vary. At one extreme the tutor may collaborate in the writing itself.
At a less involved level, the tutor may teach specific stylistic points,
diagnose problems, or suggest alternative ways of structuring and
organizing the material. Minimally the tutor listens and prompts to
help the student make explicit the processes involved in writing and
to develop the student's capacity to use them.
Conferencing has implications for the distribution of tutor time.
Extra tutorials may be needed during the time the student is
planning and writing, but less time may be needed for feedback on
the finished product. It should also be remembered that conferencing does not *guarantee* the internalization of writing skills and
strategies any more than other methods of study skill teaching.

However conferencing may well be an improvement on traditional
methods of providing feed-back.

EXAMPLE 8.7

Which is the 'better' piece of writing and why?

Version H

All our experiments showed that the distributions did not depend on
time. This has been shown by most previous work on liquid distribution, and it suggests that the flow pattern in the packed bed is stable.

We thought it would be interesting to know to what extent this
flow pattern depends on bed structure and to what extent it depends
on the random movement of the initial liquid particles making
wetted paths through the packing. In any given packing arrangement, re-packing or 'stirring' might be expected to change the
structure of the bed; complete overloading of the bed with a high
liquid flow-rate (pre-flooding) might be expected to alter a flow
pattern, depending on which paths through the pattern were wetted.

So we used salt tracer methods to measure liquid spread before
and after stirring (using half-inch rings) and before and after pre-
flooding. Other conditions – packed height and liquid rate – were
kept constant. Both stirring and pre-flooding affected the stable flow
pattern, but stirring had much greater effect than pre-flooding;
obviously, the structure of the bed is mainly responsible for the
stable flow pattern.

Version R

All the experiments showed the distributions to be time-independent.
This has been noted by most previous workers on liquid distribution.
It indicates the existence of a stable flow pattern in the packed bed.
This flow pattern may be dependent on two factors. The first is bed
structure, the second is purely random movement of the initial
liquid particles producing wetted paths through the packing. It is of
interest to determine to what extent flow pattern is dependent on
these two factors. For a given arrangement of packing it could be
expected that complete overloading of the bed by a high liquid flow-
rate (pre-flooding) would alter a flow pattern. For the same arrangement, re-packing or 'stirring' the bed would be expected to cause
changes in the structure of the bed. Liquid-spread measurements
were undertaken to test this. They were carried out before and after
either pre-flooding the packed bed or changing the bed structure by

stirring. Half-inch rings were utilized for the latter purpose. Other conditions, namely packing height and liquid rate, were kept constant. Salt tracer experiments were used. Both pre-flooding and stirring influenced the stable flow pattern. The effect of re-packing, however, was substantially greater than that of pre-flooding. This means that stable flow pattern is determined mainly by bed structure.

EXAMPLE 8.8

Modify this extract from an essay on study skills.

Studying skills is a very important part of the life of a student and studying may be divided into public and private bits. The public bits are in lectures tutorials and laboratory classes and the private parts are to do with reading, revising and writing such things as projects or even essays and sometimes lab reports and problem solving. These are the most important, very time consuming and so you should think about all the ways in which you could help yourself to improve your approaches to impriving your studying techniques and your use of time.

Your version:

EXAMPLE 8.9

Sketch a plan or 'map' for an essay or short paper on one of the following topics. Compare your plan with that of a few other students. Discuss with them how you set about formulating your plan.

1 The likely effects of computerization on life in Britain during the 1990s.
2 Acid rain.
3 The arguments for and against animal experimentation.
4 The nature of measurement in science.
5 The role of imagery in literature.
6 How could unemployment in Britain be reduced.
7 The Mirror is but a reflection of the Times . . .

IMPROVING PROBLEM-SOLVING

In this section we suggest some ways to develop the problem-solving strategies of students, particularly in science-based subjects and the social sciences. Given the rich variety of problems encountered in academic subjects it is hardly surprising that there is no one specific strategy of problem-solving. Indeed if there was, there would be no problem . . .

The suggestions we offer draw upon three sources. First, the writers on problem-solving such as Wickelgren (1938), Polya (1945, 1962), de Bono (1967, 1968, 1969, 1973), and Wertheimer (1961). Wickelgren and Polya were particularly concerned with problems based on mathematics and logic. De Bono is also concerned with more open-ended problems. The second source is the experience of providing workshops on problem-solving for students and colleagues. This experience has taught us that although different subject areas are concerned with different problems there are some general strategies which seem to apply across all subjects. The third source is research on problem-solving. Some of this research is based upon computer-aided modelling of mental processes and has become known as AI (artificial intelligence) (Johnson-Laird and Wason 1977; Newell and Simon 1972; Kahney 1986). Other work is based upon problem-solving experiments with human subjects (Johnson-Laird 1983) and studies of thinking (Wittrock 1986). Much of the research has been concerned with logical confusions and errors. As yet, this research has not been used to teach problem-solving in academic subjects.

A first step in teaching others how to solve problems is to reflect upon how you, the lecturer, tackle problem-solving. A second step is to tackle some problems and check whether you do what you claim to do. It is useful to consider not only the solutions but also the false starts, the loops in thinking, and the clues you used.

These activities can also be incorporated into workshops and seminars on problem-solving for students so that they become aware of their own processes of thinking and they can begin to analyse those processes. When students have analysed and discussed their processes of solving problems you can introduce them to a model of problem-solving which identifies the usual stages in problem-solving. Such a model is given in Figure 8.5. It may, of course, be modified for use in different subjects. Alternatively students can be invited to develop their own 'private' models of problem-solving and then compare these to the model we propose.

Figure 8.5 Problem-solving strategies and tactics

STRATEGIES				TACTICS
First Stage				
I	S	D	E	Unpick wording
D	T	I	X	Specify goal(s)
E	A	S	P	Distinguish key points
N	T	S	L	Represent graphically/figuratively
T	E	E	O	Search for implicit information
I		C	R	Look for problem within problem
F		T	E	Play with different combinations of key
Y				concepts, variables
				State 'nub' of problem
Second Stage				
P	S	R	S	Scan memory for possible procedures
L	E	E	T	Distinguish similarities/differences
A	A	L	R	from previous cases
N	R	A	U	Break down into sub-parts, simplify
	C	T	C	Consider and evaluate alternative
	H	E	T	courses of action
			U	
			R	
			E	
Third Stage				
D				Work back from answer
O				Work back and forward from midpoint
				Solve sub-parts
				Treat sequences of steps as single units
				Use trial and error systematically
				Use 'evaluation' function
				Use proof by contradiction
				Select and apply course of action with best fit; obtain feedback
Fourth Stage				
T	A	L	R	Check results by logical deduction and
E	P	E	E	inference
S	P	A	F	Check result by different method
T	L	R	L	Use solution; search for corollary
	Y	N	E	Analyse problem-solving process(es)
			C	used
			T	Check if alternative/simpler method
				Evaluate solution against goals and values

PROBLEM-SOLVING STRATEGIES AND TACTICS

Four stages may be identified in the model (Figure 8.5). These approximate to the questions: 'What is the nub of the problem?', 'Have I met a similar problem before?' 'What approaches can I use?', 'How should I check the solution?'. Within each stage are a set of strategies and associated tactics which can be used as guidelines for improving problem-solving.

At the outset it is stressed that problem-solving is not always sequential. You may move backwards and forwards across the stages. Progressing from hypothesis to proof in Euclidean style may be the most common mode of presentation. It is not always the way in which problems are actually solved. Nor should you assume that describing a model of problem-solving to students will in itself improve their problem-solving strategies. To improve your problem-solving skills you need practice, guidance, constructive feedback, and opportunities to reflect upon the processes involved.

EXAMPLE 8.10

Before reading on, try this problem. Before looking up the answer in notes and comments, think about how you tackled the problem.

Are there more nephews in the world than male (first) cousins? Try to solve this problem and at the same time keep a record of what strategies you tried and rejected and what led you to your solution. Compare your approaches to the problem with those of a colleague. What strategies did you use?

Stage 1: What is the nub of the problem?

The nub of the problem may be another problem which may be more simple or complex than the problem presented. In science-based subjects, at undergraduate level, the core problem is often simpler than the problem presented. In social sciences and law the nub of the problem may be a deeper problem on which there are views rather than answers. As well as problems within problems nubs may be conflicts – I want to do X and I want to do Y – or an apparent contradiction – it cannot be X and Y simultaneously so what is it?

In any of the above cases the task is going beyond the surface characteristics to the core. For many students this is the most difficult part of problem-solving. They may be proficient at reasoning and calculating but quite unable to penetrate the data given to the underlying problem. Hence the importance of practice at this stage of problem-solving. Useful tactics are reading for meaning or underlying terms, or picking out words that look crucial. Restating the problem in your own words can help this process. So too can drawing the problem as a figure or diagram. Graphical representation can suggest relationships between given concepts or variables, and picturing the problem mentally can provide clues to the embedded problem or paradox.

Stage 2: Have I met a similar problem before?

In this stage an active memory search is required. If a similar problem has been encountered you have to recall the method of solution or appropriate formulae. Having done this you often leap to the next stages. If the problem still remains intractable then you have to consider in what ways it is similar and different from previous problems encountered. The use of analogies and metaphors can be useful in this stage for they can provide clues for action. Sometimes the analogies may be a simpler version of the problem – which you can try to solve – or an analogy drawn from a different topic or subject. Metaphors may provide powerful insights into a problem and indeed have often led to the solution of quite deep problems of structure and design.

Stage 3: What approaches can I use?

Stages 1 and 2 may lead immediately to a known approach. This is particularly true of problems with which you are familiar. It is often true also of problems requiring insight. For insight itself is essentially the act of creating new links within the data given in a problem and between the data given and prior knowledge. Once these links are established the problem often becomes soluble.

However some problems are less tractable. Indeed you may have to go back to Stages 1 and 2 or resort to experimenting with problem-solving tactics. Such experimenting may involve several tactics from systematic trial and error through to methods of *reductio ad absurdum*. These tactics are the heart of the process of problem-solving so they are discussed here in some detail.

Problem-solving tactics can be likened to climbing up a tree which has several major branches, each forking in turn into smaller branches (Duncker 1945; Wickelgren 1938). The difficulty for the climber is knowing which branch to take each time there is a decision point or fork. Systematic trial and error is one possible tactic. When you reach a dead end [sic] you climb back to an earlier fork and set off up again along the alternative route.

Duncker (1945) showed this process in action when he posed to subjects the problem of a patient with an inoperable stomach tumour, and of rays that can destroy organic tissues including tumours if they hit it with sufficient intensity. By what procedure could the rays be used on the tumour without destroying the healthy organic tissue surrounding it? The problem was tackled initially by setting off along one of three branches: avoiding contact between rays and healthy tissue; desensitizing the healthy tissue; or lowering the intensity of rays on their way through healthy tissue. Each of these branches yielded further alternative routes. For example subjects who took the second branch then decided between injection of a desensitizing chemical or 'immunization' by adaption to weak rays. However only the third branch yielded the feasible solution – focusing several weak rays from different angles in such a way that they converged, and therefore intensified their effect, only at the point of the tumour.

To use systematic trial and error effectively, a student needs to draw up a complete list of alternatives which are mutually exclusive, and apply each one in turn. However, trial and error can be laborious and in some cases overwhelming. If there are too many possible routes to take, and a large number of variables to work with, it is more sensible to try other tactics.

Working backwards from the answer is useful here. The tactic is particularly appropriate where there is a uniquely specified goal (e.g. in a proof problem) and where the operations can easily be reversed (where there is a single input to achieve a single output) (Wickelgren 1938). Backward working is less helpful where the goal is not clearly specified (e.g. in many 'find' problems) and where the operations require multiple inputs to obtain the output.

A second useful way to cut down the number of possible choices and routes is to define a likely subgoal that will have to be achieved en route to solving the whole problem. Having identified a suitable middle point, a student can then work backwards from this point to the 'given' and forward from the subgoal to the final solution, if necessary using dummy variables. An analogy for this strategy is building a bridge by establishing a central pillar in the middle of the river and working from that towards the banks on either side – rather than trying to build the bridge out unsupported from either bank alone. This technique is obviously of most use where it is fairly easy to see what subgoals are needed, but even with more complex problems, it may be worth a student's spending a little time thinking about and deriving likely subgoals.

A third and related way is to prune the 'decision' tree to a reasonable size by considering the problem in terms of sequences or categories of steps needed, rather than the individual steps themselves. If a number of individual steps can be grouped together and considered as a single unit, it may be possible to reconceive the decision tree as requiring a much smaller number of decisions between these aggregated units. The problem then becomes more manageable.

Having cut down the number of decisions to be made by one strategy or another, the student still has to devise a satisfactory way of testing and comparing their usefulness in reaching the solution. This is where an 'evaluation function' can be effective (Wickelgren 1938).

Evaluation functions are not usually given in a problem and they may therefore need to be thought out by the student. The purpose of the evaluation function is to provide a computable measure against which the results from two or more courses of action can be compared to see which approximates closest to the desired goal.

In some problems it may be necessary to compare the desirability of routes after two steps have been taken rather than one, and the student may also need to define the 'evaluation' function in terms of more than one dimension. (By analogy, the goal of a car journey may be to get from town A to town B in the least number of miles, but on a route which gives pleasant views and has no steep gradients.) Working step by step through a problem or through a list of alternative choices, using an evaluation function as a guide is a useful and powerful strategy provided that the problem does not require lengthy detours in its solution and/or has not been designed to require non-optimal choices at an early or middle stage.

With certain problems (especially 'to prove' problems), however, there is a strategy which can be useful – indirect proof or proof by contradiction, that is the truth of something is established by showing that its opposite is false. In addition to a single true/false proposition this strategy can be used where there are a small number of alternative solutions offered, only one of which is correct (e.g. in multiple choice questions with three to five items). Where the number of alternative goals is large but finite, or even potentially infinite, then the individual goals need to be classified according to some category system and the indirect proof method applied to the categories.

Closely allied to indirect proof is the technique of *reductio ad absurdum* whereby the falsity of a proposition is demonstrated by deriving statements from it which are obviously absurd. If X is true, Y is true, and Z is true, but Z is absurd so X can't be true.

Stage 4: How should I check the solution?

The final stage of problem-solving contains two separate but related processes. The first is to check the solution in some way. 'Does it feel right?', 'Is it congruent with my perception of the problem?', 'Are the inferences made sound?', 'If I went about it in a different way would I get the same result?'. The second is to reflect on the tactics used to solve the particular problem to see what can be learned from it both in terms of corollaries of the solution and in terms of applying a similar strategy to other problems. This second process may be neglected by students, yet it is the one which most contributes to development of their problem-solving skills.

Getting stuck

A common frustration encountered by problem-solvers is 'getting stuck'. This can be experienced as 'going round in circles', 'running out of ideas', 'not seeing what to do next'. Figure 8.6 offers some simple tactics for getting unstuck; you may like to modify these or describe new ones for your own students or, better still, invite students to pool their suggestions.

Figure 8.6 Getting unstuck

- Hold one part of the problem constant, but change the rest.
- Simplify or select and solve one part of the problem.
- Work on a related problem.
- Check you've used all information given, both explicit and implicit.
- Redefine evaluation function.
- Go a step or two further before rejecting a choice of method/ procedure. Don't reject too quickly.
- Restate the problem to take account of whatever progress has been made.
- Analyse the procedures used so far, not the problem.
- Go away and do something else for a while.
- Work on a completely different or unconnected problem/topic, then see if any of the procedures/ideas can be transferred.
- Make the problem apparently more complex – see if a route then emerges.
- Go back and see if something which was right at the time could now be changed to take the problem forward.
- Generate alternatives to 'right' decisions.
- Take an unlikely looking or 'wrong' path for a while.

One of the reasons for getting stuck is a phenomenon known as 'functional fixity'. The student is stuck with one perception of a problem and can see only one way of using the available data or materials. Unfortunately this mental 'set' the student has towards the problem is not the one which will lead to the solution. Sometimes too, the student makes unwarranted (often subconscious) assumptions about how the problem has to be solved, and sets off on the wrong track, within self-imposed and unnecessary constraints. Loosening-up perception, making assumptions explicit, and generating alternative perspectives on a problem are part of creative problem-solving. Example 8.11 contains a classic simple problem which requires some 'lateral' thinking (Reid 1951).

EXAMPLE 8.11

How can you construct four equilateral triangles out of six matches, where each side of a triangle is equal in length to the length of the matches?

De Bono is probably the best-known exponent of creative approaches to problem-solving. Although many of the problems he poses are ingenious puzzles his suggestions are designed to be applicable to 'real' problems in daily life. He argues that the traditional logico-deductive approach to problem-solving needs to be supplemented with strategies and tactics of a less orthodox nature that help you to break out of established ways of thinking and see alternatives. Among these is the deliberate use of discontinuities, bypasses, and 'intermediate impossibles', i.e. logically incorrect stepping stones which lead nevertheless to new ideas that do make sense. He also suggests the use of brainstorming and the juxtaposing of random nouns against concepts in the problem to stimulate new images and ideas.

The activities and suggestions given in this section go some way towards helping students to develop their problem-solving strategies. Tutors might also develop activities based upon problems that are central to their own subject. Some of these activities should be concerned directly with analysing and discussing the processes of problem-solving and some with problems that require students to eschew old approaches in favour of newer, more powerful approaches.

Finally it is worth pointing out to your students that by improving their problem-solving they can deepen their knowledge and understanding of a subject and by deepening their knowledge and understanding they can improve their problem-solving.

Effective Teaching in Higher Education

ADDITIONAL ACTIVITIES ON PROBLEM-SOLVING

Try the following problems and reflect upon the strategies you used
to solve them. Consider the unsuccessful as well as the successful
strategies and see if you can relate your approach to the suggestions
in the text. The notes and comments section contains a brief
discussion of each problem. After solving the problems, read
through the section on problem-solving again. This will help you to
deepen your understanding of the processes of problem-solving.

8.12 If one theatre ticket at the Playhouse, Nottingham, costs £4.50
      what do ten theatre tickets cost?

8.13 Here is a water-measuring puzzle. Three jars of the capacities
      (in mls) given are to be used to measure out a required amount
      of water (in mls).

	A	B	C	Required
1	29	3	–	20
2	21	127	3	100
3	14	163	25	99
4	18	43	10	5
5	9	42	6	21
6	20	59	4	31
7	23	49	3	20
8	15	39	3	18
9	28	76	3	25
10	18	48	4	22
11	14	36	8	6
12	10	25	6	10

8.14 Two tribes who inhabit the same area have only one major
      distinguishing feature. One tribe always tells the truth and the
      other always tells lies. You meet a male member of one tribe.
      You have one question to find out whether he will lie or tell the
      truth. What is your question?

      The vicar said to the verger, 'How old are your three children?'
      The verger replied, 'If you add their ages you get the number
      on my door. If you multiply their ages together you get 36.'
          The vicar went away for a while but then came back and
      said he could not solve the problem. The verger said, 'Your son
      is older than any of my children.' Then the vicar told the
      verger the ages of the verger's children.

Use the above information to find the ages of the verger's children.

8.16 For this problem you need twenty-one matches and a partner. Take it in turns to pick up the matches. Either player may pick up from one to three matches. The player who picks up the last match loses the game. What is the best strategy for winning?

8.17

Take the numbers one to eight in the above diagram and reinsert them so that you end up with no consecutive numbers next to each other, either horizontally, vertically, or diagonally.

8.18 One of the intractable problems of the 1851 Great Exhibition in the Crystal Palace was bird shit. The excrement fouled the exhibits, the people, and the building. Cleaning was very expensive, it was impossible to prevent the birds entering the building, and it was not possible to shoot them because of the glass in the building. Offer a realistic solution which would minimize the problem.

8.19 Thirty-two teams enter a knock-out competition. Assuming there are no replays how many games will it require to obtain the winning finalist? How many games if the initial entry was 2,048?

8.20 (a) Here are five equal squares. Make four similar squares out of the five by moving three sides.

(b) Here are seven equal squares. Make only five by moving three sides.

(c) Here are four equal squares. Make only three by moving three sides.

(d) Here are five equal squares. Make only four by moving three sides.

(e) Here are five equal squares. Make only four by moving two sides.

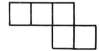

8.21 How can you tell if a hard-boiled egg is, indeed, hardboiled without breaking the shell?

8.22 A very tall building was built in which it was quickly discovered that the lifts were too slow for the office staff. There were several complaints. Extra lift shafts were impossible. More powerful motors would increase the speed of the lifts but they would be very expensive and put the lifts out of action for months. Offer a possible solution to the problem.

8.23 A factory is making oven doors for cookers. When the doors have been cast they have to be given a protective coating. This coating has to be bonded on to the doors by being heated at high temperature. There are two furnaces available for doing this. However, there is a problem. In order to bond the coating to the thick central section of the door, the door has to be left in the furnace for 20 minutes. Unfortunately by this time, the coating on the thin edges of the door has got too hot, has 'run', and formed ridges. The ridges make it difficult to fit the door on to the oven properly, and there are a lot of rejects.

How could the problem be solved?

8.24 How would you set about making an approximate estimate of how much it cost to build the Tyne Bridge in 1928? (You may assume that the exact figure is nowhere recorded.)

8.25 Throughout this book we have offered activities and suggestions for you to try on different aspects of teaching and learning. Now it is your turn . . .

Design a workshop or seminar for students on some aspect of learning in your subject such as problem-solving, writing, reading, or learning through discussion. Give the workshop and collect comments from the students about the workshop. Redesign it, if necessary, and give the workshop again.

Notes and comments

CHAPTER I

1.1 and 1.2 are to start you thinking about the nature of research and teaching and how these might be assessed. There is a considerable overlap in the skills required to do research and to teach effectively. Both involve thinking, planning, and communicating. Assessing research and teaching ability involves a mixture of objective and subjective estimates.

1.3 'Spoonfeeding' is one of those emotive terms which has little meaning but often a powerful impact in an argument. Ask a few colleagues to write down their description of spoonfeeding. Often they write down examples and descriptions which would help a student to learn more easily and effectively. Effective teaching is also concerned with helping students learn more easily and effectively. So spoonfeeding may have *some* part to play in effective teaching?

1.4 Your answer to this depends on your values and in particular your confidence in handling your subject material and various sizes of group. Some lecturers prefer lectures because they have greater control in lectures. Some prefer small group teaching because they enjoy discussion. Some even prefer it on the dubious(?) grounds that 'one doesn't have to prepare seminars – the students do'.

1.5 If you can write down characteristics of effective teaching then you are well on the road to assessing teaching . . . !

1.6 These dimensions often evoke controversy in groups drawn from various faculties. Often arts lecturers value 'stimulating' more highly than 'systematic'. The reverse seems true of science lecturers. Students vary similarly, although as examinations approach many students favour 'systematic' and 'caring'. Discussing the dimensions with students can be a useful springboard for discussion of teaching and learning. Comparing your self-estimates, probable student estimates, and, if possible, actual student estimates is an interesting exercise. The results give you some appraisal of your teaching but the dimensions don't, of course, provide you with specific guidelines for improving it. Subsequent chapters provide more detailed guidelines.

1.7   Only if the teaching has no effect upon the students.

CHAPTER 2

2.1   to 2.4 require you to reflect upon your current practices and to relate them to the information given in the chapter. By thinking and discussing these apparently simple questions you become aware of the processes of lecturing and learning from lectures – and of your strengths, weaknesses, and assumptions about lecturing. Such reflection and discussion provide a useful preliminary to reading Chapter 3.

2.5   is challenging. It is also most valuable. It provides you with a sample of your verbal, non-verbal, and extra-verbal messages to 'students'. More important it gives a real example of how you structure an explanation. The important feature of the activity is not whether you commit any errors in giving an explanation but whether you can perceive those errors and develop strategies to minimize them. Chapter 3 is designed to help you to improve your explaining and lecturing. So it is worthwhile repeating Activity 2.5 when you have tackled the content and activities in that chapter.

Five-minute explanations may seem 'artificial'. Yet in lectures each subtopic of the whole lecture may take only five minutes. A common error in tackling this activity is to attempt to compress content rather than select key principles or facts. The same error occurs in whole lectures – covering too much too quickly. The activity forces you to think and select as well as structure and present. The activity may also be used to assist research students to present brief papers at conferences.

This activity is the basis of a training programme in explaining which yielded significant changes in the quality of explaining by participants (Brown 1982).

CHAPTER 3

3.1   The repeat of the activity provides an opportunity for learning from the first experience of attempting an explanation and from reading Chapter 3. The activity can be tackled after doing 3.2 to 3.10 since each of the activities contributes to effective explaining.

3.2 It is often useful to generate your own check-lists and then identify your own strengths and weaknesses on the basis of your own check-lists.

3.3 and 3.4 These activities are designed to help you to pitch different levels of explanation. In carrying out the activities lecturers often find that explanations for more sophisticated audiences are broader as well as deeper.

3.6 Most people think that the second attempt is marginally better than the first.The structure of explanations can be described as:

Explanation 1
1 Why are nude mice important to biologists?
2 What is the thymus?
3 What does the thymus do?
4 Why is the natural condition preferable to the surgical condition?
5 How does the nude mouse come into this?

Explanation 2
1 Why are nude mice important to biologists?
2 What is a nude mouse?
3 What are its characteristics?
4 Why is the absence of its thymus useful to biologists?
5 That's why nude mice are important to biologists.

Explanation 1 contains more details but the lecturer leapt from nude mice to thymus without indicating why. (The lecturer had just completed his PhD on nude mice.) Explanation 2 has structure but is low on content. A combination of 1 and 2 would yield:

1 Nude mice have no hair because they do not have a thymus.
2 The thymus also controls the defensive responses of the body to infections.
3 So nude mice do not have defensive responses to infections.
4 This allows infecting organisms to be studied in the nude mouse with no interference from defensive responses.

(NB This type of activity is also useful for analysing the structure of brief research papers and articles.)

3.7 Thinking of examples is not always easy yet it is worth the attempt if only because it clarifies meanings and definitions.

3.10 Colleagues argue over these. The lecture on Freud is thought by some to be totally unstructured and worthless, by others to be stimulating, and by yet others to be so poor as to drive the students actually to read Freud. The opening of the Marx lecture is usually thought to be well-structured. The lecturer establishes rapport and provides clear guidelines. Opinions differ as to whether the rest of the lecture will be good or simply pedestrian.

3.11 This activity invites the participants to recall, share, and then analyse their experiences. Such an approach extends and lifts the quality of discussion. The general approach is therefore of value in a wide variety of tasks.

3.13 This is a challenging activity which has almost always been successful. Its success is due, probably, to the confidence it gives participants and to their recognition that underlying structures can be worked on even if they are unfamiliar with the content.

3.14 This activity is most usefully done in groups of three or four. Allow about 15 minutes per participant. A common error in this activity is to try to compress content matter rather than select and structure it. The strategies described in Lecture preparation and Activity 3.13 are relevant to this activity. Paradoxically, familiar material is sometimes more difficult to structure than unfamiliar material.

3.15 This is a time-consuming activity but it is certainly a powerful learning task. It may be simplified by preparing only the structure of the lecture.

CHAPTER 4

4.1 gives you and your students a way into thinking about what goes on (and doesn't) in your small group sessions. With students it can also lead to a discussion of how they might gain more from small group work through their own efforts. It is also possible to lead gently towards an informal contract with the students on the conduct of small group work.

4.6 highlights three common management problems in small group teaching. Each of the mini-cases generates various comments and strategies. A frequent general comment is that the tutor should not have let the situation get out of hand. While this is true it is not relevant. The situation is out of hand so what should the tutor do?

The conflict in the 'silent student' is that you may need to correct what is wrong while at the same time encourage the student to contribute. The 'know-it-all student' may need to be told to be quiet, there may need to be a discussion about sharing, he or she may need to be given a role such as minute-taker or summarizer. The nub of the problem in the case of the 'aggressive student' is whether his or her views are representative of the group or an individual view. A problem the tutor has to consider is what is more important: sorting out the problem or continuing with the planned important topic.

In these cases and in similar problems it is important to:

1 Diagnose the problem – is it an individual or group problem?
2 Consider the nature of the group – is it supportive, aggressive, co-operative, competitive?
3 Consider the management task – is it appropriate? Is it more important than the well-being of the group?

4.8   can generate a lot of discussion. 'Recall' and 'thought' seem easy to understand when you are reading. They are more difficult to identify in practice – partly because you have to take account of the content. As stated in the chapter what may require thought by first-year students may require recall by more advanced students.

Prompts and probes can also be difficult to identify in practice. Furthermore, probes usually require students to think. So a question may be classified as a probe if you are considering tactics in questioning and as a 'thought' question if you are considering levels of thinking.

4.9   usually generates thoughtful discussion of questions and their classifications. It is a good activity in a workshop. Often colleagues find generating 'thought' questions difficult – because we are unused to it. The activity also introduces the notion of thinking about a topic as a preparation for small group teaching. An alternative activity based on empirical, conceptual, and value questions is also useful.

If the material is familiar, that is you have existing categories to which to relate the information, then the task is relatively easy. Sometimes the listener's explanation is better than the explainer's. If the information is unfamiliar, categorizing, storing, and recalling is more difficult. The use of questions by the 'listener' enables him or her to search actively for points of contact between what he or she already knows and the information given. Even within three minutes one might microsleep and thereby miss an important point.

4.10 is related not only to levels of listening – skimming, surveying, searching, and studying – but also to your strategies of information processing.

4.11 The mapping exercise certainly gets most people thinking. Often, using it as a basis for discussion with a group of students reveals areas which they have not considered and, occasionally, areas you have not considered. It is also interesting to compare which parts of the maps were explored by the different groups of students.

CHAPTER 5

5.1 This activity is difficult for it requires you to put in order of priority your values, to reflect upon your existing laboratory teaching, and consider alternative approaches. The exercise is particularly valuable if you are rethinking and redesigning your lab course – although it does not consider individual experiments. The use of the matrix of objectives and experiments is also useful for the task of redesigning a lab course (see Activity 5.4). When the activity is done in groups drawn from different branches of science and engineering, different priorities emerge and this can generate discussion. When a group is from the same department, there *tends* to be a consensus. The activity clarifies the values of individual colleagues and this can assist in decision-making about lab courses.

5.4 A surprising number of experiments are at levels 0 and 1. Levels 2 and 3 are more likely to stimulate a student to think and develop as an experimentalist. Level 4 is more likely to occur in projects and postgraduate research – but even at this level it does not occur frequently.

5.7 1 is an experimental exercise which contains implicitly the answer. 2 is a structured enquiry which requires the student to think and design an experiment.

5.8 Frequently colleagues assert that lab work is important. It is certainly expensive. But marks assigned to lab work tend to be relatively low. The reasons often given are: marking of lab work is unreliable, practical work is difficult to assess, marks do not reflect the real value of lab work. (Students may feel this too!) These arguments are probably rationalizations of poor assessment procedures.

CHAPTER 6

6.1 This activity often reveals wide discrepancies of views on approaches, on relative responsibilities of supervisor and student, on the nature of a PhD, and even on the nature of research. By discussing the question posed you become aware of your own values and taken-for-granted assumptions. Neither of these may necessarily be fully shared by your immediate colleagues or those outside the department.

6.2 This activity provides a framework in which to explore the different aspects of research supervision and the values involved. There are usually differences in viewpoint between different subjects on choice of topic, contact, and contributions to the thesis. Some people try to avoid taking decisions on value by questioning the scales provided. They could be invited to modify the scales and then assign their value. Others claim that they can't generalize since it depends very much on the student and the project. They should be asked to relate their ratings to one particular student.

The activity may be used in a group of supervisors and students or with students alone. There are sometimes differences between the views of groups of supervisors and groups of students. There are also differences between first-year research students and those about to submit a PhD – particularly on statements concerned with thesis writing.

6.3 This activity invites you to generate simple direct hints. We have found that a light, humorous list is enjoyed and remembered more than a solemn litany of dangers. It is useful to discuss and try out the list with students who have just completed their research.

6.4 This is easier than 6.3. It does reveal divergences of opinion. It will provide the basis of a set of hints to give to research students.

6.5 Time-management was the most frequently cited problem by research supervisors in our workshops – in other words, finding time to do your personal research and writing it up. The common problems that students were reported to have were subject related. Arts and some social science students spent too long on choosing and refining a topic. Some social science and science students spent too long on data collection and had

difficulties in discussing and interpreting (not analysing) results. A common problem across all subjects was writing-up.

6.6   Two common ploys of colleagues in discussion of case studies
of overseas students are 'It's not my responsibility' and 'The
tutor should not have let it happen'. Both may be used as
springboards for discussion. 'It's not my responsibility' leads
naturally to a discussion of roles and responsibilities of supervisors who have overseas students. 'The tutor should not let it
happen' can be used to open up a discussion of how you should
structure research and monitor student progress.
      Neither of the above ploys should however be allowed to avoid
discussion of the cases presented. All of the cases generate
discussion on a wide range of issues. The case of the Indian
student is a deep cultural and interpersonal problem. As usual,
you would like more information before making a decision on
what to do, if anything, for the student. What is certain is that
whatever counselling or discussion is provided by you (or a
qualified counsellor) should be directed at helping her to make
her own decision.
      The case of the Saudi student raises the question of how you
tackle the problem of helping someone to improve their style of
writing. Correction of specifics may not be enough. Again the
issue of responsibilities of the supervisor will appear in dis-
guised form.
      The case of the Tanzanian student raises the issue of what
you should do about a student who may not be capable of a
PhD – and the deeper questions: 'How can you be sure of what
is the standard of a PhD?', 'Should the supervisor teach the
student again?', 'Should he or she do the data analysis for the
student?'.

6.7   and 6.8 provide a way of evaluating your research tutorials.
As well as structure, look at the proportion of talk by you and
your student, at student-initiated questions, and at the kinds
of questions raised. A common weakness observed in research
tutorials is wandering far from the issue under discussion. A
little wandering can be helpful but too much leads to frustration.
      Listening to (or viewing) and discussing the recording of a
tutorial with the research student can lead to a consideration of
the skills that he or she needs in the tutorial. For some students
(and supervisors!) this notion is surprising. The recording can
also be used to open up a discussion of expectations and of
anxieties and problems which the student may be experiencing.
      A more sophisticated method of identifying tutorial structure

is given in Appendix 1. This may be used as an alternative to Figure 6.10.

6.9   The information in Chapter 6 on reading a thesis and giving a viva will be helpful for this task. Even if you disagree with our approach, it does give you some ideas to react against.

6.10   Opening up discussion of research supervision in a seminar or workshop is a useful way of getting supervisors and students involved in improving supervision and research. But it is important for the seminar to have purpose and structure otherwise the seminar can simply become a vehicle for airing (well-rehearsed?) prejudices. Follow-up activities between each seminar can be used to involve students or supervisors and to help them develop their approaches to research and research supervisions.

CHAPTER 8

Examples

8.1   Practice on brief 'lectures' followed by comparisons (in small groups) of notes taken has proved to be a useful and valued exercise. The use of POKE EARS enhances the activity but you should stress that there will be some disagreements on categories of lecturer talk. The transcripts in Appendix 2 can be used as the basis of live demonstrations or simply as transcripts. Excerpts should be chosen which are relevant to the group's subjects.

8.2   This activity sensitizes listening and develops responding. The participants have to think how they can link what they wish to say with what has already been said. The examples of contentious issues have been used successfully with students of different disciplines. The activity can be difficult for students (and colleagues). Sometimes groups get so involved in the topic that they forget to build on others' ideas. Quite often the discussions end in good-humoured banter. Do leave time at the end of the activity to discuss the point of the discussions – to develop listening and responding skills.

8.3   This experimental task has often proved challenging to students and colleagues. To maximize control, the best approach is for the experimenter to hold the top of the rule on the wall, the experimental 'subject' should place his finger at the bottom of the rule, not quite touching it. The visual signal is the experimenter's hand movement when she releases the rule. The distance dropped by the rule gives an estimate of reaction time. To estimate reaction time to touch, the experimental subject should place his free hand on top of the experimenter's hand which is holding the rule. The other hand should be not quite touching the bottom of the rule and his eyes should be closed. Generally the results obtained indicate that tactile reactions are faster than visual reactions. The discussion of the task can be quite lively – particularly about whether the task is an experiment. The activity has been used with students and colleagues from science, medicine, and engineering. It should be stressed to the groups that this is an example of a 'simple' experiment involving thinking and experimental design. A useful follow-up activity is for small groups of participants in related disciplines to try to design a 'simple' ingenious experimental task in their own subject.

8.4 A possible diagram is:

Minerals (rough classification)

Metals				Stones		
Noble	*Rare*	*Common*	*Alloys*	*Precious*	*Semi-precious*	*Masonry*
gold	lithium	iron	steel	diamonds	?	granite
silver	uranium	copper	brass	emeralds		marble
platinum		aluminium	bronze	sapphires		limestone
						slate

Note: The diagram makes the classification easier to remember and also reveals the absence of examples of semi-precious stones. The combination of metals in alloys is not given.

Similar 'hierarchical' tasks can be set in many subjects.

8.5 There are various possible solutions. The best is probably as follows:

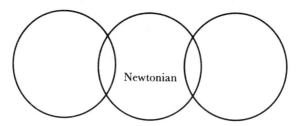

The key elements appear to be size of particle, strength of field, speed of particle. Probably the best diagram is:

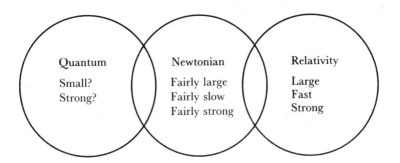

The article did not clearly specify the nature of quantum mechanics. Nor is it clear whether quantum and relativistic mechanics both explain fully Newtonian mechanics. (If they both do then Newtonian mechanics would be contained in each of the circles representing Quantum and Relativity.) Incidentally the fundamental task in mechanics may be represented visually as attempting to produce one circle which contains all three types of mechanics.

8.10 The answer is that there are more nephews. This example is a useful opening task in a workshop – particularly if you are going to go through the stages of problem-solving with the participants. The nub of the problem is the relationship [sic] between the definitions of nephew and male (first) cousins. Nephews necessarily have uncles and aunts. Uncles and aunts don't necessarily have children.

You may recall a similar problem in Chapter 4. Are there more grandfathers than fathers? This was solved by considering whether the 'set' of father included the 'set' of grandfather, or vice versa. Once you identify the type of problem, the solution is relatively straightforward.

8.11 Matchstick problems such as this one and Example 8.16 may seem trivial but they often exemplify essential principles. This example is no exception. Most people on first encountering the problem assume it is in two dimensions. In three dimensions the solution is easy – a tetrahedron. The problem illustrates the importance of examining your assumptions and considering whether you have become too fixed on a particular strategy.

8.12 There's obviously a catch but what is it? The arithmetical answer is £45. The actual answer is £40 because a discount is given on ten or more tickets.

8.13 This puzzle often induces 'functional fixity'. Problem 1 is solved easily as $A - 3B$. Problems 2 to 6 are solved by applying $B - 2C - A$. Problems 7 and 8 may be solved in this way but also, more easily, without the use of B, i.e. $A - C$ and $A + C$ respectively. Problem 9 cannot be solved by $B - 2C - A$. People often get stuck until they see that $A - C$ yields the answer. Problems 10 and 11 can be solved as $B - 2C - A$ or 10 as $A + C$ and 11 as $A - C$. In problem 12 A already contains 10 mls – the required amount – but people often attempt to solve it in a complicated way.

The puzzle often reveals the processes of problem-solving and getting stuck. Once you have become stuck with a process which is not working you have to step back and look for a different approach – and sometimes you forget to do this.

8.14 This problem sometimes causes confusion because it is simple. The easiest solution is 'Are you female?'. Some people attempt complex questions such as 'If you were a member of the other tribe and I asked you whether you told lies, would you say yes?'. These complex questions are sometimes put forward because the 'solver' is aware of encountering a similar but more complex problem. Another possibility is that the solver does not believe the solution can be that simple. This is where evaluation functions and checking whether the solution works come into play. If it almost always works and it's simple, then do it that way – unless the consequence of being wrong is a nuclear disaster . . .

8.15 This problem is tricky because most people do not use all the information given. It combines trial and error with inference. The solution is that the verger's children are aged 1, 6, and 6. The process of solving first involves working out the eight combinations of numbers that yield 36 when multiplied together, that is 3, 3, 4; 2, 3, 6; 1, 6, 6; 2, 2, 9; 1, 4, 9; 1, 3, 12; 1, 2, 18; and 1, 1, 36. At this point most people get stuck. If you re-read the problem you might note that the vicar could not solve the problem even though he knew the number on the verger's door. Why? Because two of the right sets of numbers add up to the same number, 13, which is presumably the number on the verger's door. These sets are 1, 6, 6 and 2, 2, 9. The vicar still could not do the problem until the verger said the vicar's son was older than any of the verger's children. Given that the two possible solutions are 1, 6, 6 and 2, 2, 9 *and* the problem was solved, then the vicar's son must be 7 or 8 and the verger's children are 1, 6, and 6. If the vicar's son had been older than 9, the problem would still not have been solved. This problem is tricky for most people because you have to use all the data given for trial and error and for inferences.

8.16 This is an example of working 'backwards' from the given solution. In a workshop provide matches or cocktail sticks and let the participants play the game before introducing the task of identifying the winning strategies. After the activity you can introduce participants to the EIA procedure:

- Explore
- Invent (a solution/strategy)
- Apply (check and test).

The EIA cycle may be used on a wide range of problems concerned with materials. The exploratory stage enables the learner to tune in, recall known strategies, and play with new alternatives. The apply stage brings into play 'evaluation' functions and so ensures the solution is valid. (See Karplus *et al.* 1977; Carmichael *et al.* 1980).

The nub of the problem is the relationship between the two rules of the game:

1 The person who picks up the last matchstick loses.
2 You can only pick up a maximum of three matchsticks.

Therefore to win you must leave your opponent five matchsticks. To do this you must leave your opponent nine matchsticks, thirteen matchsticks, seventeen matchsticks, twenty-one matchsticks. So the best strategy is to let him or her start and aim for leaving seventeen, thirteen, etc. If you start also aim for leaving seventeen, thirteen, etc. Various minor Machiavellian strategies can be devised to obscure your grand strategy.

8.17 This is an example of a trial and error problem. Some people, initially, attempt a random trial and error. After playing with the numbers they may come to recognize that the problem is best tackled by considering the major constraints first. In this problem the major constraints are the central two squares since they each touch six other squares. So fill these squares with numbers which give you most freedom. These numbers are 1 and 8 since they each have only one neighbouring number (2 and 7). Apply the same strategy to each of the middle row of numbers. Check your solution. It should be:

	3	5	
7	1	8	2
	4	6	

(or a mirror image)

If a problem has severe constraints, deal with them first and preferably in a way which leaves you with flexibility.

8.18 This is an example of a problem within a problem. It was not the excrement but the producers of the excrement which were the problem. To minimize the number of 'producers' the Duke of Wellington suggested the use of sparrowhawks to kill the sparrows. The suggestion worked quite effectively.

8.19 The answers are 31 and 2,047. The first part can easily be worked out as sixteen matches in the first round, eight in the second round, and so on. A similar procedure can be used for 2,048 competitions but it is becoming cumbersome. An alternative approach is to refocus the problem. If there are thirty-two competitors and only one winner there are thirty-one losers, so thirty-one matches are required. The same principle can also be applied to 2,048 competitors. It can also be applied to any number of competitors providing you allow byes in the early rounds. Refocusing or recasting a problem is often helpful. Experimenting with a simpler problem and looking for an underlying principle is also helpful. Of course you also have to check out whether the strategy works.

8.20 The solutions are:

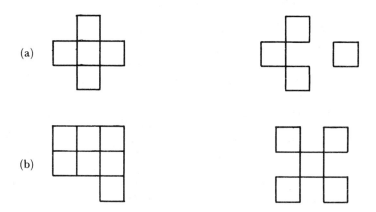

(a)

(b)

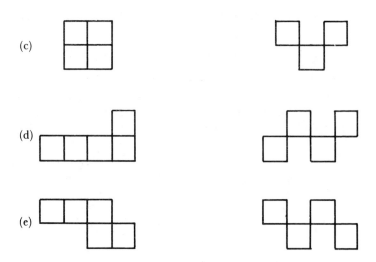

(c)

(d)

(e)

The problems are from Katona (1940).

Two principles can be used. One 'arithmetical' and one 'spatial'. The arithmetical principle is to maximize the number of squares for a given number of matchsticks, ensuring that the squares are adjacent. To decrease the number of squares, make sure they are not adjacent. The spatial principle focuses upon the 'holes' created. To decrease the number of squares you open up the holes; to increase them you reduce the holes. Katona found that the spatial principle was marginally better than the arithmetical principle for transfer to new problems but both were superior to rote-drill of existing solutions.

The activity introduces the notion of analysing and searching for guiding principles rather than simply solving each problem. Ask the participants to discuss how they tackled the problem and what guiding principles, if any, they developed. Point out too the importance of always reflecting on how you solved a problem.

8.21 The nub of the problem is the difference between a hard-boiled egg and a raw egg. A hard-boiled egg is solid, a raw egg contains liquid, a yolk, and space. X-rays could do it – but that solution is expensive and inconvenient. Are there any differences between a solid object and a shell container? One difference is spin (or inertia). The hard-boiled egg will spin faster than the raw egg at a given force – because the inside of the raw egg will not start to spin immediately, thereby slowing the outside down. Since seeing is believing, the solution should be demonstrated.

The problem may be used to illustrate the importance of looking for comparators and then working towards a solution which is based on the differences and is, preferably, simpler.

8.22 Another example of refocusing. Given that the lifts could not be changed, then you might focus on reducing the impatience of the staff. Three possibilities are music, mirrors in the lift, and humorous notices to read. These solutions may seem trivial but they are relatively effective and cheap.

8.23 One solution would be to remove the doors from the furnace part way through the bonding time and let them cool before returning them to the furnace to finish off. During the cooling time, the thin sections would lose heat faster, and cool more, than the thick sections. When returned to the furnace, the thick sections would come back up to temperature quickly, while the thin sections would take longer – thus preventing over-heating. An alternative would be to call in the designer to redesign the component parts so that the problem did not arise . . .

8.24 Some people tackle this problem holistically and others serially. The holistic approach is to ask what a comparable bridge would cost today, check on the overall change in prices since 1928, and adjust the estimate accordingly. The serial approach is to identify the material used, the labour needed, the land requisitioned, and so on, and cost these individually. This is much more time-consuming but probably more accurate. Underlying this problem is the question – how much time and money are you prepared to invest for precision?

Appendix 1:
The structural phases of the tutorial encounter

The following may be used to identify aspects of the research tutorial. It may be used to obtain global impressions or as a precise instrument to record the appropriate category at fixed time intervals (for example every 5 seconds).

1 REVIEWING

Included here are statements of past goals, earlier content and decisions, progress to date, reiteration of earlier problem identification.

Watch out for evaluation which is properly category 9.

2 PURPOSE

Concerns the identification and clarification of the purpose of the encounter usually in fairly general terms.

Watch out for more specific considerations that are likely to move into such categories as 3 and 4.

3 STRUCTURE

Only of concern here are statements, proposals, decisions relating to the *organization of this encounter*, and the means of dealing with the purposes.

Watch out for organization of student project and problem-solving work which are really categories 8 or 6.

4 PROBLEM

Included here are all descriptions, clarifications, explorations, qualifications, and discussions related to the problem.

Watch out for quite sudden moves which begin to consider solutions 5 or 6.

5 ALTERNATIVE SOLUTIONS

Included here are all references and explorations relating to possible solutions to the problem and all discussions regarding a single solution until that solution is agreed.
Watch out for signs of agreement regarding a particular solution when a move to category 6 is implied.

6 SPECIFIC SOLUTION

Concerns all discussion, clarification, exploration of a specific *agreed* solution.
Watch out for final statements relating to what has been agreed which more properly will be category 7 or even 8.

7 SUMMARIZING

Relates only to summaries of agreements, decisions, discussions, content within *this* encounter.
Watch out for summary of earlier work, which is category 1, and more formalized summaries which may be category 8.

8 CONTRACTING

Likely to take place at the end of the encounter and be a formal statement (either written or verbal) relating to goals, progress, process, that are to take place *outside* the encounter to which *the student agrees*.

9 EVALUATING

Relates to considerations of feasibility decisions, contingency plans, criteria for assessment, proposals for evaluation of future success as well as actual evaluation of achieved progress, content, results.

10 SOCIAL

Concerns all interaction that is non-task-specific – health, wealth, weather, and so on.
(Based on Shaw 1987.)

Appendix 2:
Some transcripts of explanations

ARCHITECTURE: HEIGHTS OF BUILDINGS AND COST

My subject is architecture, and I'm going to show you one way in which the height of a building, the height you decide a building is going to be, has a significant effect on its cost. In fact, as we'll see, a building gets a lot more expensive as it gets higher.

Imagine you have a fairly large office building, and you start off by deciding, well, it should be about five storeys high [draws on board] – a sort of aerial view of the building, ground floor, and four upper storeys.

Now, if you took out one of these upper floors and looked at it in plan you would see that in addition to the area that the client actually pays for, the office space that he can get rent from or whatever that might be, there's a lot of service area, and in fact going up through the building there are three distinct tubes of services. There are two staircases, two fire escape staircases, stuck one at each end of the building, two stair wells enclosed in a concrete shaft with an own fire protection, fire resistance, and a lift well.

Now, suppose you try the experiment of saying 'Well, let's take this office accommodation and put it over ten storeys, instead of five'. Chop the building in half and then look at one of these floor plans [draws on board], you'll see that it comes to something like this – adopting the same sort of basic layout.

Half the area of usable office space but still the same area, more or less, of concrete tubes going up the building. Do it again, make it a twenty-storey building instead of a ten-storey building so you get a very long thin structure [draws] twenty storeys high – just a little bit higher than the one down the bottom end of the university, you find that the floor plan is pretty well dominated by these essential elements of vertical circulation, that the area taken up by the staircases and the lifts is an enormous percentage of the whole thing. In other words, if you start off by saying 'My client wants a hundred – a hundred thousand square metres of office space' then to get this he would have to pay in addition the cost of maybe 10 per cent extra in terms of circulations and services.

If you spread it over twenty storeys then the proportion of useless office space, useless space, goes up two or three times [draws on board].

Putting some actual numbers to it, if you look at plans of five-storey buildings you might find that something like 15 per cent or 16 per cent of this space inside the building was taken up with staircases and lifts. In a twenty-storey building that might be 30 per cent more. And, what is worse, this area of the lift well doesn't stay constant as you make the building higher because you have a higher percentage of people using the lifts for their normal day-to-day movement about the building and they've got to travel further, so you need more lifts, you need faster bigger lifts so instead of having this, in fact [indicates] on a five-storey building, to get to the ten or twenty storeys the actual plan area of the lift shaft might be two or three times as big. Even though the staircases might be just a little bit smaller [writes on board].

BIOLOGY: MICRO-ORGANISMS

The topic I decided to briefly explain was the reasons why micro-organisms are suitable systems for industrial exploitation as opposed to higher organisms.

Now, there's three – basically three features.

In the first place the speed of metabolism, of micro-organisms [overhead projector].

They have a very, very high metabolic rate in comparison with, say, a higher plant or a higher animal. This, in essence, is an expression of the very high surface to volume ratio that micro-organisms have. Er – obviously life processes are a lot to do with the exchange of materials across a surface and the higher the surface volume ratio because of their very small size they have a high surface volume ratio – the higher it is the faster these processes can take place.

I have actually a statistic, a comparative productivity statistic between a bullock, a soy bean plant, and yeast. In the 10 cwt bullock over 24 hours one would get about 0.5 kilograms of protein. Er – in the soya bean which is perhaps the most productive protein source in higher plants one would get about 40 kilograms which is roughly about a hundred times as much as in the bullock, and in the 10 cwt of yeast under ideal conditions of course which is something that is difficult to achieve one would get about 50,000 kilograms which is about twenty times I think – which is a hundred thousand times as much as in the bullock.

The second feature one can perhaps describe as variability of metabolism [overhead projector].

Micro-organisms produce a lot of unusual secondary metabolites which you don't find in other organisms. The classic example would, in fact, be an example which was mentioned in the previous talk penicillin or other antibiotics which of course have great industrial uses.

And the third feature which one can exploit is what I have called for want of a better description adaptability metabolism [overhead projector].

Micro-organisms can grow on very unusual substrates – er this is particularly true with reference to carbon sources which is the one example I've put up here. For instance waste products of other industrial processes in the sugar industry – molasses, it is used as a waste product for microfungitational processes and in recent years some very unusual carbon sources, for instance methane from North Sea gas, is used in a bacterial process and the production of food yeast on hydrocarbons, that is petrol, has got to the point in France where it is an actual established industrial process now. The organism responsible is a thing called *candida upolitica* which is a yeast and grows specifically on C_{11} to C_{19} hydrocarbons, which in fact is a fraction which is not very much used in other processes.

ENGLISH: REVENGE DRAMA

Well, I'm not going to introduce myself because we've met already. And what I'm going to talk about is something – er probably slightly separate from you namely revenge drama, which is probably separate from you because it is associated with the seventeenth century. If I, however, mention Hamlet and say that Hamlet is a play which fits in the revenge genre then you are more likely to be with me.

A revenge play, basically, follows the adventures of a guy or a girl engaged in the process of seeking retribution for a crime done against him or her or their family. The play tends to begin with the initial crime – kicking hell out of somebody, killing them. Then follows the machinations of the revenger through to the end of the play which usually is a blood bath involving the death of the revenger, all the closest of kin, all the friends and usually half the political system within which he exists.

Mm – I'm not going to use Hamlet as an example because Shakespeare was a very provocative so and so and didn't write a very good revenge play in Hamlet.

There's another dramatist, Thomas Kydd, who you won't have heard of and many students of literature wish they hadn't heard of him either, but he wrote quite a good revenge play where – mm – this guy's son is killed at the beginning and hung up in the orchard which is all very erotic and the father spends the rest of the play ranting in wonderful blank verse, full of tremendous poetry and eventually seeks the death of all the people who he thinks committed the crime. And the king, and the dukes and anybody else who happens to be around at the same time dies.

It would be irresponsible of me to leave that essential pattern of crime, process, destruction – it would be irresponsible of me to leave that without pointing out the effective moral behind it which made it so acceptable to the Elizabethan stage.

The moral behind it is – it's assumed somebody who takes into their own hands a course of action which involves their own and the death-destruction of half the political system, that course of action is assumed to be unhealthy. In other words it's wrong to take the law into your own hands. What you are meant to do is trust in heaven or the state system as it exists. An idea, a moral that was amazingly attractive to the very authoritarian Elizabethan police state, that it is wrong to take the law into your own hands.

So there you are, the pattern of the crime, the revenger speaking very poetically, with whom we sympathize perhaps emotionally, the final destruction and consequent disapproval of this act of taking the law into your own hands. It's the attractive bloodiness combined with the effective moral point which made it such a successful dramatic medium.

SOCIAL STATISTICS

I'm concerned with one of a number of difficulties which we encounter when we try to interpret the meaning of statistics, which are quoted from social surveys.

Mm – the particular problem which I'm going to talk about is called the problem of the shifting definition [writes on board].

Right. The problem of the shifting definition.

Now, basically what we mean by a shifting definition is the way that we cate . . . that we define a category in one survey different from the way that the same category is defined in another.

In other words the definition of a term has shifted from one survey to another.

Now this is a very simple concept on the surface but if it is not considered when we are looking at social surveys we can find that it leads to disastrous results.

Mm to take a simple example. (If you look at unemployment.)

Now, the 1966 census on unemployment defined a person as unemployed if he was out of work on the Monday before census day [writes on board]. So in 1966 an unemployed person was a person who was out of work on the Monday before census day.

Now in the 1971 census the definition had shifted. This time a person was considered unemployed if he had been out of work for the entire week before census was taken.

Now we can see how there's a problem here when we are trying to assess the amount of real unemployment and how this might be used for political purposes. If for example it was found that in 1971 unemployment had, quote, 'dropped by 30 per cent', we have no way of telling whether in fact things are much better or whether because unemployment is defined as being out of work for a longer period of time we are just finding fewer people unemployed.

Now, to take a slightly more cagey example, mm – we can look at the police department in New York. In 1950 the commissioner of the police was replaced by a fellow named Murphy who you probably heard of and about two months after he came into power it was reported in the local press that the degree of crime had risen by about 34 per cent. There, of course, were gasps. You know New York is getting to be a worse place to live, crime is on the increase, what will we do? Well as it transpired there wasn't an increase in

crime at all it was just that the definition of crime had changed, it
had shifted. In 1949 previously the degree of crime was defined as
the number of criminal acts which had in fact been investigated and
which had been solved. Now this, in fact, left out a good deal of
crime which was uncovered when Commissioner Murphy came in,
because he didn't consider only crimes which had been solved as
crimes but all crimes that had been reported – that includes possible
crimes as well as solved crimes.

So you can see again that the definition employed in a survey can
shift from one survey to another and that this does make a great deal
of difference in what we consider to be important.

So the basic point is that [laughs] the important point of the shifting
definition is in fact when we are looking at statistics we must be very
careful, firstly to decide what the researcher has actually meant
when he defined the problem and to see whether that definition has
shifted from one time to the next.

SOCIOLOGY: THE DIFFERENCE BETWEEN SOCIAL CLASS AND SOCIO-ECONOMIC GROUPS

I'd like to explain the difference between social class and socio-
economic groups.
   This – er – confusion that often occurs here has arisen – er – from
different attempts to measure social stratification – mm – or the
different rankings of people in a community.

Now, social class as defined by the Registrar General – mm –
consists of a rank of occupations which are ranked by prestige. So,
for example, postmen would be ranked below university lecturers
because the prestige rating of those two occupations – mm – is–is–is
– turns out to be like that when people are asked to put one above or
below the other. Mm – and there – er – are five groups – er – which
the Registrar General uses for his measurement of social class.

But on the other hand, socio-economic groups are groups of people
who have economical social conditions in common, not just necessarily occupation, but also their educational attainment, their leisure
interests, and so forth. And the groups themselves are not necessarily
– they are not in fact ranked in any order of prestige – although we
ourselves may judge that some of the groups are higher than others.
So, an illustration of two occupations in one socio-economic group
would be for example clergymen and school teachers – mm –

because they more or less have the same kind of salary and the same kind of educational attainment. Mm – but in fact on the prestige ranking – er – used in measurements of social class – er – clergymen are still ranked number one whereas school teachers are ranked number two.

Well, I could give other illustrations but I haven't time. So, I just want to repeat the main point there that social classes are occupational groups ranked in terms of prestige whereas socio-economic groups are collections of people who have similar social and economic factors in common, but the difference between different socio-economic groups is not necessarily ranked.

PHARMACOLOGY: HOW PENICILLIN KILLS BACTERIA

I'd like to explain to you how penicillin kills bacteria.

Now, I'm sure that at various times in your life you've – you've both had gastro-enteritis – you've had pains in your stomach. And you go along to the doctor and he – he tells you that you've got gastro-enteritis and the way to get rid of it is to take penicillin. So you go along to the chemist, you get some penicillin, you take the penicillin, and eventually the pain disappears. This is because in your gut you have bacteria which are growing and as they grow they produce poisons or toxins which result in you experiencing pain. And when you take penicillin, penicillin kills the growing bacteria.

Now, in order for you to understand how penicillin kills bacteria – mm – you need to know something of the structure – of a bacterium.

Now, a bacterium looks very like a balloon [blows up a balloon]. You can get bacteria of different sorts, different sizes, and different shapes. Some of them are rod shaped, like this balloon, some of them are circular – spherical, some of them are spiral – so I could have chosen any balloon to describe any particular bacterium. But they are all similar in that they contain a cell wall – in this case represented by the balloon itself, and cell contents, in this case represented by the air inside. And they grow [inflates balloon]. As they grow they take up nutrients from the environment by an active process – they synthesize new cell contents, and they synthesize new cell wall. So that as the bacterium gets bigger [inflates] its cell wall stays in the same thickness. Because it is synthesizing new cell wall it doesn't get any thinner. Of course this isn't the case with the balloon because as I blow up the balloon it stretches and it gets thinner.

Now, what happens in the presence of penicillin.

In the presence of penicillin cells still grow, they still take up nutrients from the environment, they still synthesize new cell contents, but they cease to synthesize new cell wall. So that as the bacterium gets bigger [inflates], the wall gets thinner [inflates] until eventually [balloon bursts] the cell bursts.

And that is how penicillin kills bacteria. It kills bacteria by inhibiting cell wall synthesis.

Appendix 3:
Suggestions for
organizing workshops

The term 'workshop' has many different meanings and connotations. For us, a workshop is a structured set of activities which provide opportunities for learning through thinking, practice, and discussion. It is not a rambling seminar nor is it specifically concerned with emotions and feelings.

To plan a workshop we suggest you begin with goals, work through activities, inputs, timing, order, and review the goals. The cycle is this:

GOALS

These should be expressed relatively briefly. They are for the benefit of the participants as well as the planners so couch them in down-to-earth terms.

'This workshop is concerned with lecturing. In it you will have an opportunity to reflect upon your approach to lecturing and to discuss your approach with others. You will be introduced to some recent research on lecturing styles which you can match against your own style. You will be given an opportunity to try out some approaches to lecture preparation which have been found useful by colleagues in other universities . . .'

The goals are descriptions of the content and processes of the workshop. This approach seems, to us, preferable to the use of behavioural objectives such as 'By the end of the workshóp you will be able to identify five distinctive styles of lecturing and state explicitly three methods of lecturing'.

ACTIVITIES

Given that the primary purpose of workshops is discussion and thinking, it is important to begin with activities or tasks for the participants. There are several examples of activities in this text. Bligh (1986) contains ideas which can be converted into activities in small group teaching and Cryer (1986) provides a wealth of activities on various teaching methods. Think through these activities, consider how they relate to the expressed goals, and try to anticipate the discussion points which might be raised. Do not over-use plenary discussions. On the other hand, do leave opportunities for some general discussion. But, above all, vary the type of activity used.

INPUTS

These are brief lectures given by the workshop leader. They are used to summarize the points made in discussion, to provide new information and expertise, and perhaps to introduce a different aspect of the workshop. Some colleagues say that inputs are not necessary and that experiential learning is enough. Our view is that experiential learning is necessary but not enough. If you are invited to give a workshop it can be assumed that the participants expect the workshop leader to be knowledgable and well informed. Participants are likely to feel cheated if the leader never provides any inputs.

TIMING

Having worked out a set of activities and inputs it is important to estimate the time requirements for each section of the workshop. Remember to leave time for tea or coffee, for changeover of activities, a little time for unanticipated discussions, and some time for an evaluation of the workshop. At this stage you often have to exclude activities and inputs so check that what remains does match the goals.

ORDER

Look through the sequence of activities and inputs and check whether the order could be improved. Sometimes you find that the last activity you thought of might be the best one to begin with. Sometimes an activity does not link satisfactorily with the next input so do check the links.

Having completed the cycle of goals, activities, inputs, timing, and order, return to the goals to check whether they are still appropriate; if not, change the goals or change the activities and inputs. Your next step is preparing the appropriate written materials and other aids for the workshop. Then you should consider again how you are going to open the workshop. Last but not least think about how, at the end of the workshop, you will draw the themes of the workshop together.

When you have given the workshop look through the evaluation sheets to see in what ways the workshop might need changing. But do not rely only on these evaluations. Consider also what *you* think of the workshop.

Further reading

USEFUL GENERAL TEXTS

Beard, R. and Hartley, J. (1984)
Teaching and Learning in Higher Education, 4th edn, London: Harper & Row.
This provides a valuable overview of research and contains suggestions on all aspects of teaching, learning, and assessment.

McKeachie, W. J. (1986)
Teaching Tips: A Guidebook for the Beginning College Teacher, 8th edn, Lexington, Mass: D.C. Heath.
A deservedly popular American text which gives useful snapshots of different aspects of teaching, learning, and assessment. The bibliographies are also useful.

Rowntree, D. (1977)
Students: How Shall We Know Them?, London: Harper & Row.
Although this text is primarily concerned with assessment, it is full of insights into the organization of teaching and learning.

LECTURING

Bligh, D. A. (1972)
What's the Use of Lectures?, Harmondsworth: Penguin.
This describes research evidence on learning from lectures, and on lecturing. It also shows various methods of preparing, structuring, and giving lectures.

Gibs, G., Habeshaw, S., and Habeshaw, T. (1983)
53 Interesting Things to do in Your Lectures, Bristol: Technical and Educational Services Ltd.
This contains ideas and suggestions for bringing variety into your lectures.

SMALL GROUP TEACHING

Jaques, D. (1984)
Learning in Groups, London: Croom Helm.

A thorough and comprehensive text, it combines a review of research with practical suggestions for organizing and running small group sessions.

LABORATORY TEACHING

Boud, D., Dunn, J., and Hegarty-Hazel, E. (1986)
Teaching in laboratories, London: SRHE/NFER-Nelson.
This reviews research on laboratory teaching and provides suggestions on laboratory design.

RESEARCH SUPERVISION

Moses, I. (1985)
Supervising Postgraduates, HERDSA Green Guides no. 3, Sydney: Higher Education Research and Development Society of Australia.
A down-to-earth, practical guide to supervision which is based on a combination of personal experience and research.

Rudd, E. (1985)
A New Look at Postgraduate Failure, Guildford: SRHE/NFER-Nelson.
This book is based on a piece of research which examined the various factors which contribute to failure to complete, or to late completion.

STUDENT LEARNING

Marton, F., Hounsell, D., and Entwistle, N. (1984)
The Experience of Learning, Edinburgh: Scottish Academic Press.
This provides an outline and discussion of relevant research on learning both in formal settings and in private study; a good starting-point for anyone wishing to explore student learning more deeply.

References

Abercrombie, M. L. J. (1969) *Varieties of Small Group Teaching*, Guildford: Society for Research in Higher Education.

Abercrombie, M. L. J. and Terry, P. (1978) *Talking to Learn: Improving Teaching and Learning in Small Groups*, 4th edn, Guildford: Society for Research in Higher Education.

Abrami, P. C., Leventhal, L., and Perry, R. P. (1982) 'Educational seduction', *Review of Educational Research* 52:446–64.

Adderly, K., Ashwin, L., Bradbury, P., Freeman, J., Goodlad, S., Green, J., Jenkins, D., Rae, J., and Uren, O. (1975) *Project Methods in Higher Education*, London: Society for Research in Higher Education.

Andrews, J. D. (1980) 'The verbal structure of teacher questions: Its impact on class discussion', *POD Quarterly* 2:130–63.

Argyle, M. (1983) *The Psychology of Interpersonal Behaviour*, 4th edn, Harmondsworth: Penguin.

Aspden, P. and Eardley, R. (1974) *Teaching Practical Physics – The Open University Approach*, mimeo, Milton Keynes: Open University.

Atkinson, M. (1984) *Our Master's Voice*, London: Methuen.

Ausubel, D. P. (1968) *Educational Psychology: A Cognitive View*, New York: Holt, Rinehart & Winston, 127.

Ausubel, D. P., Novak, J. S., and Hanasian, H. (1978) *Educational Psychology: A Cognitive View*, 2nd edn, New York: Holt, Rinehart & Winston.

Baddeley, A. (1983) 'The working party on postgraduate education', *Bulletin of the British Psychological Society* 32, April:129–31.

Barnes, C. P. (1980) 'Questioning: the untapped resource', paper presented at annual meeting of American Educational Research Association, Boston, Mass.; discussed in Dunkin, M. J. (1986) 'Research on teaching in higher education', in M. C. Wittrock (ed.) *Handbook of Research on Teaching*, London: Collier Macmillan, 754–77.

Barrass, R. (1984) *Study!*, London: Chapman & Hall.

Battersby, D. and Battersby, K. (1980) 'In the eye of the beholder: Results from a New Zealand survey of education students' view on postgraduate research supervision', in A. H. Miller (ed.) *Freedom and Control in Higher Education*, Sydney, Australia: Higher Education Research and Development Society of Australasia, 88–101.

228   Effective Teaching in Higher Education

Baum, T. (1980) 'The PhD octopus revisited', Proceedings, *Improving University Teaching*, Sixth Annual Conference, Lausanne, July: 717–22.

Baumgart, N. L. (1976) 'Verbal interaction in university tutorials', *Higher Education* 5: 301–17; see also Baumgart's unpublished doctoral dissertation (1972) 'A study of verbal interaction in university tutorials', Macquarie University, Sydney, Australia.

Beard, R. and Hartley, J. (1984) *Teaching and Learning in Higher Education*, 4th edn, London: Harper & Row.

Beaugrande, R. de (1984) *Text Production: Toward a Science of Composition*, Norwood, NJ: Ablex.

Becker, H. S. (1961) *Boys in White*, Chicago, Ill.: University of Chicago Press.

Becker, H. S., Geer, B., and Hughes, E. C. (1968) *Making the Grade: The Academic Side of College Life*, New York: John Wiley.

Biggs, J. B. (1978a) 'Individual differences in study processes', *Higher Education* 8: 381–94.

—— (1978b) 'Individual and group differences in study processes', *British Journal of Educational Psychology*, 48: 266–79.

Black, P. J. and Whitworth, R. W. (1974) 'Unit laboratories in the department of physics at Birmingham University', in Nuffield Foundation (1976) *Studies in Laboratory Innovation*, London: Nuffield Foundation.

Bligh, D. A. (1972) *What's the Use of Lectures?*, Harmondsworth: Penguin.

—— (1980) 'Methods and techniques in post-secondary education', *Educational Studies and Documents*, 31, Paris: UNESCO.

—— (ed.) (1986) *Teach Thinking through Discussion*, London: NFER-Nelson.

Bliss, J. and Ogborn, J. (eds) (1977) *Students' Reactions to Undergraduate Science*, London: Heinemann.

Bloom, B. A. (1956) *Taxonomy of Educational Objectives*, New York: David McKay.

Boud, D., Dunn, J. G., Kenworthy, T., and Walker, M. (1978) *Laboratory Teaching in Tertiary Science: A Review of Recent Developments*, Sydney: HERDSA.

Boud, D., Dunn, J., and Hegarty-Hazel, E. (1986) *Teaching in Laboratories*, London: SRHE/NFER-Nelson.

Bransford, J. D. (1979) *Human Cognition: Learning, Remembering and Understanding*, Belmont, Calif.: Wadsworth.

Brewer, I. M. (1985) *Learning More: Teaching Less*, London: NFER-Nelson.

Brock, W. H. and Meadows, A. J. (1977) 'Physics, chemistry and higher education in the UK', *Studies in Higher Education* 2(2): 109–24.

Broudy, H. (1963) 'Historic exemplars of teaching methods', in N. L. Gage (ed.) *Handbook of Research on Teaching*, Chicago, Ill.: Rand McNally, 1–43.

Brown, G. A. (1978a) *Microteaching: A Programme of Teaching Skills*, revised edn, London: Methuen.

—— (1978b) *Lecturing and Explaining*, London: Methuen.

—— (1979) *Learning from Lectures*, Nottingham: University of Nottingham Press.

—— (1981) 'Analysing small group teaching', in K. Cox and C. Ewan (eds)

—— (1982) 'Two days on explaining and lecturing', *Studies in Higher Education* 2:93–104.

—— (1985) 'How to make and use video in teaching', *Medical Teacher* 7(2):139–50.

—— (1986) 'On lecturing', in T. Hudson and N. Postlethwaite (eds) *International Encyclopaedia of Education*, Oxford: Pergamon.

—— (1987) 'Studies of lecturing', in M. J. Dunkin (ed.) *International Encyclopaedia of Teacher Education*, Oxford: Pergamon.

Brown, G. A. and Armstrong, S. (1984) 'On explaining', in E. C. Wragg (ed.) *Classroom Teaching Skills*, London: Croom Helm.

Brown, G. A. and Atkins, M. J. (1986) 'Explaining in professional contexts', *Research Papers in Education* 1:60–86.

Brown, G. A. and Bakhtar, M. (eds) (1983) *Styles of Lecturing*, Loughborough: Loughborough University Press.

Brown, G. A. and Daines, J. M. (1981a) 'Learning from lectures', in E. Oxtoby (ed.) (1981) *Higher Education at the Crossroads*, Guildford: Society for Research in Higher Education.

—— (1981b) 'Can explaining be learnt? Some lecturers' views', *Higher Education* 10:573–80.

—— (1983) 'Creating a course on lecturing and explaining', *Programmed Learning and Educational Technology* 20:64–9.

Brown, G. A. and Edmondson, R. (1984) 'Asking questions', in E. C. Wragg (ed.) *Classroom Teaching Skills*, London: Croom Helm, 97–120.

Brown, G. A. and Hatton, N. (1982) *Explaining and Explanations*, London: Macmillan.

Brown, G. A. and Shaw, M. (1986) 'Social skills in education', in P. Trower and C. Hollins (eds) *Handbook of Social Skills*, Oxford: Pergamon Press.

Brown, G. A. and Tomlinson, D. (1980) 'How to improve handouts', *Medical Teacher* 2(5):215–21.

Buzan, T. (1982) *Use Your Head*, revised edn, London: BBC Publications.

Calfee, R. and Drum, P. (1986) 'Research on teaching reading', in M. C. Wittrock (ed.) *Handbook of Research on Teaching*, London: Collier Macmillan, 804–49.

Carmichael, J. W., Hassell, J. W., Hunter, J., Jones, L., Ryan, M. A., and Vincent, H. (1980) 'Project SOAR (Stress on Analytical Reasoning)', *American Biology Teacher* 42:169–73.

Chapman, P. (1974) 'On academics and student supervision', *Australian and New Zealand Journal of Sociology* 10 (2):147–9.

Clanchy, J. and Ballard, B. (1983) *How to Write Essays*, London: Longman.

Clark, R. E. and Salomon, G. (1986) 'Media in teaching', in M. C. Wittrock (ed.) *Handbook of Research on Teaching*, London: Collier Macmillan, 464–78.

Cohen, P. A. (1981) 'Student ratings of institution and student achievement: A meta analysis of multisection validity studies', *Review of Educational Research* 51:281–309.

Cohen, S. A. and McVicar, M. L. A. (1976) 'Establishing an undergraduate research programme in physics', *American Journal of Physics* 44(3):199–203.

Collier, K. G. (1969) 'Syndicate methods: further evidence and comment', *Universities Quarterly* 23, autumn:431–6.

230   Effective Teaching in Higher Education

Collier, K. G. (1985) 'Teaching methods in higher education: The changing scene with special reference to small group work', *Higher Education Research and Development* 4 (1): 3–27.

Cornwall, M., Schmitals, F., and Jaques, D. (eds) (1978) *Project Orientation in Higher Education*, London: UTMU (now Centre for Staff Development in Higher Education, University of London Institute of Education).

Cox, K. and Ewan, C. (eds) (1981) *The Medical Teacher*, Edinburgh: Churchill Livingstone.

Cryer, P. (1986) *Activities for Teachers in Higher Education* vol. 3, Guildford: Society for Research in Higher Education.

Cryer, P. and Rider, J. G. (1977) 'A "do it yourself" demonstration laboratory', *Physics Education* 12(6): 384–93.

CVCP (1985) *Postgraduate Training and Research*, London: Committee of Vice-Chancellors and Principals.

Dahlgren, L. O. (1978) 'Students' conceptions of subject matter: An aspect of learning and teaching in higher education', *Studies in Higher Education* 3: 25–35.

Daines, J. M. (1986) 'Self-assessment in a laboratory course on dispensing', unpublished PhD, University of Nottingham.

Dansereau, D. F., Collins, K. W., McDonald, B. A., Holley, C. D., Garland, J., Dickhoff, G., and Evans, J. (1979) 'Development and evaluation of a learning strategy training program', *Journal of Educational Psychology* 71(1): 64–73.

Davies, E. R. (1977) 'Using a unit laboratory format to teach electronics', in J. Ogborn (ed.) *Practical Work in Undergraduate Science*, London: Heinemann.

—— (1978) 'Helping postgraduate demonstrators in the laboratory', *Studies in Higher Education* 3: 81–9.

De Bono, E. (1967) *The Use of Lateral Thinking*, Harmondsworth: Penguin.

—— (1968) *The Five-Day Course in Thinking*, Harmondsworth: Penguin.

—— (1969) *The Mechanism of Mind*, Harmondsworth: Penguin.

—— (1973) *PO: Beyond Yes and No*, revised edn, Harmondsworth: Penguin.

Delamont, S. and Eggleston, J. F. (1983) 'A necessary isolation?', in J. F. Eggleston and S. Delamont *Supervision of Students for Research Degrees*, Birmingham: BERA, 23–46.

Dowdeswell, W. H. and Harris, W. D. C. (1979) 'Project work in university science', in D. McNally (ed.) (1979) *Learning Strategies in Science*, Cardiff: University of Cardiff Press.

Dubin, R. and Taveggia, T. C. (1968) *The Teaching–Learning Paradox: A Comparative Analysis of College Teaching Methods*, Eugene, Oreg.: Center for the Advanced Study of Educational Administration, University of Oregon.

Duncker, K. (1945) 'On problem solving', *Psychological Monographs* 58(270): 1–113.

Dunkin, M. J. (1983) 'A review of research on lecturing', *Higher Education Research and Development* 2: 63–78.

—— (1986) 'Research on teaching in higher education', in M.C. Wittrock, (ed.) (1986) *Handbook of Research on Teaching*, London: Collier Macmillan, 754–77.

(1981) *The Medical Teacher*, Edinburgh: Churchill Livingstone, 45–54.

Dunkin, M. J. and Biddle, B. J. (1974) *The Study of Teaching*, New York: Holt, Rinehart & Winston.

Ellis, R. and Hopkins, K. (1985) *How to Succeed in Written Work and Study*, London: Collins.

Ellner, C. L. (1983) *Studies of College Teaching: Experimental Results, Theoretical Interpretations and New Perspectives*, Lexington, Mass.: D. C. Heath.

Elton, L. R. B. (1984) 'Evaluating teaching and assessing teachers in higher education', *Assessment in Higher Education* 9(2): 97–114.

Ennis, R. H. (1969) *Logic in Teaching*, Englewood Cliffs, NJ: Prentice-Hall.

Entwistle, N. J. and Hounsell, D. (1975) 'How students learn: Implications for teaching in higher education', in N. J. Entwistle and D. Hounsell (eds) *How Students Learn*, Lancaster: University of Lancaster Press.

Entwistle, W. and Ramsden, P. J. (1983) *Understanding Student Learning*, London: Croom Helm.

Entwistle, N. J., Hanley, M., and Hounsell, D. (1979) 'Identifying distinctive approaches to studying', *Higher Education* 8: 365–80.

Entwistle, N. J., Hanley, M., and Ratcliffe, G. (1979) 'Approaches to learning and levels of understanding', *British Educational Research Journal* 5: 99–114.

Entwistle, N. J., Percy, K., and Nisbet, J. B. (1971) *Educational Objectives and Academic Performance in Higher Education*, Lancaster: University of Lancaster Press.

ESRC (1985) see Turney, J. (1985) 'ESRC cracks down on PhD rates', *Times Higher Education Supplement*, 1 November: 1–2.

Flanders, N. A. (1970) *Analysing Teaching Behaviour*, New York: Addison-Wesley.

Foster, P. J. (1981) 'Clinical discussion groups: Verbal participation and outcomes', *Journal of Medical Education* 56: 831–8.

Fransson, A. (1977) 'On qualitative differences in learning: IV – effects of motivation and text anxiety on process and outcome', *British Journal of Educational Psychology* 47: 244–57.

Gall, M. D. (1970) 'The use of questioning in teaching', *Review of Educational Research* 40: 707–21.

Galton, M. (1983) *British Mirrors*, 2nd edn, Leicester: University of Leicester School of Education.

Gardner, G. and Stanley, G. (1974) 'Student supervision and joint author-ship: The "all my own work" myth', *Australian and New Zealand Journal of Sociology* 10(2): 145–7.

Gassin, J. (1982) 'The learning difficulties of the foreign student and what we can do about them', *HERDSA News* 4(3): 13 and 16.

Gibbs, G. (1981) *Teaching Students to Learn*, Milton Keynes: Open University Press.

Gibbs, G., Habeshaw, S., and Habeshaw, T. (1983) *53 Interesting Things to do in Your Lectures*, Bristol: Technical and Educational Services Ltd.

Goldschmid, B. and Goldschmid, M. L. (1974) 'Individualising instruction in higher education: A review', *Higher Education* 3: 1–24.

Goldschmid, B. and Goldschmid, M. L. (1976) 'Peer teaching in higher education: A review', *Higher Education* 5:9–33.

Graves, D. H. (1978) *Balance the Basics: Let them Write*, New York: Ford Foundation.

Habeshaw, S., Habeshaw, T., and Gibbs, G. (1986) *53 Interesting Things to do in Small Group Teaching*, Bristol:Technical and Educational Services Ltd.

Hale, Sir E. (chair) (1964) *Report of the Committee on University Teaching Method*, London:HMSO.

Hamilton, E. R. (1928) *The Art of Interrogation*, London: University of London Press.

Harden, R. M. and Cairncross, R. (1980) 'Assessment of practical skills: The objective structures practical examination (CSPE)', *Studies in Higher Education* 5:187–96.

Hargie, O. (ed.) (1986) *Handbook of Communication Skills*, London:Croom Helm.

Harri-Augstein, S., Smith, M., and Thomas, L. (1982) *Reading to Learn*, London:Methuen.

Hartley, J. (1984) *Designing Instructional Text*, London:Kogan Page.

—— (1986) 'Improving study skills', *British Educational Research Journal* 12(2): 111–24.

Hartley, J. and Burnhill, P. (1977) 'Fifty guidelines for improving instructional texts', *Programmed Learning and Educational Technology* 14:65–73.

Hartley, J. and Knapper, C. (1984) 'Academics and their writing', *Studies in Higher Education* 9(2):151–67.

Hayes, J. R. and Flower, L. S. (1980) 'Writing as problem solving', *Visible Language* 14(4):388–99.

Hegarty, E. H. (1978) 'Levels of scientific enquiry in university science laboratory classes: Implications for curriculum deliberations', *Research in Science Education* 8:45–57; see also Hegarty's unpublished doctoral dissertation (1979) 'The role of laboratory work in teaching microbiology at university level', University of New South Wales, Sydney, Australia.

—— (1982)'The role of laboratory work in science courses', in M. B. Rowe (ed.) *Education in the 80s: Science*, Washington, DC:National Education Association.

Hegarty-Hazel, E. (1986) 'Research on laboratory work', in D. Boud, J. Dunn, and E. Hegarty-Hazel *Teaching in Laboratories*, London:SRHE/NFER-Nelson.

Hegarty, E. H. and Lee, A. (1979) 'How to organise effective laboratory teaching in medicine', *Medical Teacher* 1(5):227–34.

Heron, J. (1975) *Six Category Intervention Analysis*, Mimeo, Guildford: Centre of Adult Education, University of Surrey.

Hilgard, E. R. (1963) 'A perspective on the relationships of learning theory and education practice', in his (ed.) *Theories of Learning and Instruction*, Chicago, Ill.: National Society for the Study of Education 63rd Yearbook.

Hodgson, V. (1984) 'Learning from lectures', in F. Marton, D. Hounsell, and N. Entwistle (eds) *The Experience of Learning*, Edinburgh:Scottish Academic Press.

References 233

33

Hofstein, A. and Lunetta, V. N. (1982) 'The role of the laboratory in science teaching: Neglected aspects of research', *Review of Educational Research* 52(2):201–17.

Homans, G. C. (1951) *The Human Group*, London:Routledge & Kegan Paul.

Hounsell, D. (1984a) 'Understanding teaching and teaching for understanding', in F. Marton, D. Hounsell, and N. Entwistle (eds) *The Experience of Learning*, Edinburgh: Scottish Academic press.

—— (1984b) 'Essay planning and essay writing', *Higher Education Research and Development* 3(1):13–31.

Humes, A. (1983) 'Research on the composing process', *Review of Educational Research* 53:201–16.

Hyman, R. T. (1974) *Teaching: Vantage Points for Study*, New York:Lippincott.

Jaques, D. (1984) *Learning in Groups*, London:Croom Helm.

Johnson, H., Rhodes, D. M., and Rumery, R. E. (1975) 'Assessment of teaching in higher education. A critical retrospect and proposal', *Higher Education* 4:173–99.

Johnson-Laird, P. N. (1983) *Mental Models*, Cambridge:Cambridge University Press.

Johnson-Laird, P. N. and Wason, P. C. (eds) (1977) *Thinking: Readings in Cognitive Science*, Cambridge:Cambridge University Press.

Joyce, B. and Weil, M. (1972) *Models of Teaching*, Englewood Cliffs, NJ: Prentice-Hall.

Kahn, B. (1986) *Computers in Science: Using Computers for Learning and Teaching*, Cambridge:Cambridge University Press.

Kahney, H. (1986) *Problem Solving: A Cognitive Approach*, Milton Keynes: Open University Press.

Karplus, R., Lawson, A. E., Wollman, W., Apel, M., Bernhof, R., Rusch, J., and Sullivan, F. (1977) *Science Teaching on the Development of Reasoning: A Workshop*, Berkeley, Calif.:Regent of the University of California.

Katona, G. (1940) *Organising and Memorising: Studies in the Psychology of Learning and Teaching*, New York:Columbia University Press.

Kelley, H. H. and Thibaute, J. W. (1970) *The Social Psychology of Groups*, New York:John Wiley.

Kerry, T. (1982) *Effective Questioning*, London:Macmillan.

Kohlan, R. G. (1973) 'A comparison of faculty evaluations early and late in the course', *Journal of Higher Education* 44(8):587–95.

Kozma, R. B., Belle, L. W., and Williams, G. W. (1978) *Instructional Techniques in Higher Education*, New Jersey:Englewood Cliffs Educational Technology publication.

Kulik, J. A. and Kulik, C.-L. C. (1979) 'College teaching', in P. L. Peterson and H. J. Walberg (eds) *Research on Teaching: Concepts, Findings and Implications*, Berkeley, Calif.:McCutcheon, 70–93.

Kulik, J. A., Kulik, C.-L. C., and Cohen, P. A. (1979) 'A meta-analysis of outcome studies of Keller's personalized system of instructions', *American Psychologist* April:307–18.

Land, M. L. (1985) 'Vagueness and clarity in the classroom', in T. Husen and T. N. Postlethwaite (eds) *International Encyclopaedia of Education: Research Studies*, Oxford:Pergamon.

234   Effective Teaching in Higher Education

Laurillard, D. (1979) 'The processes of student learning', *Higher Education* 8:395–410.
Lindsay, P. H. and Norman, D. A. (1972) *Human Information Processing*, New York: Academic Press.
Luker, P. A. (1987) 'Some case studies of small group teaching', unpublished PhD, University of Nottingham.
McAleese, R. and Welsh, J. (1983) 'The supervision of postgraduate research students', in J. F. Eggleston and S. Delamont (eds) *Supervision of Students for Research Degrees*, Birmingham: BERA, 13–22.
McCleish, J. (1976) 'The lecture method', in M. L. Gage (ed.) (1976) *Teaching Methods*, Chicago, Ill.: National Society for the Study of Education 75th Yearbook.
McKeachie, W. J. (1974) 'The decline and fall of the laws of learning', *Educational Researcher* 3:7–11.
—— (1986) *Teaching Tips: A Guidebook for the Beginning College Teacher*, 8th edn, Lexington, Mass.: D. C. Heath.
McKeachie, W. J. and Kulik, J. (1975) 'Effective college teaching', *Review of Research in Education* vol. 3, Itascu, Ill.: F. E. Peacock.
MacKenzie, N., Eraut, M., and Jones, H. (1970) *Teaching and Learning: An Introduction to New Methods and Resources in Higher Education*, Paris: UNESCO.
MacLennan, R. (1974) 'How well do you see the case method?', *Industrial Training International* 9:323–4 and 348–50.
Maddox, H. (1967) *How to Study*, London: Pan.
Main, A. (1984) 'Reflection and the development of learning skills', in D. Boud (ed.) *Reflection and Learning*, London: Kogan Page.
—— (1986) 'Every academic a study counsellor', *SRHE International Newsletter* 6, April: 21–9.
Malec, M. A. (ed.) (1971) *Attitude Change*, Chicago, Ill.: Markham.
Marsh, H. W. (1982) 'Students' evaluation of tertiary introduction: Testing the applicability of American surveys in an Australian setting', *Australian Journal of Education* 25(2):177–93.
Marshall, L. A. and Rowland, F. (1983) *A Guide to Learning Independently*, Milton Keynes: Open University Press.
Martin, E. and Ramsden, P. (1987) 'Learning skills or skills in learning?' In J. T. E. Richardson, M. W. Eysenck, and D. Warren Piper (eds) *Student Learning*, Milton Keynes: Society for Research in Higher Education and Open University Press, 155–67.
Marton, F. (1975) 'How students learn', in N. J. Entwistle and D. Hounsell (eds) *How Students Learn*, Lancaster: University of Lancaster.
Marton, F. and Saljo, R. (1976) 'On qualitative differences in learning', *British Journal of Educational Psychology* 46:4–11.
Marton, F., Hounsell, D., and Entwistle, N. (eds) (1984) *The Experience of Learning*, Edinburgh: Scottish Academic Press.
Mathias, H. (1976) 'BSc by thesis: A degree of evaluation', *Chemistry in Britain* 12(8):258–61.
Merlino, A. (1977) 'A comparison of the effectiveness of three levels of teacher questioning on the outcomes of instruction in a college biology

course' (doctoral dissertation, New York University, 1976), *Dissertation Abstracts International* 37:5551-A.

Miller, C. M. and Parlett, M. R. (1974) *Up to the Mark: A Study of the Examination Game*, Guildford:Society for Research in Higher Education.

Moore, W. G. (1968) *The Tutorial System and its Future*, Oxford:Pergamon.

Moses, I. (1982) *Postgraduate Study: A Select Annotated Bibliography*, Brisbane, Australia:Tertiary Education Institute, University of Queensland.

—— (1984) 'Supervision of higher degree students – problem areas and possible solutions', *Higher Education Research and Development* 3(2):153–65.

—— (1985) *Supervising Postgraduates*, HERDSA Green Guides no 3, Sydney: Higher Education Research and Development Society of Australia.

Newell, A. and Simon, H. A. (1972) *Human Problem Solving*, Englewood Cliffs, NJ:Prentice-Hall.

Nightingale, P. (1984) 'Examination of research theses', *Higher Education Research and Development* 3(2):137–50.

Nisbet, J. and Shucksmith, J. (1984) *The Seventh Sense*, Edinburgh:Scottish Council for Research in Education.

Norman, D. (1977) *Teaching Learning Strategies*, San Diego, Calif.:University of California.

—— (1980) 'Cognitive Engineering in Education', in D. J. Tumo and S. Reis (eds) *Problem Solving and Education*, Hillsdale, NJ:Lawrence Erlbaum.

Nuffield Foundation (1974) *Studies in Laboratory Innovation*, Group for the Study of Research and Innovation in Higher Education, London:Nuffield Foundation.

—— (1976) *Small Group Teaching*, London:Nuffield Foundation.

O'Connell, S., Penton, S. J., and Boud, O. J. (1977) 'A nationally designated laboratory mini course', *Programmed Learning and Educational Technology* 14:54–161.

Ogborn, J. (ed.) (1977) *Practical Work in Undergraduate Science*, London: Heinemann.

Open University (1979) *Preparing to Study*, Milton Keynes:Open University Press.

Palinscar, A. S. and Brown, A. L. (1984) 'Reciprocal teaching of comprehension – fostering and monitoring activities', *Cognition and Instruction* I:117–75.

Palmer, R. and Pope, C. (1984) *Brain Train*, London:E. & F. N. Spon.

Pask, G. (1976) 'Styles and strategies of learning', *British Journal of Educational Psychology* 46:12–25.

Pask, G. and Scott, B. C. E. (1972) 'Learning strategies and individual competence' in J. M. Whitehead (ed.) *Personality and Learning I*, London: Hodder & Stoughton.

Pear, T. J. (1933) *The Psychology of Effective Speaking*, London:Kogan Page.

Phillips, M. (1981) 'Early history of physics laboratories for students at the college level', *American Journal of Physics* 49:522–7.

Pirianen-Marsh, A. (1985) 'The lecture as discourse', unpublished thesis, Studies in Philology, University of Oulu, Finland.

Polya, G. (1945) *How to Solve it*, 2nd edn (1957), New York: Doubleday.

Polya, G. (1962) *Mathematical Discovery, vol. 1: On Understanding, Learning and Teaching Problem Solving*, New York: John Wiley.

Ramsay, H. P. (1973) 'The demonstration laboratory – teaching aid in biology', *Journal of Biological Education* 7:19–24.

Ramsden, P. and Entwistle, N. J. (1981) 'Effects of academic departments on students' approaches to studying', *British Journal of Educational Psychology* 51:368–83.

Reid, J. W. (1951) 'An experimental study of "analysis of the goal" in problem solving', *Journal of General Psychology* 44:51–69.

Richardson, J. T. D. (ed.) (1986) *Cognitive Processes in Student Learning*, London: NFER-Nelson.

Robinson, L. G. (1957) 'The research student and his supervisor', pamphlet, London: London School of Economics and Political Science.

Rogers, D. (ed.) (1980) 'Assessing teaching', *FERN* 1, Leicester: Further Education Research Network, Leicester Polytechnic.

—— (1986) 'BIAS: A programme for assessing teaching', *FERN*, Leicester: Further Education Research Network, Leicester Polytechnic.

Rossum, E. J. van and Schenk, S. M. (1984) 'The relationship between learning conception, study strategy and learning outcome', *British Journal of Educational Psychology* 54(1):78–83.

Rowntree, D. (1977) *Students: How Shall We Know Them?*, London: Harper & Row.

Rudd, E. (1975) *The Highest Education*, London: Routledge & Kegan Paul.

—— (1981) 'No running away from the sands of time', *Times Higher Education Supplement* 23(1):81.

—— (1985) *A New Look at Postgraduate Failure*, Guildford: SRHE/NFER-Nelson.

Rudduck, J. (1978) *Learning through Small Group Discussion*, Research into Higher Education Monograph, Guildford: Society for Research in Higher Education.

Rutherford, E. (1918) Quoted at the Conference of Universities, referred to by Simpson, R. (1983), *How the PhD Came to Britain: A Century of Struggle for Postgraduate Education*, Guildford: Society for Research in Higher Education, 154–5.

Scardamalia, M. and Bereiter, C. (1986) 'Research on written composition', in M. C. Wittrock (ed.) *Handbook of Research on Teaching*, New York: Macmillan, 778–803.

SERC (1982) *Research Student and Supervisor: A Discussion Document on Good Supervisory Practice*, London: Science and Engineering Research Council.

Shaw, M. (1987) 'The tutorial: An analysis of skills', unpublished PhD, University of Nottingham.

Sheffield, E. F. (ed.) (1974) *Teaching in the Universities: No One Way*, Montreal: Queen's University Press.

Short, A. H. and Tomlinson, D. R. (1979) 'The design of laboratory class work', *Studies in Higher Education* 4(2):223–42.

Shulman, L. S. and Tamir, P. (1973) 'Research on teaching in the natural sciences', in R. M. W. Travers (ed.) *Second Handbook of Research on Teaching*, Chicago, Ill.: Rand McNally.

Simpson, R. (1983) *How the PhD Came to Britain: A Century of Struggle for Postgraduate Education*, Guildford: Society for Research in Higher Education.

Skinner, B. F. (1954) 'The science of learning and the art of teaching', *Harvard Educational Review* 24:88–97.

Smith, R. V. (1980) *Development and Management of Research Groups*, Austin, Tex: University of Texas Press.

Spence, R. B. (1928) 'Lecture and class discussion in teaching educational psychology', *Journal of Educational Psychology* 19:454–62.

Sprott, W. J. H. (1957) *Human Groups*, Harmondsworth: Penguin.

Stenhouse, L. (1971) 'Teaching through small group discussion: formality, rules and authority', *Cambridge Journal of Education* 21:18–24.

Svensson, L. (1977) 'On qualitative differences in learning: III – study skill and learning' *British Journal of Educational Psychology* 47:233–43.

Swinnerton-Dyer, P. (chair) (1982) *Working Party Report on Postgraduate Education*, London: HMSO.

Tabberer, R. (1987) *Study and Information Skills in Schools*, Windsor: NFER-Nelson.

Thompson, N. (1979) 'The assessment of candidates for degrees in physics', *Studies in Higher Education* 4(2):169–80.

Turney, C., Eltis, K. J., Hatton, N., Owens, L. C., Towler, J., Wright, R., Cairns, L. G., and Williams, G. (1983) *Sydney Microskills Redeveloped*, Sydney: University of Sydney Press.

Turney, C. (ed.) (1984) *Skills of Supervision*, Sydney: University of Sydney Press.

UKCOSA (1982) *Overseas Students – Who Learns What?* and *The Teaching and Tutoring of Overseas Students*, 60 Westbourne Grove, London: UKCOSA.

Walford, G. (1980) 'Why physics students start doctorates', *Studies in Higher Education* 5(1):77–80.

Weinstein, C. F. and Mayer, R. F. (1986) 'The teaching of learning strategies', M. C. Wittrock (ed.) *Handbook of Research on Teaching*, New York: Macmillan, 315–28.

Wells, J. C. (1986) 'The initiation of a study skills programme in a lower 6th form', unpublished PhD, University of Exeter.

Welsh, J. (1978) 'The supervision of postgraduate research students', *Research in Education* 19:77–86.

—— (1979) *The First Year of Postgraduate Research Study*, Guildford: Society for Research in Higher Education.

—— (1980) 'Predicting postgraduate performance', *Notes on University Teaching* 1:1–4, University of Aberdeen, Scotland.

—— (1981) 'The PhD student at work', *Studies in Higher Education* 6(2):159–62.

Wertheimer, M. (1961) *Productive Thinking*, London: Tavistock.

White, R. T. and Tisher, R. P. (1986) 'Research on natural science', in M. C. Wittrock (ed.) (1986) *Handbook of Research on Teaching* 3rd edn, New York: Macmillan, 874–905.

Wickelgren, W. A. (1938) *How to Solve Problems*, revised edn (1974), San Francisco: Freeman.

Wilson, A. (1980) 'Group sessions for postgraduate students', *British Journal of Guidance and Counselling* 8(2):237–41.

Wilson, G. M., Lever, R., Harden, R. M., Robertson, J., and Macritchie, J. (1969) 'Examinations of clinical examiners', *Lancet* 2:37.

Witton, R. (1973) 'Academics and student supervision: apprenticeship or exploitation?', *Australian and New Zealand Journal of Sociology* 9(3):70–3.

—— (1974) 'Apprenticeship or exploitation: an unresolved issue', *Australian and New Zealand Journal of Sociology* 10(3):192–234.

Wittrock, M. C. (1986) 'Students' thought processes', in M. C. Wittrock (ed.) *Handbook of Research on Teaching*, New York:Macmillan, 297–314.

Wright, J. (1986) *Improving Submission Rates of the PhD*, mimeo, Counselling Unit, University of Reading.

Yorke, D. M. (1981) *Patterns of Teaching*, London:Council for Educational Technology.

Young, R. E. (1976) 'Invention: A topographical survey', in G. Tate (ed.) *Teaching Composition: Ten Biographical Essays*, Fort Worth, Tex:Christian University Press.

Zimbardo, P., Erbeson, E., and Maslach, C. (1977) *Influencing Attitudes and Changing Behaviour*, Massachussets:Addison-Wesley.

Zuber-Skerritt, O. (1985) 'Helping students overcome barriers to dissertation writing', *HERDSA News* 7(3):8–10; see also 'Problem definition and thesis writing: Workshops for the post-graduate student', *Higher Education* (forthcoming).

—— (1986) 'The integration of university students' research skills in postgraduate programmes', unpublished monograph, Griffith University, Australia.

Name index

Subject index

Subject index

Subject index   245

UKCOSA 128–9

writing 177–83; helping students with 181–3; process of 177–80; research papers 125–6, 138–9